Contemporary French Political Parties

Contemporary French Political Parties

Edited by
David S. Bell

ST. MARTIN'S PRESS NEW YORK

© 1982 Croom Helm Ltd
St. Martin's Press, Inc., 175 Fifth Avenue,
New York, N.Y. 10010
Printed in Great Britain
First published in the United States of America in 1982

Library of Congress Cataloging in Publication Data

Contemporary French political parties
  1. Political parties – France. 2. France –
Politics and government – 1969. I. Bell,
David Scott.

  JN299 1982.C66   324.244   81-21301
  ISBN 0-312-16662-1   AACR2

CONTENTS

Preface   vii

Introduction   1
David S. Bell

PART ONE: THE RIGHT   7

1   The Giscardians and Party Politics   9
    Ella Searls

2   Gaullism, Advanced Capitalism and the Fifth Republic   24
    Philip G. Cerny

3   'Nouvelle Droite': Cultural Power and Political Influence   52
    Michalina Vaughan

PART TWO: THE LEFT   69

4   The Strategies of the French Left: 71
    From the 1978 Defeat to the 1981 Victories
    Neill Nugent

5   The French Communist Party and 'Class Alliances':   89
    Intellectuals, Workers and the Crisis of Social Ideology
    Jolyon Howorth

6   The Unified Socialist Party (PSU) Since 1968   108
    Vladimir Claude Fišera and Peter Jenkins

PART THREE: DETAILED STUDIES   121

7   The CERES in Two Departments – Political Compromise   123
    on Aude and Vilaine?
    David Hanley

8   The Play of Tendencies: Internal Politics in the SFIO   138
    Before and After the Second World War
    B.D. Graham

9   The French Left and the European Community   165
    Joy Bound and Kevin Featherstone

Appendix: The French Legislative Elections 1981   190

Notes on Contributors   192

Index   193

PREFACE

This book is a collection of essays written during 1981. Its origins are in the SSRC conference on French political parties in Leeds University Politics Department in January 1981 and most of the earlier drafts of these papers were presented to that conference and discussed there. These were research papers presenting the findings of the contributors and outlining research problems and directions. Since that time there have been two elections and France has moved, again, into a new political situation so the chapters of this book have been re-written to take this upheaval into account and to provide, where possible, analyses of various aspects of it.

Thanks are therefore due to the SSRC for their help in setting up the Leeds conference on French political parties and to their indulgence with our administrative difficulties. Thanks are also due to those who contributed to that conference - with papers, as the 'chairs' in discussion, or as discussants - but who are not represented here.

D.S.B.
Leeds.

INTRODUCTION

This book is organised into three separate parts dealing with the Left, the Right, and with particular detailed problems. Although the French parties are evolving rapidly under the impact of the Socialist victory of 1981 the book does take into account the legislative elections of June. However the French party situation is still essentially fluid and it is not possible to go into the prediction business at quite this stage. Nevertheless people who want a 'tour d'horizon' of the French party set-up at the time of Mitterrand's victories will find that parts I and II are useful as they analyse the forces at work on the parties.

Thus the aspects chosen by the authors are of contemporary concern and range across the entire spectrum of French political parties. The only omissions are the two marginal formations of the extreme revolutionary Left and the extreme revolutionary Right (though the 'Nouvelle Droite' is the subject of Chapter 3) which are not central to the preoccupations of the 1980s as the Fifth Republic becomes Socialist. There is, naturally, given the current situation, an emphasis on the Left and the subjects covered here are the Socialist Party, the Communist Party and the PSU, though there are, in Part III, studies of CERES, factionalism and the EEC as an issue on the Left. Broadly speaking though, the book reflects the research interests of the various researchers represented here.

Part I deals with the Right, that is the parties and forces of the 'ex-majority'. France has been dominated for 23 years or thereabouts by the Right and since 1962 the Gaullist Party has played the key role in Fifth Republic politics to the extent that it almost seemed that post-1958 French politics were synonymous with the Right just as, say, Swedish politics were synonymous with social democracy; however, as in Sweden, the apparent immobility was broken after a long period. For French politics, therefore, the Right remains of importance and the future of French politics will depend, to some extent, on whether the opposition can find its lost unity, to present a united front to the Left in forthcoming elections.

There are three essays in this part: the first, by Dr Ella Searls, is entitled 'The Giscardians and Party Politics' and it deals with the ex-Giscardian supporters; the second, by Dr Phil Cerny, is called 'Gaullism, Advanced Capitalism and the Fifth Republic', and it analyses the current position of the Gaullist Party; and the final chapter is by Professor M. Vaughan, 'Nouvelle Droite: Cultural Power and Political Influence', and discusses the importance and

1

influence of this, essentially 1970s, pressure group.

Dr Searls discusses the development, cohesion – or otherwise – of the centre group known as Giscardian in the 1970s. In fact a heterogeneous group, the Giscardians have not been as successful as the election in 1974 might have led them to believe. Giscard in fact lacked a party group for part of his term of office and the remaining Centrists in Parliament in 1981 do not readily lay claim to Giscard's mantle. They are none the less an important group and have not disappeared with the Socialist election victory of 1981 (they are bigger than might have been expected) but they are disorganised, leaderless, suspicious of Jacques Chirac and, debilitating for a Fifth Republic group, without a conspicuous 'presidential' figure in their midst yet.

The Fifth Republic cannot be described or explained without reference to the Gaullist Party which, for almost 20 years, has been the biggest of the French political parties as well as being part of the governing coalition. In Chapter 2 Dr Cerny, who has been researching Gaullism – and in particular de Gaulle's foreign policy – discusses the RPR and its antecedents. With the Gaullist Party, even now, being the main force in the parliamentary opposition, organised around the main figure on the Right, Jacques Chirac, the RPR will remain a central force in French politics whatever the future brings for the centre UDF.

However, Jacques Chirac was instrumental in Giscard's downfall. Whether this was a 'politique du pire' or not remains a moot question, but the effect was to leave the Gaullist Party as the best organised and largest party of the Right organised around a potential presidential figure – Jacques Chirac. It is by no means clear that Chirac can overcome divisions on the Right to create a coherent opposition because he is regarded by many Centrists as having caused the downfall of President Giscard. Chirac has overcome difficulties of this nature before and may be able to transcend them again.

Phil Cerny discusses the divisions on the Right and the Gaullist contribution to those divisions as well as the Gaullist position on the Right and their highly distinctive style. He also discusses Gaullism today as an ideology (as one commentator has asked, 'How is it possible to be a Gaullist when everybody is now a Gaullist?') and the new-found Gaullist views of economics (supply-side economics was featured by Chirac in his presidential campaign). The future for a party which was above all a party of the regime is analysed in a concluding statement.

Professor Vaughan in the 'Nouvelle Droite' (ND) studies the shape, influence and potential of this small intellectual coterie known, perhaps, more than anything else as a philosophical group with journalistic leanings and associations with the 'Figaro' magazine. This group has, however, an evangelistic aim centred around 'new' analyses of politics, society and literature. In addition the 'Nouvelle Droite' has been self-consciously 'entryist' and aspired to, in fact seemed to have, influence in elite circles where small numbers could achieve great influence through 'cultural power'.

As Professor Vaughan points out, this cultural power is based
on the redissemination of ideas which were generally neglected at
the end of the war: they fight egalitarianism and the Left with
elitism, state unity, scientism and a toughness of thought which
is quasi-racial. It would be wrong to dismiss the 'Nouvelle Droite'
as either 'Fascist' or an intellectual fad because they have been
careful to demarcate themselves from the extreme political fringe
of the Right (despite the extremist use of 'Nouvelle Droite' themes)
and because they are an extension of the philosophies of competition and market process. Their influence and extension has already been enduring enough to dispose of the idea that they are
a form of ephemeral intellectual gimmick.

Professor Vaughan shows the overlap between the policies
advocated by the 'Nouvelle Droite' and those put into effect by
the Giscardians particularly the Haby education reforms. Anti-
Marxist to a degree, but above all publicists for their own distinctive views, the 'Nouvelle Droite' has been influential within the
ex-majority despite the contrast with liberal Giscardianism. The
recirculation of old ideas with a new found intellectual respectability and in a self-consciously political framework is almost
bound to be influential, particularly in a Right which is trying to
find its bearings once again: Professor Vaughan notes the possibility for these ideas to become part of the mainstream ideology.

Part II is devoted to the parties of the Left and is centred on
the Socialists, the Communists and the small PSU (Unified Socialist
Party). Now that the Left is the majority in the Fifth Republic
the anatomy and functioning of these parties had become of even
greater significance. With the victory of François Mitterrand and
the subsequent all-conquering Socialist Party victory the forces
which shape politics on the Left will become the forces which help
shape the Fifth Republic. In this part there are chapters by Neil
Nugent, 'The Strategies of the French Left: For the 1978 Defeat
to the 1981 Victories 4', by Jolyon Howorth, 'The French Communist Party and "Class Alliances" ', and by Peter Jenkins and
Vladimir Fišera on the 'Unified Socialist Party (PSU) since 1968'.
These chapters cover the Left from a party perspective and are
intended to take various themes and aspects of party function on
the Left for individual analysis.

The first chapter in part II by Neill Nugent analyses the strategies involved in bringing the Left to power in the Fifth Republic.
This means, in particular, looking at the strategy of 'Union of
the Left' which was cemented in June 1972 with the signing of the
'Common Programme of Government' and which broke down in
September 1977. For years it was said that the Left 'won the
opinion polls but never the elections' and Neill Nugent discusses
both the Left's inability to seize power during the 1970s as well
as the Mitterrand and Socialist victory of 1981. The relation of
this victory to the defeats of Left union forms one of the subjects
of discussion in that chapter as does the problem of alternative
paths to power, third force strategy, and the internal structure
of the Socialist Party itself. Thus the main figures in the party

and the views grouped around them are shown: François Mitterrand, Michel Rocard, Pierre Mauroy, and the left-wing group CERES are related to the forces within the party and the French Left's differing perspectives. This chapter sets the French Left against the background of quarrels of personality and policy during the 1970s.

Chapter 5 by Jolyon Howorth deals with one of the most sensitive subjects for the French Communist Party: its relationship with the intellectuals. In 1981 the elections served to show the difficulties of this part of the party's political line as the Marchais candidature caused many intellectuals to desert the PCF and the party took steps to exclude a number of them (including Jean Elleinstein, the herald of mid-1970s 'Eurocommunism'). Partially, this was due to the brutal and merciless Communist application of internal discipline around the anti-Socialist, anti-Left union line taken by the party until the first round of the 1981 presidential elections. However, the French Communist Party, unlike the Italian Party, has not been able to work out a stable relation to intellectuals even while it has had prestigious people - like Picasso - in its ranks.

Jolyon Howorth relates this to the 'ouvriérism' of the PCF, its obsession with all that is 'genuinely' working class and its unwillingness to countenance anything outside that circle, and its peculiar attempts to come to grips with what really is working class. It is pointed out that this excessive 'ouvriérism' was a feature of the Marchais election campaign in 1981, but at the same time it was unable to find a way of appealing to the 'new working class' of France. The French Communist Party appeals to intellectuals using a language which is almost 'guesdiste' in its accents but at the same time, so the chapter argues, the PCF cannot decide on the strategy that it is trying to pursue. In this respect the difficulties of the party's intellectual sector and the intellectual journal 'Révolution' are revealing: these have suffered splits and quarrels of considerable intensity but were not resolved before the April 1981 elections.

Whatever the fortunes of the PCF in government - and one of its ministers, J. Ralite, was concerned with cultural affairs - the party will need to be rebuilt (if it can be) from its current shambles. A new vitality in the intellectual life of the party would be a sign of this if it is able to do it.

Chapter 6 is by Vladimir Fišera and Peter Jenkins who write about the history of the small non-Communist left-wing party, the Unified Socialist Party (PSU). This party has been an irritant or gadfly on the Left since its foundation but it has never been more than a limited parliamentary representation. In 1969 Michel Rocard was its presidential candidate and in 1981 its candidate was the university teacher Huguette Bouchardeau. The candidatures of these two people show something of the PSU's role in the French system over the past ten years or so: presenting ideas and policies which the other parties would not, or could not, take up themselves.

Although the PSU got only just over 1 per cent of the vote in the 1981 presidential elections and its major figure, presidential candidate Huguette Bouchardeau, just failed with PS support to get onto the second legislative ballot, the party is not going to disappear. This is because the PSU is served by a number of dedicated activists who constitute a fairly large network and, above all, because it is active in the trade unions (CFDT in particular). It was this link with the unions which was important to Michel Rocard – and which he to some extent brought with him to the PS in 1974 – and it remains so today despite the growth of the Socialist Party.

Vladimir Fišera and Peter Jenkins describe the trajectory of the PSU from its post-1968 period when it appeared to be indissociable from the name of Michel Rocard to its rather late entry into the 1981 presidential elections. They analyse the so-called 'autogestion' of the PSU, which it brought to French attention along with others, and its work in the difficult margins of French politics.

Part III of this book is devoted to individual, in-depth studies of particular problems in French political parties. These reflect the current research interests of the authors involved who have been doing fieldwork on these particular problems for some years. As it happens, these are all studies of the parties of the Left – which may well reflect current academic interests – but this is particularly apposite for a France which has just turned to the Left with the 1981 elections.

The chapter (7) by David Hanley deals with the local implementation and activity of the left-wing group CERES in the French Socialist Party départements of the Aude and in Vilaine. It is often stated that local politics is of particular importance in the French political system but this has never been analysed in detail nor have the local-national connections been explained. David Hanley's study reveals that these are much more complicated and varied than is often assumed.

Ille-et-Vilaine and the Aude are quite contrasted départements: one is a new département where the Socialist implantation is recent and the other is an old SFIO area. David Hanley shows that the view of the 'Leninist style assault-squad' led by a centralised Paris oligarchy belongs strictly to the realms of political myth in these two areas. The CERES conquests of the local political scene here are based on a long-haul, hard work, and local political realities, rather than on the takeover of the party, federation by federation.

Chapter 8 is Bruce Graham's study of internal socialist politics. French Socialism is commonly accused of being excessively prone to internal disputes, splits, schisms and arguments 'à l'outrance' on doctrinal points; this chapter discusses the dynamics of the process and provides a model of the way French Socialists interact on matters of conflict which is of relevance to contemporary French Socialism. Professor Graham's chapter compares the internal conflicts which beset the French Socialist Party in 1938 and

1946 when the party, having participated in government, found itself forced to accept a severely limited ability to influence events which caused many to call for a fresh start.

This chapter shows that the sources of dissent were intense and multifarious and that networks of intellectuals, of local leaders and activists, etc., could be quickly constructed. The interaction between intellectual networks and local activists could occur in various ways but, if the occasion was propitious, the sectarian groups could create broad coalitions by articulating grievances or interests within an ideological framework. It is argued that the Popular Front set in motion a game of tendencies in which populist and revolutionary groups challenged the central leaders who were forced to rely on unity and discipline as ways of maintaining their support.

The final chapter (9) is a policy oriented study of the Left's view of the Common Market. This is an issue of unusual conse-quence to the French Left: a sticking point for many years, it was used by President Pompidou to try to split the crystallising Left union, and recently resurfaced at the 1979 European elections in another form (enlargement) as a contentious area of policy. It is also, of course, of interest to readers who need some guide to the future intentions of the Left in Europe and the likely pressures on the Mauroy government as it starts to tackle foreign policy and European reforms (see Mitterrand's propositions 41-44).

In Chapter 9 the authors review both Socialist and Communist Party policies on the Common Market. They discuss the develop-ment of policy, the forces at work in shaping policy and the diffi-culties of the Common Market issue for the Left in France. With the signing of the Common Programme, policies came somewhat into line but they then diverged again. The authors discuss this as well as the continuing points of convergence on the EEC issues, the major problems still facing the parties on the Market and the Community as an issue on the French Left. This chapter is of interest both for its views on the EEC issue in France and the pressures on the Mitterrand presidency and for its insights into the way the Left handles policy-making, discussion, etc.

This book therefore provides an overview of the French Party system at a crucial time in the history of the Fifth Republic: as the leader of the Socialist opposition to the governments of the Right becomes President and as the Socialist Party becomes the majority in the Assembly. It would not be correct or accurate to say that the face of the Fifth Republic has changed or that, now the Left forms the French government, the institutions of the Fifth Republic have reached a sort of plateau of stability and therefore the description of the forces at work on and within political parties given in this volume will form the parameters for the next seven years. It is hoped that although this is a book of research work done by various academics over the last few years its contemporary relevance will make it useful and interesting to students of France and to the interested reader.

PART ONE: THE RIGHT

1   THE GISCARDIANS AND PARTY POLITICS

Ella Searls

CONTEXT OF RESEARCH

This Chapter briefly analyses the nature and development of the non-Gaullist Right during the Fifth Republic, with particular reference to the relationship between the Presidency of Giscard d'Estaing and the Giscardians. The Right in general has changed considerably since 1958, in electoral strength, organisation, coherence and discipline. The impact of presidentialism has been one of the main factors which has channelled the direction of this change. The nature of this impact ranges from the formation of the explicitly presidential alliance, the Union pour la Démocratie Française, to more subtle changes in the structure, ideology and power relations of the parties of the Right. This chapter covers the following areas:

(i)   Introduction: The Impact of Presidentialism;
(ii)   The Development of the 'Giscardians' 1962-81;
(iii) The Internal Structure of the UDF;
(iv)   Conclusions: UDF - Federation or Party?

It should be noted that although considerable research has been carried out by the author on the central organisation and structure of the UDF and on the relationship between the Giscardians and the Presidency, research on the Republican Party and the UDF at constituency level is as yet at an embryonic stage.

INTRODUCTION: THE IMPACT OF PRESIDENTIALISM

It is commonly held amongst commentators on the Fifth Republic that presidentialism has had a considerable impact on the party system and on individual parties. However, the nuances of this relationship have not been subject to much close analysis. The influences of presidentialism are very varied; they range, for example, from the intentional manipulation of coalitions by Presidents, to more subtle side effects such as the impact which presidential patronage has had on the role of parties as recruiting agents for the national political arena. Obviously, other factors such as the electoral system, which has tended to clarify (if only superficially) the party system, and the changing social structure, are not without their impact on political parties, but they will not be discussed at any length in this chapter.

Before discussing the needs of Presidents and elaborating the institutional and pragmatic reasons for the impact of presidentialism on parties of the Right, it is worth observing that a distinction can be made between the effect of Presidents as 'inspirators' of 'their' parties and the effect of Presidents as Presidents. For de Gaulle was, in effect, the founder, spiritual leader and inspirator of the Gaullists; similarly, Giscard d'Estaing was the founder of the Independent Republicans, and in 1981, remains the guiding light of the Republican Party and provides the ideological 'raison d'être' of the UDF. Although Pompidou was readily accepted by the Gaullists as de Gaulle's favoured son, he did not benefit from the same paternal bonding with a party as the other two Presidents. The importance of de Gaulle and Giscard as mentors of their respective parties permeated all other types of relationships which they had with the parties.

The implications of the Fifth Republic Constitution and its subsequent development have been very well documented and analysed. Only a cursory glance at the institutional and constitutional framework is therefore necessary in order to set the scene for evaluating the political needs of the President. The constitution of the Fifth Republic established a mixed parliamentary/presidential regime, which has moved in the years since 1958 towards a presidential system, in that the bulk of decision-making is in the hands of the President. Parliament, although potentially important, has come to play a subservient role both in the articulation of interests and in the control of the government. The reasons for this swing towards presidentialism are many: de Gaulle's pre-eminence in dealing with the foreign and colonial problems facing the early Fifth Republic, the subsequent dominance of the government by de Gaulle, his manipulation of the Constitution and the election of the President, since 1962, by universal suffrage, are all key factors in the strengthening of the office. In addition, the existence of an initially confused and subservient Parliament and since 1962 the development of a 'majority' - a phenomenon virtually unknown in the Fourth Republic - within the National Assembly, which has broadly supported Presidents, has contributed to a sound power base. As Duverger convincingly argues,[1] the more support the President gets from a majority in the National Assembly, the more his power is reinforced; the less support he has from the National Assembly, the more he will have to rely on his constitutional and institutional prerogatives (such as the use of the bloc vote) to reinforce his power. The logical conclusion of this argument, Duverger points out, is the check-mate situation where the President has no coherent support from the National Assembly. Presidents have tended to try to build up majorities and coalitions within the National Assembly to give them support for their programmes, and in this sense the regime is not unambiguously presidential. Additionally, since 1974, it has become clear that Presidents have needed party support and the benefits of electoral machines to put (if not to keep) them in office. This chapter will now consider these two areas: first, the need for party support in the

National Assembly; and second, the need for an electoral machine.

The Need for Support within the National Assembly
It is interesting to note that whilst the Fifth Republic has seen an enormous increase not only in the power of the President but also of the Executive as a whole at the expense of Parliament, Presidents still maintain close links with their support bases in Parliament, and have become increasingly dependent on them. Although de Gaulle claimed that he was 'above party politics' he was not above reaping the benefits of the support of the Gaullists in the National Assembly, who had developed into a stable parliamentary majority following the 1962 general election. Pompidou, a shrewd politician, realising that his position as President was built on rather different ground to that of de Gaulle, was more concerned than his predecessor with building up his electoral position (both in legislative and presidential terms).[2] Consequently, after his accession to power in 1969 he pursued a policy of integrating the Independent Republicans of VGE and leading Centrists into the government majority, in the face of opposition from the Gaullist 'barons'. Giscard (VGE) was elected to office with a very thin margin over Mitterrand in 1974, and, as head of the Independent Republicans who were a minority within the Right holding 55 seats compared to the 183 of the Gaullists, found himself being 'from the majority but apart from it'. Although there is much similarity between the Gaullists and the Giscardians, there are differences in policy – for example, over European affairs, foreign policy, control of the economy and defence – and, more importantly, there are important territorial conflicts highlighted by the competition between the two parties in the 1981 presidential elections.

The mechanics of this situation have led Giscard to be continually concerned with the shape of his power base in the National Assembly and to pursue an explicit coalition policy. Initially Chirac, a leading Gaullist, was Giscard's Prime Minister, and a substantial minority of government ministers have always been Gaullist. However since 1976, Giscard has placed more emphasis on integrating the non-Gaullist Right, as a counterbalance to the Gaullists, whilst at the same time trying to ensure that the Gaullists are not too alienated from the government as he is dependent on their support. During the first two years of his presidency Giscard's strategy took the form of attempting to strengthen and widen the Independent Republicans into a 'parti du président'.[3] However, despite being re-formed in 1976 into the Republican Party, the growth of the party was slow, and this in conjunction with the logistics of the Giscardian 'majorité' led to the formation in February 1978 of the Union pour la Démocratie Française – a loose electoral federation which principally incorporated the Republican Party, the Centre Democrats and the Radicals who together constituted the non-Gaullist majority. The subsequent development of the UDF and the role which it has played has been considerably shaped by the needs of the President. As well as providing a structure for the Giscardian deputies the UDF also serves as an electoral machine for the President and it is to a discussion of this aspect of the President's needs that we will not turn.

The Need for an Electoral Machine
In 1962, the mode of election of the President changed from indirect election by an electoral college, to direct election by universal suffrage. This change meant that in order to be elected, Presidents had to engage in political manoeuverings of a different complexion, and it has, in recent years, increased the need for presidential 'electoral machines'. If de Gaulle was able to win 'mass' appeal by his leadership qualities (skilfully transmitted through the media), lesser mortals such as Giscard d'Estaing have relied more explicitly on marketing techniques and resources for mobilisation of the electorate.

However, whilst Presidents need an electoral base, all three Presidents have tried to go beyond their parties in their election campaigns. They have tried to show themselves as representatives of the national interest and above party politics, in order to be elected. Although de Gaulle is cited as the classic example of this phenomenon, and indeed set the scene for future Presidents, with his emphasis on legitimacy, and representation of the national interest outside of party wranglings, both Pompidou and indeed Giscard have made appeal to higher virtues (stability, legitimacy, pluralism, liberalism and freedom) than those normally espoused by parties. There are several reasons why Presidents have found it an important tactic to go beyond parties in order to be successful.

(i)   The spirit of the office of the presidency, as conceived in the Constitution, was that of an arbiter above the political institutions. Although this role as arbiter has been far overstepped by all three Presidents, it remains important in the conception of the office.

(ii) Presidential politics are in many senses personalised politics in Fifth Republic France. The President is elected as an individual and not as a leader of a political grouping. Rather it is the reverse - that is to say political groupings have grown in electoral strength on the coat-tails of presidential power.

(iii) The party system in the Fifth Republic, particularly in the 1970s, has broadly consisted of four politically relevant parties, whose electoral support has been roughly equal.[4] It is therefore important for Presidents not to tie their appeal too closely to that of one party.

(iv) The electoral system for the President is a two-ballot system with the two candidates who obtain the most votes at the first ballot proceeding to the second ballot. The logic of this system is that the presidential candidate must continually be prepared to overstep the boundaries of his traditional party support, to try to attract voters across the political spectrum on the redistribution of votes at the second ballot.

(v) The final reason for the non-partisan image of the three
     Presidents (and of several presidential candidates) is a
     more general explanation linked to the nature of right-
     wing politics in France. A strong element within conserva-
     tive politics is the appeal to the non-ideological and the
     non-partisan. Conservative politics is based around the
     view on 'man as he is' without recourse to ideological
     fervour. This trend is very apparent in French right-
     wing politics and is linked to the traditional disdain which
     many voters on the Right feel for party organisation and
     discipline. In this context Presidents have stressed the
     non-ideological nature of their 'programmes' and have
     attempted to carry out non-partisan campaigns.

This contradiction and ambiguity in the attitude of Presidents
towards parties obviously has implications for the demands which
are put on parties. Parties are essential for candidates, but may
be a burden for Presidents. Whilst using party resources,
presidential candidates are also trying to divorce themselves from
parties. Thus the structures evolved for organising the elections
and the people used to advise the candidate in the campaign
although largely drawn from the party are often chosen by the
candidate rather than by the party. This often proves to be irksome
for both party members and leaders as an election campaign is
a source of great psychological, practical and ideological gratifi-
cation for the activist and to be denied this by being pushed into
the background by the organiser of a supporting committee or a
presidential adviser may lead to many tensions. For example during the 1981 Presidential campaign there were many tensions in
the UDF. For although the UDF formed the key to the Giscardian
campaign, the role which it played was inevitably discreet, which
alienated many of the militants in the party[5] who felt that the role
of the UDF should have been more evident. There were further
tensions in the party headquarters of the UDF between those who
had been chosen to work at Giscard's campaign headquarters and
those who had not.

Conclusion
The framework of presidentialism has had many repercussions on
all parties within the political spectrum as well as on the structure
of the party system. Apart from the obvious benefits which presidentialism has brought parties of the Right all parties have tended
to be constrained in their activity by the exigencies of the presidential system. Hugues Portelli in a recent article[6] usefully dis-
tinguishes three areas of party life which have been affected by
presidentialism - the organisational, the ideological and the sociological. In the first area he argues that presidentialism has affected the structure and power relations in individual parties; in the
second, he contends that many parties have become ideologically
weaker to the extent that they have become the mouthpieces of
presidential candidates; and in the third, he points out that tradi-

tional party elites are losing their importance as they become ousted in favour of the new breed of technocrats surrounding many presidential candidates. He argues convincingly that presidentialism has led to a weakening of parties. The present author agrees with many of his conclusions. The fact that presidentialism has given the Right more access to political power and has strengthened, at least temporarily, the electoral base of the Right tends to be overshadowed by the manipulation of the parties by the President and the constant pressure on the parties to respond to the needs of the President. It appears that parties, such as the Republican Party, have little impact on policy-making except to the extent that they are used by the President. This domination of the Giscardians by the President will be discussed further below.

THE DEVELOPMENT OF THE 'GISCARDIANS' 1962-81

The nature of the development of the Giscardians as a political grouping has been discussed in detail elsewhere,[7] and the initial part of this section gives only a brief synthesis of the development of the Giscardians prior to the formation of the UDF in 1978.

The present Republican Party was formed in 1976 from the National Federation of Independent Republicans (FNRI). The FNRI itself had begun life as a group of deputies who had broken away from the pro-government bloc in 1962, led by the then young Finance Minister, Giscard d'Estaing. The group consisted mainly of CNIP deputies from the Fourth Republic, moulded in the traditional of 'notable' independent right-wing politics. VGE gradually built up the party (particularly after he had left governmental office in 1966) both nationally and in the country, but the process was a slow and laborious one as he was faced with the dual problems of amalgamating and disciplining deputies who were used to functioning as Independents and trying to widen the base of the party amongst an electorate who were traditionally suspicious of political parties. These problems were compounded by VGE's divergence over policy with many in his party; for Giscard's then 'liberal', 'reformist' approach (particularly in social affairs) alienated many of the hardliners within the party. Nevertheless the party grew considerably and by 1974 there were 55 deputies and party organisation in all 'departéments'. The future of the party changed in 1974 with VGE's accession to the Presidency, and since then the President has pursued a policy of renovating, liberalising and popularising the party. In May 1977 the party was reformed into the Parti républicain under Jean-Pierre Soisson with a more liberal mass and popular image.

However the balance of power was such in the National Assembly, that Giscard wanted to bring together all the non-Gaullist majority parties into one grouping - at the same time he hoped to attract some deputies from the opposition Centre. Negotiation for the formation of the UDF took place between the leaders of the potential constituent parties during 1977, in preparation for its eventual launching in February 1978 for the legislative elections.

Summary of Reasons for the Formation of the UDF
- (i) VGE was still unhappy with his own party, the Republicans - despite their recent formation into the PR.
- (ii) It was easier to have a new political grouping than to try (continually) to reform the old one.
- (iii) He wanted to have a counterbalance to the Gaullist Party which in 1976 had been revitalised and reformed as the RPR under Chirac.
- (iv) Giscard was searching for a coalition strategy which would sustain him as President.
- (v) VGE had long hoped to build a large Centre party (an idea echoed by Poniatowski) which would embrace different political groupings. This aim was based on his liberal view of French society as a diverse and pluralist.

The UDF principally brought together the Parti républicain (Secretary General, Jacques Blanc), the Centre des démocrates sociaux (President, Jean Lauarmet), and the Parti républicain radical et radical socialiste (President Jean-Jacques Servan-Schreiber). These three parties had different histories, philosophies and policies. Both the Centre Democrats and the Radicals had long political histories, stemming from the Third Republic (although both had been restructured due to splits under the Fifth Republic), whilst the Republican Party was in many ways a more 'modern' party, born under the Fifth Republic though rooted in the Independent tradition. The Radicals represented a secular, conservative tradition in French political life, whereas the Centre Democrats were the inheritors of French Social Catholicism - both were fiercely independent. The Republican Party, which overshadowed the other two parties in its parliamentary strength and in its electoral support, was itself a mixture of economic and social liberalism, and rigid conservatism. The parties potentially differed on economic and social policy as well as on European policy and the role of France in the world. The UDF, therefore, was attempting to bring together ideologically diverse groups which had historically been in competition, particularly at local level, as well as deputies who traditionally resented any form of organisation. The UDF also included two smaller groupings - the Mouvement Démocrate et Socialiste Français (President, Max Lejeune) a small centrist grouping, and the political clubs, Perspectives et Réalités (President, Jean Fourcarde) which were sympathetic to, but not directly affiliated to, the Republican Party.

The UDF is basically a federation which co-ordinated parties and groupings who supported the actions of Giscard d'Estaing, as Article 2 of the party statute states,

L'union pour la Démocratie Française a pour objet de cordonner l'action des partis politiques, associations et adhérents indi-

viduels qui la composent, en vue de l'ouvrir pour l'unité
nationale, le progrès et la justice. Elle affirme son attachement
aux institutions de la Verne République et aux orientations de
pensée et d'action du Président de la République, telles qu'elles
sont exprimées dans 'Démocratie Française'.

Initially, the organisation of the UDF was very light, consisting
of a council, a 'Délégué Général' - Michel Pinton (who was appointed by Giscard) - a President - Jean Lecanuet - and a small
central organisation. After the 1978 election further national
bodies were created, a parliamentary group and UDF organisations
at departmental level. In addition the UDF began to recruit direct
members, which swelled the ranks of affiliated members from the
constituent parties. That is to say that the UDF began to take on
features of a 'normal' party organisation.

The main 'raison d'être' for the UDF was, and remains, to provide a structure which effectively co-ordinated support for Giscard and his policies as expounded in the bible of the movement
'Démocratie Francaise'. This is illustrated by a quote from the
party newspaper - UDF scope - which appeared shortly before
the 1981 presidential election.

> . . . la vocation de l'Udf: être an centre de l'échiquier politique,
> le mouvement de la raison et de l'imagination, le mouvement qui
> soutient l'action de VGE et son projet de société, 'Démocratie
> Française'.[8]

Support for the President is, it is claimed by the activists, the
'glue which holds the parts together'. If this is the case, it is
sometimes ineffectual. For although on the surface the UDF has
had many successes, particularly as an electoral machine - for
example in the 1978 legislative elections and 1979 European elections
- and in organising the 'Giscardian' Deputies in the National
Assembly under the skilful leadership of Roger Chinaud (it has
had less success in the Senate), there are within it many under-
currents of problems and discontent. Many of these problems stem
from the ambiguous nature of the federation and in its relations
with the constituent parts, which will be discussed in the final
section.

There are, very briefly, several areas of discontent: conflicts
over territory, policy differences, differences over the tactics
which the federation should pursue, and finally, differences of
opinion over the nature of the UDF.

Conflicts over Territory. Quite naturally, like individuals, parties
which are thrown together into an alliance, compete for space and
territory. This occurs for two reasons. Firstly, the smaller parties,
fearful for their loss of identity, are often hostile to the PR,
particularly at the local level. Secondly, the PR itself, is often
uneasy within the federation as, since 1974, they have, albeit
under a different label, seen themselves as the 'parti du président'

and they therefore resent the role played by the UDF and the minor parties within it.

Policy Differences.   As mentioned above, there are often divergences over the policy which the UDF should pursue. Areas which prove particularly troublesome are foreign policy, European policy and social policy. These policy differences are often worked out beyond closed doors, but may come out into the open, as for example the reaction of the CDS to Giscard's attitude to Europe during the 1979 European election (the CDS resented his 'Gaullist' European line as they themselves favoured a more federalist Europe).

Divergence over Tactics.   Some dissension in the UDF occurs over the tactics which the union should be following. For although the UDF form a substantial part of the 'majorité', it has in theory the alternative of moving towards the Centre Left or firming up alliances with the Gaullists.[9] A liberal element within the party who are concerned with the reduction of social and to a certain extent economic inequalities – for example, Stoléru, Foucarde, Bariani and Stasi, and Pinton – identify the Giscardians as a movement of the Centre and follow a move towards the Centre Left. Others, such as Blanc, are inclined to favour a strengthening of unity with the Gaullists, both for ideological reasons and on the grounds of 'better the devil you know'.[10] Although such disputes over tactics tend to be submerged they are obviously of considerable significance for the future development of the UDF.

Conflict over the Nature of the UDF.   Finally, the most fundamental conflict is that over the very nature of the UDF. The spirit of the UDF was that it was to be an electoral alliance, federating the parties which supported Giscard. It has clearly become more than this, and to a certain extent has begun to usurp the function of the constituent parties. The question at stake is whether this trend should continue, resulting in a fused structure or whether the UDF should remain a co-ordinating body. As one would expect, it is mainly the leaders of the constituent parties, for example, Blanc, Stasi and Diligent, who favour the latter solution – that is, a limited UDF – whereas the founders of the movement, Lecanuet, Soisson, Foucarde and in particularly Pinton, favour the former solution of a fused UDF. The actual course which the UDF takes will depend not so much on the views of its leaders, or on its success, but on the needs of Giscard d'Estaing.

   To conclude, the precarious and undecided future of the UDF and the disparate nature of its composition make it inevitable that the constituent parties will emphasise their own separate identities. From time to time, therefore, each party within the UDF flexes its muscles to demonstrate its autonomy. This can take place in a variety of ways – at party congresses, in the National Assembly or at elections.[11] For example, the poor showing of the UDF in the early December 1980 by-election led to a reappraisal of the nature

and success of the UDF by leaders of the constituent parties and
a reassertion of their autonomy. However to date (spring 1981)
these shows of strength have not threatened the nature of the
UDF, for as its leaders know the constituent parties have, on the
whole, more to gain from staying in the movement than from moving outside of it.

THE STRUCTURE OF THE UDF

The internal structure of the UDF was created within a federal
perspective. Thus, in principle all the main constituent elements
are represented equally in most organs of the party. This federalist approach was explicitly pursued by the organisation's
founders (VGE, Soisson, Pinton, Lecanuet and Foucarde) in order
to minimise competition and conflict between the component parts.
In particular, it was designed to safeguard the interests of the
two smaller parties, the Radicals and the Centre Democrats who
were anxious about losing their identity within the new organisation. The structure of the party was also a manifestation of the
principle of 'pluralism with unity' which VGE had expounded in
his work 'Démocratie Française'. The UDF tries to be sufficiently
flexible to represent the independence of its integral parts and
strong enough to maintain unity. However, in practice, 'pluralism'
has often meant disharmony and 'unity' has necessitated the super-
vision and intervention from the centre in order to achieve political balance at local level and resolve personality clashes, for,
as in many other spheres, conflicts between individuals and
groups over issues such as power and territory are rarely solved
through structural mechanisms. An analysis of the internal organisation of the party is illuminating, for the structure is, in many
senses, a microcosm of the UDF as a movement: the problems posed
by the functioning of the organisation reflect many of those faced
by the movement as a whole.

The membership of the UDF consists of the affiliated members
of the membership of the three main parties and also of direct
members, who the UDF claimed had reached 80,000 by March 1981.
Both the affiliated members and direct members have a certain
representation in the decision-making bodies, but as in the PR
it is the parliamentarians and local office-holders, and above all
the leadership, who dominate the parties. Party congresses for
the activists are held yearly (Paris 1979, Orleans 1980). They
are centred around certain themes which are produced for discussion by work groups - for example in 1980 ten themes were
discussed including 'the social effort of the nation', 'liberties',
'growth' and 'planning'. In addition to the congresses, mass
rallies are now held yearly ('fêtes de la Liberté') which include
cultural and musical attractions as well as a discussion of politics.

Central Organisation
The national structure of the UDF which is paralleled at departmental and circonscriptional levels, consists of the Convention,
the National Council and the Executive Bureau. The Convention
is the representative body of the UDF which in principle 'defines
the policies of the movement'. It consists of all Council members,
UDF parliamentarians, UDF and local and regional politicians and
a number of representatives from the constituent parties. It meets
at least every two years, or when called by the President. In
practice it seems to have little influence on the leadership. It
brings together the party loyal and is used by the leadership as
a forum for explaining policy. For example the second convention
of the UDF which met in a dispirited mood prior to the spring
1981 presidential elections did little more than discuss the party
leadership's explanation of the role which the UDF was to play in
the presidential election campaign.

The council of the UDF meets monthly to 'direct the policies of
the Union'. It is responsible for appointing the President, Vice-
Presidents, 'Délégué Général' and Treasurer of the Union, although
to date (April 1981) the Council has merely notified the initial
choices of Lecanuet as President and Pinton as 'Délégué General'.
The Council consists of a maximum of 25 members (although normally it has 20 to 22) including 3 representatives of each of the 3
main parties, 1 representative of the Mouvement Démocrate et
Socialiste, 1 representative from the Clubs, and the Presidents of
the parliamentary groups.[12] The additional members are chosen
with care (they either come from one of the constituent parties,
or are eminent people supporting the UDF) in order not to upset
the political balance. The Council nominates from its midst the
Executive Bureau which consists of at least seven members – the
President of the Union, the three Vice-Presidents, the Délégué
Général, and the Presidents of the two parliamentary groups. It
meets at least twice a month to 'implement council decisions' but,
in practice, it appears to be the key decision-making body.

The UDF also has well-developed central services consisting of
a series of commissions and study groups (normally presided over
by members of the Council) and a growing army of paid officials
who carry out the daily work of co-ordinating and marketing. The
services cover such areas as: elections, federations, direct
membership, candidate 'formation' and publicity.

Local Organisation
In early 1981 Unions existed not only in the 'départements', but
also at circonscriptional level, and the UDF central organisation
planned to extend the movement to cantonal level. The attempt at
balance between the different political elements comprising the
Union is echoed at local level. However, the balance is hampered
not only by personal and political competition but also in some
cases by the lack of personnel to fill the elected offices. For often
the constituent parties are ill-organised and lacking in personnel,
and it appears that militants sometimes do not have the time and

energy to carry out what is often seen as 'duplicate' work in the UDF. A departmental delegate is appointed by the central organisation 'in collusion' with the Departmental Council and the delegate liaises between the centre and the localities. He is used by the centre to keep an eye on the political problems of the Departmental Unions and to ensure their smooth functioning. He also liaises with the centre over the choice of UDF candidates and tactics.

The membership of a Departmental Council (which varies in number from thirty to 100) consists of at least one representative from each constituent party, representatives of the direct membership and the UDF parliamentarians, general councillors and mayors of the 'département'. The Departmental Council elects a President, Vice-President and Executive Bureau of between five and ten members. In principal these posts are shared between the constituent parties - for example if the President is from the Republican Party ideally the Vice-President should be a member of the CDS and the Treasurer should be a Radical; however, in practice, as noted above, this may be difficult to achieve.

On the whole the degree of success of the Departmental Unions of the UDF is dependent on the nature of the constituent parties - the activists and the leaders. In some areas the federation may have very little impact on the constituent parties, in others, such as the Pas de Calais, it is highly successful and tends to dominate the other parties. The central Union, for its part, tries to channel the direction which the local federations take, and attempts to stimulate their growth. If, as it is claimed, the UDF is a forum of ideas and a haven of internal democracy, these are very much constrained by the needs and domination of the centre.

CONCLUSIONS: UDF - FEDERATION OR PARTY?

As discussed above, the original idea of the UDF was that it would act as a light co-ordinating body which federated the constituent parties. Assurances were made by its founders in the secret negotiations of 1977 conducted between presidential advisers and the leaders of the future component parties[13] that it was not, or would not become a political party. To a certain extent this has remained the case as the constituent parties have kept their separate organisations, identities and activists. However, the longer the UDF has stayed in existence, the more it has taken on the function and characteristics of a party in its own right, although at the time of writing (spring 1981) it still remains a Union both by its structure and its statutes.

First, it fights elections. Although UDF candidates kept their own party labels they stood under the UDF label in the 1978 legislative elections.[14] Furthermore, the UDF stood as the UDE in the 1979 European elections. In the 1981 presidential elections, the UDF, for reasons already explained, played a fairly low-key role, although it was the UDF rather than the constituent parties around which the 'comités de Soutien' evolved and the UDF played a vital role in organising the campaign. Secondly, the UDF plays a substantial role in selecting and forming potential parliamentary candidates. This is a key area of dispute between the UDF and the constituent parties who jealously guard this role, and argue that they are best placed to achieve it. Thirdly the UDF is increasingly involved in mobilising the electorate and widening the power base of presidential support. It is increasingly building up the services and personnel to achieve this. Fourthly, it organises at the parliamentary and senatorial level and the leaders of legislative groups are involved in the party machinery - that is to say the UDF is more than a legislative clique. Finally it could be argued that it has a distinct political identity in the eyes of the electorate.

Having identified some functions of the UDF which are similar to those carried out by a political party, it should be noted that the constituency parties argue that in reality they perform many of these functions which are merely directed or channelled by the UDF. For example, they argue that the UDF has no local resources and that in reality it is the activists of the local parties who provide the manpower and expertise. There is, it appears, a great deal of ambiguity in the respective roles and a great deal of duplication in the work carried out.

In addition I would add some provisos to identify the UDF as a party. First, it does not itself provide a source of recruitment to political leadership - this is partly because of the nature of the impact of presidentialism on recruitment which has been discussed elsewhere - partly because the UDF is in this sense still a marketing organisation which grooms and markets candidates from the other parties and partly from lack of independent personnel. This does appear to be changing with the growth in the number of specifically 'UDF' men and women. Secondly, it has no clear ideology or set of principles except those expounded by VGE in 'Démocratie Française' - however this is not necessarily a drawback to parties on the Right, and hence is not necessarily a useful criteria for assessing the UDF as a political party. Finally, despite prediction of increasing clarity and stability, the world of French right-wing politics remains kaleidoscopic in its nature, and it is therefore unwise to generalise about the future development of a political grouping. To date (spring 1981) the future of the UDF is tied to the needs of Giscard as President, but as the experience of the Gaullists have shown, this does not necessarily mean that its continued existence is dependent on political office.

POSTSCRIPT: 1981 ELECTIONS

The defeat of Giscard in the presidential elections and of the Right in the legislative elections has inevitably had a traumatic impact on the UDF. Many of the problems of the Union which have been discussed above have come to the fore in the 'débâcle' of the election period. The former covert squabbling between personalities and factions over strategies and direction have come out into the open.

Following Giscard's defeat as President, the UDF and the RPR hastily formed themselves into an electoral alliance of the Union pour la nouvelle majorité (UNM) in order to fight the legislative elections on a (superficially) united front. However, the two parts of the alliance chose to sit as autonomous groups within the new National Assembly. Both were severely defeated – the Gaullists obtaining 83 seats as compared to 155, and the Giscardians 61 seats as compared to 119 in the previous Parliament. At present (June 1981) the UDF still remains an alliance of Republicans, Centrists and Radicals – the latter two groups staying within the alliance if for no other reason than they are not in themselves large enough to form parliamentary groups. The Union is, given the complexion of the government, much more firmly placed on the Right than many of its members would choose. Political strategy necessitates the submergence of any factions which favour a soft approach towards the Socialists.

Finally, many of the leading personnel of the UDF have been defeated in the election. Party leaders such as Deniau, Lecat Chinaud and Bassot have been ousted from their political seats, and consequently new 'leaders' will have to be found. Most importantly, Giscard's departure has robbed the UDF of its prestigious position; Giscard's influence within the possibly 'new style' UDF is uncertain. To sum up, the present position of the UDF looks bleak. Not only are they out of office, but, whilst publicly underestimating their plight, they are demoralised, disorganised and humiliated. They face not only the Socialists in government but the Gaullists within the opposition. Their future is linked not only to the Right in general, but to their ability to revitalise and restructure their organisation.[15]

NOTES

1   See M. Duverger, 'L'Echec au Roi', Pans, 1978.
2   For a synopsis of this strategy, see M. Anderson, Political Strategies and Coalition Building in France, unpublished paper.
3   For a more detailed analysis see E. Searls, The Republican Party in 'Giscard, Giscardians and Giscardism', ed. V. Wright, Allen and Unwin, forthcoming.
4   This, of course, was not the case in the 1981 legislative elections.
5   See 'Le Monde', 8/9 March 1981.
6   H. Portelli, La présidentialisation des partis français, 'Pouvoirs', 14, 1980.
7   See for example, J. Colliard, 'Les Républicains Indépendants', Paris, 1972; J.C. Colliard, Le Giscardisme, 'Pouvoirs', 9, 1979; M. Anderson, 'Conservative Politics in France', London, 1974, and C. Ysmal, Le chemin difficile du parti Républicain,

'Projet', 118, September – October 1977.

8 'UDF Scope', 18 April, 1981.

9 Interviews.

10 For a discussion of these different currents see J.L. Thiebault, Le Paradoxe de l'Udf Cohésion et Conflits, 'Revue Politique et Parlementaire', 889, November – December 1980.

11 See 'Le Monde', 9 December 1980.

12 Additional members should also reflect the political balance of the Council.

13 In particular Pinton, Soisson, Lecanuet, Griotteray, Ridacci, Bariani.

14 See examples of election literature in 'Programmes et Engagements Electoraux; Elections générales des 12 et 19 Mars 1978', 3 vols, Assemblée Nationale.

15 I am indebted to the SSRC and to Newcastle University for various grants which have enabled me to carry out this study. Much of the material in this chapter came from interviews with party leaders and activists, conducted in 1980 and 1981.

2 GAULLISM, ADVANCED CAPITALISM

AND THE FIFTH REPUBLIC

Philip G. Cerny

The 1981 presidential and parliamentary elections have demonstrated that Gaullism, despite its decline in the late 1970s and its
losses this year, still plays an important part in French party
politics. It is the only party of the broad Right in France to have
a mass-based membership, an efficient national organisation, a
slick campaigning style in the American mould, and a long-term
presidentialist strategy based on the populist leadership of Jacques
Chirac. It provides a contrast with the diffident yet haughty style
of the former President of the Republic, Valéry Giscard d'Estaing,
and the loose coalition of 'cadre' parties[1] which supported him. It
is currently the 'motor force' of a rather disorganised right-wing
coalition, still shell-shocked by the unexpected defeat of Giscard,
and dependent since the beginning of the Fifth Republic upon
the existence of a right-wing President in office for an organisational focus.

However, although the Gaullist Party - named, since 1976, the
Rassemblement pour la République (RPR), the Rally for the Republic - still retains some of the aura of legitimacy surrounding
the founding father and first President of the Fifth Republic,
General Charles de Gaulle (a national leader who emerged to
create a French government-in-exile during the Second World War
and worked thereafter to establish a presidential regime), today's
'neo-Gaullism' has undergone a considerable metamorphosis in its
attempt to adapt to the post de Gaulle era. The party system has
changed; no longer is Gaullism the 'dominant party' of the Right
- much less of the party system as a whole.[2] The occupant of the
presidential office in the Elysée Palace - for the second consecu-
tive seven-year term - is a non-Gaullist; since last May, the post
has been held by Socialist Party leader François Mitterrand. The
electoral appeal of Chirac is limited and the policy proposals of
the RPR are a vague combination of restrictions on public expenditure and reflationary expansionism. And many politicians of the
non-Gaullist Right are biding their time, waiting for their revenge
on a Chirac whose forceful opposition to Giscard on the first of
the two ballots of the presidential election in 1981, followed by
lukewarm support on the second, is seen by them to be the single
most important factor in the former president's defeat.

Thus Gaullism's long-term future will depend upon the party's
capacity to confront obstacles at several levels from the 'grass
roots' upwards. Chirac's potential success as a presidential candidate in 1988 - the 'sine qua non' of any genuine Gaullist revival -
is by no means assured, nor even likely. But the party remains,

24

thrust once again into the leading role on the Right, in the short
term at least, and certain to retain a major voice in any restructuring of the right-wing coalition at the local level, in the National
Assembly, in the formulation of the opposition's economic strategy
and in the campaign to recapture the presidency later on. This
chapter will attempt to examine the reasons for Gaullism's early
success - laying particular stress upon economic and social context which facilitated Gaullist dominance of the first decade of the
Fifth Republic along with the legacies of this so-called 'État UDR'
- and will then consider the problems and prospects of Gaullism
in the 1980s.

GAULLISM AND THE TRANSITION TO THE ADVANCED
CAPITALIST STATE

Gaullism has a privileged place in the history of the Fifth Republic.
The word itself represents a phenomenon of great diversity. Not
merely a political party, it also represents a wider social movement growing out of the Second World War and expressing a view
held across much of the political spectrum that the parliamentary
system - the political institutions of the Third and Fourth Republics - had failed to deal effectively with social, economic and
international changes during the twentieth century, and that
priority had to be given to modernising the French state. Furthermore, as the name implies, Gaullism in action is historically linked
to the leadership of one man: as the organisational vehicle for de
Gaulle - particularly as, in his later years in power, he attempted
to 'routinise' his charismatic authority and to create a state which
would be stable and durable after his own departure.[3] Gaullism
as a political party claimed to be more than just a party, but
rather the organisational embodiment of the new Fifth Republic
itself.[4]

Its 'étatiste' ideology[5], its development in the 1960s into what
was then judged to be a 'dominant party', and its hegemonic
penetration into the administrative structures of the state all
seemed to make it a party different from the others. Even its fall
from power after the death of de Gaulle's successor, President
Georges Pompidou, in 1974, left it with an aura of exceptional
legitimacy, but its decline raises new questions about its historical
role in this period of transition from unstable parliamentarism to
presidentialism and from a society still in transition from a situation of very uneven social, economic and political development
into an advanced capitalist society.

Therefore the historical significance of Gaullism cannot be judged
merely by its ideological façade, its ability to retain or regain
power, nor the constitutional structures which are the most tang-
ible legacy of the era of Gaullist dominance, but needs to be
examined in the perspective of its conjunction and interaction
with the rapid development of new underlying structures in
French society. The concept of 'advanced capitalism' is complex,

and can be explained and interpreted in many different ways.[6] It
is taken here to involve a number of closely linked developments
in the economy and in society; in the 'functions' (tasks, roles,
activities)[7] which the state carries out; and in the structures of
the state itself. Gaullism, I shall argue, is best seen as a vital
linkage mechanism, previously lacking in the French polity, per-
mitting the co-ordination of changes at each of these three levels
(and between the levels) during the crucial period of transition
and enhancing the role of the state as the primary agent of
structured change. However, once the period of transition was
completed, and the advanced capitalist state constructed and set
in place, Gaullism's 'raison d'être' was diminished; however, the
party persisted, and a long period of groping towards some form
of neo-Gaullism began.

Problems of Gaullism and Advanced Capitalism
The Fifth Republic came into being during a period of rapid change
in the structures of French society and politics, structures which
had not undergone a homogeneous process of 'modernisation' from
traditional to industrial society in the nineteenth and early twentieth centuries. The transition to an 'advanced capitalist society'
involved closely interrelated processes which, in other societies
such as Britain, the United States and Germany, had been pre-
ceded by a stage of 'industrial capitalism' in which manufacturing
industry both dominated the economic sphere and dictated the
pace and direction of social and political change more generally.

These processes, as we have said, have involved a number of
changes, in France as elsewhere. In the economic sphere, some
of the features of advanced capitalism include: the concentration
and rationalisation of industrial production to adapt to the more
and more demanding exigencies of competitiveness on an international scale within a more and more interlocking world economy,
with the increasing vertical and horizontal integration of firms;
the decline of the rural sector, usually to below 10 per cent of
the workforce, along with a growing gap between large-scale
agriculture and a relatively impoverished smallholding sector; the
expansion of the service sector and of employment in the public
sector; the expansion of credit and the increasingly predominant
role of financial institutions; the crucial significance within each
of the above processes, but developing a momentum of its own,
of technological innovation and development and of the organisational structures set up to apply new technologies, etc. (The list
itself, and the relationship among the processes indicated, is of
course at the centre of theoretical controversies.)

Social corollaries of the above changes might include: urbanisation and suburbanisation; the 'proletarianisation' of much of
the previously self-employed workforce from agriculture, the
retail trade, artisan manufacture, etc.; the formal separation of
the ownership of the means of production, through shareholding,
from day-to-day management of firms; the spread of mass com-
munications media; mass education; the growth of a 'consumer

culture' and the privatisation of personal life; greater geographical mobility; secularisation of morality; and the like.

But for this chapter the most important set of features of advanced capitalism concerns the role of the state. On the one hand, the state has assumed a number of economic functions. These include production or 'supply-side' activities such as sub-sidies, investment, credit, research and development, and public shareholding in firms (including nationalisation); consumption or 'demand-side' functions such as providing public and social ser-vices, welfare provision, state procurement, and more complex forms of fiscal and monetary policy; and the expansion of state activities at international level - trade and payments, participation in international economic organisations including common markets, development aid, etc. In countries which experienced a relatively homogeneous phase of industrial capitalism, such developments on the part of the state tend to arise in an incremental fashion as trade expands, industries decline, firms demand large injec-tions of capital to achieve economies of scale in shifting world markets, and the like. In France, however, the rapidity of change after 1945 meant that the state took a leading role in promoting specific forms of change.

Indeed, in France as in other advanced capitalist societies, the major bone of contention with regard to the activities of the state - the dominant 'issue cleavage' of the advanced capitalist state - concerns the overall pattern of deployment of state policies for the expansion of industry, the protection of employment, the distribution of incomes, and the promotion of economic growth in general. The greater the range, scope and co-ordination of government measures, the more the economy is said to be 'plan-ned'; in contrast, absence of planning is supposed to give greater scope to 'free market forces'. However, property ownership generally remains in private hands, and, in a society which is still capitalist, the primary goal of planning itself is to keep the private sector profitable and expanding. On the other hand, in a liberal democracy, mass demands expressed through political parties and trade unions - as well as the demands of smaller sec-tors of society expressed through pressure groups, social net-works and strategically important economic and financial interests - will influence policy decisions in a number of ways and may set parameters for certain state activities.

Finally, these activities of the state lead to changes in the organisation of the state itself. The main tendency, of course, is for bureaucracy to grow, and this raises crucial questions con-cerning the control and co-ordination of the decision-making and administrative apparatuses. The structures of the advanced capitalist state are usually analysed in terms of two 'norms': (1) efficiency, or the capacity of the state structures to achieve the goals set for them with a minimum of complexity and waste; and (2) autonomy, or the capacity of the state to make decisions independently of the possessors of economic and financial power, and to act strategically in shaping the economy in an innovative

fashion. And it was precisely on these areas that the Gaullist
critique of the parliamentary regime of the Third and Fourth
Republics focused, and it was towards the resolution of the problems of transition to advanced capitalism through the modernisation of the state apparatus itself that Gaullist constitutional
and party-political reforms were aimed.

In pursuing their self-appointed task of 'modernising' the
French state, de Gaulle and the Gaullists were above all concerned
with establishing institutions and procedures which could be both
efficient and autonomous. Their critique of parliamentarism was
essentially that the Third and Fourth Republics had been too
divided and weak to control the production, consumption and
international functions which the state needed to assume out of
necessity in an advanced capitalist society operating within a complex world economy. Only the reform of the state itself could
provide the 'motor force' for such changes - especially given the
rapidity of change in post-war France and the leading role which
the state played in the absence of a 'modernising oligarchy'
among the industrial elite.[8]

In the process of instituting these new structures, Gaullism in
its various guises attained a position of dominance. However, unlike the dominance of its closest ancestor, Bonapartism, Gaullist
hegemony was not based on the charismatic authority of an 'heroic
leader' alone, but on liberal-democratic legitimacy.[9] In attempting
to reform the state while retaining liberal-democratic legitimacy,
Gaullism, as the dominant political party during the crucial transition to the Fifth Republic, was the key transmission belt between
the processes of economic modernisation which had taken off after
the Second World War - and which had already profoundly transformed parts of the bureaucracy - and the political institutions
of the state. In so doing, the Gaullists, although imperfectly
united on the precise role of the state, nevertheless pursued a
vision of an active state taking the lead in social and economic
transformation.

In the 1970s, as advanced capitalism became more deeply rooted
in France, the role of the state also changed, becoming less plan-
ned (if no less interventionist in a more ad hoc manner), particularly under the leadership of Giscard d'Estaing and his second
Prime Minister, Raymond Barre (1976-81). The stability of the
political institutions, moreover, is undergoing a new and crucial
test with the election of the first president not to belong to the
Right of the political spectrum in the entire history of the Fifth
Republic. So far, de Gaulle's successors - particularly in the long
period of economic recession following the oil crisis of 1973-4 -
have not been able to dominate the state in the same fashion. In
this context, Gaullism appears in a new guise - a mixture of
residual Gaullism from the early days and an organisational vehicle
for the current leadership of Jacques Chirac. Its other leaders
are divided, and its legitimacy as the party of the Fifth Republic
has been eroded under the Giscard presidency. It demonstrated
its disruptive potential on the Right in the 1981 presidential election;

whether it can reassert its leadership within the right in the new conditions is uncertain. None the less, the historical conjuncture of Gaullism with the advanced capitalist state itself - during the first years of the Fifth Republic - is now a thing of the past.

Gaullism and the Coming of the Fifth Republic

In pursuing the modernisation of the capitalist state in France, Gaullism did not simply reflect the objectives of French capitalists. It is well known that much of French capital was dragged kicking and screaming into the second half of the twentieth century. Artisan methods of production long dominated all but a few sectors of manufacturing. Even in the larger firms in textiles, steel, shipbuilding and the like, microeconomic organisation usually took the form of a particularly unadventurous type of family ownership and control. Cartellisation and market sharing restricted expansion. The lack of risk capital through conservative attitudes on the part of financial institutions, and the lack of demand for risk capital through a tradition of self-financing, combined to limit innovations. A widespread willingness among both industrial and agricultural producers to resort to tariff protection in the face of foreign competition, along with the orientation of agricultural production, services, the distributive trades and even much manufacturing to local and regional, rather than national or international, markets damped down pressures for change. Finally, the French Empire retained its mercantilist character. Thus in the century prior to the Second World War, despite some periods of expansion and structural change, the development of the French economy was slow and uneven. Indeed, its relative isolation and self-sufficiency actually mitigated the effects of the world depression of the 1930s. And the slow growth of population, exacerbated by the huge losses of the First World War (leading to an actual decline in the 1930s), reinforced this relative structural stagnation.

But the impact of the Second World War, during which Gaullism was born as a political movement, was different. Not only was the defeat of France in 1940 politically and militarily catastrophic, and the fate of the residual French war effort under de Gaulle in London subject to continuous American and British pressure to keep France in the condition of a second-class ally, but the economic organisation of the capitalist world after 1945 was shaped by American war aims and visions of free trade as a guarantor of peace. The often divergent national capitalist economies of the late nineteenth and early twentieth centuries, whose economic and political rivalry had created great empires and caused two world wars, were brought into the sphere of the Open Door, whose principle was interpenetration and interdependence (ideologically buttressed by anti-communism) and whose motor force was America's emergence as the only economic and military superpower in the post-war capitalist world. Along with economic interpenetration, funded by the Marshall Plan, went the military integration of the North Atlantic Treaty Organisation after 1949 and the institutionalisation, in the United States, of the 'National Security State', whose 'raison d'être' was the protection of the whole capitalist world.

The first manifestations of Gaullism had nothing to do with party politics, but rather with maintaining an independent French war effort, the Free French, at first in London and then in liberated Algiers and finally Paris, where it became a provisional government. But party conflict was always latent in the coalition, and after the election of a constituent assembly dominated by a Socialist-Communist coalition in October 1945, and de Gaulle's resignation as President of the Provisional Government in January 1946, pressure for a Gaullist party mounted. The adoption by a small plurality of the parliamentary constitution of the Fourth Republic in October 1946, despite vigorous opposition by de Gaulle, led to the decision to set up the Rassemblement du Peuple Français in 1947 as an anti-system movement of national unity and constitutional renovation. But, despite excellent results in local elections, the RPF could not prove itself at first at the national level because of an agreement among the pro-system parties not to call early parliamentary elections (the next statutory date being 1951).

The RPF had difficulty during this period in keeping the constitutional issue alive, and rapidly lost influence and legitimacy. The economy revived under the influence of the new Planning Commissariat and with the help of the Marshall Plan and the opening up of intra-European trade under the aegis of the Organisation for European Economic Co-operation (OEEC). New structures, both economic and political, were established on European, Atlantic and 'free world' levels, all of which drew France into the expansionary context of the new capitalist world economy. And, significantly, parts of the state apparatus - the administrative state, at least - adapted to the mixed economy and the welfare state through new processes and institutions, many of which had been initiated under the provisional government: the planning process, nationalisation of the major energy industries and of a number of key financial institutions, social security, etc. The extensive procedures for consultation between industry and the state through the Modernisation Committees of the Planning Commissariat helped to sustain a new spirit of economic expansion, despite inflationary pressures and anti-system opposition from both flanks - the RPF on the Right and the Communist Party on the Left.

At the same time, however, the parliamentary system came to resemble the Third Republic more and more. Anti-system parties - Communists and Gaullists - often acted as a 'blocking quarter' in the National Assembly, opposing governments and their policies, while the rather heterogeneous parties straddling the centre of the parliamentary spectrum - the Socialist Party (SFIO), the Christian Democratic MRP (Mouvement Républicain Populaire), the Radical Party and the various conservative and independent groups - could only reach short-term agreements and regularly demanded sacrificial lambs in the nature of the overthrow of governments. Trade unions, weak and divided, were in a running battle with virulently anti-union employers. Private capital was still dominated by traditional bourgeois elements, conservative and authoritarian, and afraid of the new winds of competition and of the demands of 'consensus politics' in a period when the Cold War was an internal conflict between French classes as well as an international conflict between East and West. The state in the 1950s went from setback to setback at home and abroad - where the colonial wars in Indochina and Algeria proved to be a disastrous drain on men, resources and morale as well as contributing to political conflict within France - all in spite of the rapid transformation of the society, the economy and much of the bureaucracy.[10]

It was, in fact, the collapse of the parliamentary system in 1958 which created a vacuum which only the Gaullists were in a position to fill. The parties which had dominated the governments of the Fourth Republic were unable to agree on a course of action, and appeared worn out and discredited. The Communist Party was not in a position to exploit the situation; both domestic anti-communism and the veiled threat of American intervention if the 'free world' were to be threatened put the PCF out of the running. No doubt General de Gaulle's skill in playing the government against the rebel army officers who had carried out a 'coup d'état' in Algiers was a significant factor; however, the fact that even their leader General Salan could think of no alternative to a public cry of 'Vive de Gaulle!' indicated the poverty of alternatives. And as the infrastructure of the Gaullist organisation, left over from the badly-eroded RPF and based on wartime loyalties, was still almost intact, the Gaullist takeover in Paris was not only outwardly legal but also efficient.

National unity and constitutional renovation, seemingly redundant in the early 1950s, once again came to the fore and, under de Gaulle, became the main objectives of the state itself. His long struggle for a strong and efficient state, and against the 'perpetual political effervescence' of the French (a weakness which he blamed for France's military inadequacy in two world wars), was now being waged from within the state rather than from without.[11] And the key element which reinforced the position of Gaullism in the state was the approval of the electorate. This approval was expressed in several different ways in the first seven years of the Fifth Republic (and to different degrees): in referendums on the Constitution itself, on de Gaulle's Algerian policy, and, in October 1962, on the question of changing the method of electing the President of the Republic from an electoral college system to universal suffrage; in parliamentary elections in 1958 and 1962, the latter of which returned an absolute majority for the pro-Gaullist coalition of the Union pour la Nouvelle République (UNR-UDT) and the Independent Republican group, and in December 1965, though in a less clear-cut fashion, in the first presidential election by universal suffrage since Louis-Napoléon Bonaparte came to power in 1848 (only to overthrow the Second

Republic and declare the Second Empire in 1851).

The Legacy of Gaullist Dominance
De Gaulle's presidential 'raison d'être' - based on deeply-held
beliefs and sustained by the profound convictions of many of his
followers (though the movement obviously contained many pragmatic and ephemeral supporters) - was the building of a state
which would be efficient, autonomous and conscious of the national
interest. It would be capable of defending the nation against military threat; it would obtain and safeguard its legitimacy through
traditional democratic means; and it would play a leading and
creative role, through public policy, in the life of a society which
he saw as having been profoundly divided since before the Revolution of 1789. Part of this vision was the sustaining of economic
'progress', which he had come to see as a necessary condition of
an effective nation-state in the modern world.[12]
    Not that de Gaulle saw himself primarily as an economic reformer;
the vague economic ideas which he did hold about a 'third way'
between capitalism and Communism did not amount to a reform
programme, and were firmly subordinated in terms of priorities
to the reform of the state itself.[13] Even his occasionally revived
schemes for 'participation', involving elements of worker shareholding in firms and of formal corporativism in certain branches
of the state, were never effectively pursued. Their resonance
among Gaullist militants and voters - as well as with more conservative Gaullist leaders like Pompidou - was limited,[14] and they
were seen by the Left to be aimed more at bypassing the trade
unions and attempting to attract the working-class electorate.[15]
And their links with the other elements of Gaullist ideology, which
revolved around a diffuse symbolic mixture of patriotism and cultural synthesis to achieve a cross-class appeal,[16] were weak and
unelaborated. Rather, the economic impact of Gaullism was indirect
and implicit, involving not the executing of the will of the capitalist class but the actual creation of a new and modern capitalist
class where one had not spontaneously evolved before. Whether
by historical accident or ingenious design, Gaullism created the
conditions in which the transition to advanced capitalism could
succeed by following the lead of the state.[17]
    These conditions took three main forms. In the first place,
Gaullism resolved, at least in the short term, the problem of the
stability of the state in a period when the administrative apparatus
of an advanced capitalist state had already begun to develop.
Although to some extent the Gaullist state represented a revival
of national capitalism and a reaction against the post-war world
capitalist system - at least in its rhetoric against American
hegemony - the most important economic decisions strengthened
France's position in that system, especially at the end of the
1950s. Two of the most salient aspects of France's stronger position
were the various economic decisions (including the devaluation of
the franc and a domestic austerity programme) which were required for successful French entry to the European Economic

Community at the time of its launching in 1958 (although France, in the longer term, exacted both economic and political concessions in return); and the political decisions involved in the setting up of the Fifth Republic itself, with the institutionalisation of a stable political authority and of clear lines of responsibility for day-to-day oversight of and intervention in the mixed economy to ensure its smooth running.

In the second place, the statist orientation of Gaullism allowed the state, in the short-run period of transformation, to take a lead in forcing French capital to adapt to advanced capitalism, particularly through such interventionist 'supply-side' measures as the promotion of 'national champions' in leading industries such as oil, steel and electronics where the state took the lead in promoting expansion and concentration with a view to enhancing the international competitiveness of French firms. De Gaulle's public praise of the planning process as an 'ardent obligation', the more vigorous use of price controls (originally instituted after the Second World War) and the acceptance of greater exposure to foreign competition (especially through the EEC) were significant examples of how existing policies could be carried out more effectively in a less unstable political context. But the adoption of strategic measures such as the restructuring of industry and the steps taken by the Agriculture Minister, Edgard Pisani, to restructure that sector (while cushioning the effects through the EEC's Common Agricultural Policy after 1962) were evidence of the beginning of a new phase of economic development which bore fruit in the rapid industrial expansion of the late 1960s and the early 1970s.

In the third place, Gaullism carefully cultivated democratic legitimacy and a cross-class national appeal which enabled it to withstand such shocks as the Events of May 1968, when a coalition of workers and students attempted to overthrow the Gaullist state and create a Socialist revolution. Not only did the UNR and de Gaulle himself in the early and mid-1960s receive a significant proportion of working-class votes, but support also came from the 'nouvelles couches', the new white-collar strata of technicians and lower and middle managers who were seen as reflecting the Gaullist objective of modernisation.[18] Thus the Gaullist Party recruited voters on a much broader basis than any previous political party in France; it was seen by Charlot as a 'catch-all' party, representative of a new kind of consensus politics characteristic of industrial democracies.[19] The conditions of social conflict which had reflected and exacerbated the 'immobilisme' of previous republics were seen to have been overtaken by visible political change rather than merely by anonymous economic forces.[20]

In a narrower sense, the period of Gaullist dominance left three legacies, each of which reflects the key characteristics of the Gaullist role in maintaining the stability and increasing the autonomy of the state during the transition to advanced capitalism. The first of these has been the Gaullist Party itself, now the RPR. In the late 1960s, the Gaullist Party - then called the UDR (Union pour la Défense de la République, 1968-9; Union des Démocrates pour la République, 1969-76) - was seen as a 'pro-system' party par excellence, distinguished from the others by its 'constituent function', its defence of the 1958 constitutional settlement per se. At the same time, following its massive victory in the June 1968 parliamentary elections and Pompidou's easy election as de Gaulle's successor in June 1969 (with 58 per cent on the second ballot), it was widely regarded to have become a 'dominant party' - i.e., strong and popular enough to remain in power almost indefinitely despite vigorous (but usually fragmented) opposition.

The strength of the Gaullist Party at the polls in the 1960s enabled the government to make policy on a wide range of subjects without fear of defeat in the National Assembly, and this con- tinuity reinforced the state's role in economic management by freeing it from the kind of divisive economic policy debates which had overturned so many governments in the Third and Fourth Republics. Furthermore, the fact that the government had majority support effectively marginalised groups opposed to its economic policies, lent the appearance of legitimacy to the government's economic strategy as material prosperity increased continuously in France's boom years up to 1973 - a period readily associated with Gaullist dominance - and seemed to represent the basis, through a progressive 'bipolarisation' of the party system, for the development of consensual and 'centripetal' politics of alter- nation in power on the model of stable capitalist democracies in the United States, Britain and Scandinavia.

The second legacy was foreign policy. The legitimacy of Gaullism, especially among those sections of the electorate most favourable to the Left opposition parties (Socialist and Communist), was solidly underpinned by the appearance (though arguably not the reality) of national autonomy and independence. Indeed, the paranoid reactions of successive American administrations to the Gaullist stance towards the Atlantic Alliance merely reinforced this appearance. The sense of belonging to a wider national culture society, embodied in the symbolic apparatus of the nation- state, had long been latent in French society, but had generally become manifest only in wartime, to be replaced in peacetime by routine, 'normal', ritual political conflict between parties and factions. De Gaulle's achievement was to harness this latent sense of identity in peacetime and use it to legitimate the institutions of the Fifth Republic - sinking his own identity into that of the regime, and, in particular, into the concept of the leading role of the President of the Republic as the representative of the 'whole' nation.[21]

Gaullist foreign policy not only emphasised the strength and effectiveness of the state, but also acted as a medium of 'consensus- building', demonstrating a widespread appeal to public opinion across the political spectrum despite vigorous criticism from opposition parties of both Left and Right.[22] Thus, by acting as a means to defuse party-political conflict, it reinforced the stability of the state itself, both enhancing the conditions for a smooth transition to advanced capitalism in the domestic economy and justifying France's more active role in the world economy. This more active role included demands for reforming the international monetary system, an increase of trade and political contacts with the Eastern European countries (including the USSR) and China, and the establishment of a neo-colonial network of economic and military relations with former French colonies not only through bilateral arrangements but also through their economic links, set up at France's insistence, with the EEC through the Yaoundé Convention.

The third legacy, and for the Gaullists the most important, was the constitutional form of the state itself. Presidential politics have become the focus of French political life, and the powers of the President of the Republic - in practice if not always in form - are considerably greater than, for example, those of his American counterpart.[23] The President came to control the work of the government, establishing his predominance over the Prime Minister in those areas in which he chose to intervene; taken in conjunction with the powers of the government with regard to the National Assembly, and the President's sole prerogative to dissolve the Assembly, the influence of the presidency could be wide indeed and not subject to extensive checks and balances in most cases. De Gaulle established the President's specific responsibility for foreign affairs, and it rapidly became clear that he had a supervisory role in determining and overseeing the broad lines of economic policy as well - a role which Pompidou and Giscard d'Estaing were to enlarge. Although he formally eschewed a direct role in party politics, de Gaulle's intervention increased in this arena as the importance of building a long-term political base through an ongoing electoral majority at parliamentary and local, as well as presidential, levels increased with the waning of his personal and charismatic appeal in the mid-1960s. Here again, Pompidou and Giscard d'Estaing were, in their different ways, even more directly interventionist in party affairs.

Therefore the President is seen by the public as responsible for what the state does in major areas of public policy. Indeed, presidential elections are the high point of the French political calendar - more so than legislative elections, the outcome of which would be less clear-cut in terms of anticipated policy decisions, intra-institutional conflict (legislative-executive and political-administrative), party coalition-building and even the psychological perception of the political process by the mass public (which socialisation studies have shown to rest particularly on the salience of the presidential image).[24] It is said that the viability of a political party depends upon whether it can field a credible presidential candidate - i.e., one who can either win or have a significant bearing on the outcome.[25] Thus presidential elections enjoy both close attention from the political class and a clear enthusiasm on the part of the electorate; abstentionism is usually lower in presidential than in other elections.

And yet this is the office which in the late 1950s was described

as being 'tailored for General de Gaulle', and often regarded at
that time as representing a neo-Bonapartist phenomenon, linked
to the historical tendency of the French political system to look to
a temporary leader in a crisis, and therefore doomed to return to
normal once the crisis had passed.[26] Now it is widely seen as a
'fait accompli', and, what is more, as the lynchpin of the Fifth
Republic. And it is certain that the dominance of the Gaullist
Party in the 1960s and early 1970s comprised the key organisational
linkage between simple control of the presidency and the ability
of a president to ensure that his writ extended throughout the
institutional structure. The basic institutional consensus, the
powers of the presidency and the organisation of the Gaullist
movement were inextricably intertwined with, on the one hand,
the stabilisation of the state after a period of political collapse and
during an era of rapid social transformation, and, on the other,
the specific policies adopted by the state to affect and to shape
the course of that transformation. The result was the peculiarly
Gaullist version of state capitalism, the État UDR. The new institutions of the Fifth Republic, underpinned by Gaullism, enabled
the state to carry out, according to the dominant ideology of its
office-holders, the new economic functions of the advanced capitalist state, with the executive embodying the top level of a new
state managerialism.

Problems of Gaullism After de Gaulle
However, once the basic structures of economic modernisation
had been set in place, and the processes of advanced capitalism
had developed their own momentum and dynamic outside the state
umbrella, Gaullism, as a linkage mechanism, became redundant
to the situation. The dominance of the presidency lasted only
until 1974, when the electorate voted in a candidate who, although
he had been a conservative Finance Minister under both de Gaulle
and Pompidou, not only was not a Gaullist, but also wanted
to develop a new centrist-conservative coalition with which to
undermine the dominance of the UDR. Giscard not only wished to
displace the Gaullists from power, but also sought to relegate the
UDR to the position of just another right-wing faction – and a
rather extremist one at that (at least in comparison with his own
'advanced liberal' policies). Having lost the presidency, the UDR
also lost the post of Prime Minister in 1976 when their new leader,
Chirac – who had broken with other Gaullist leaders in 1974 by
supporting Giscard – resigned after extensive feuding with Giscard
over prime ministerial autonomy and over economic policy. Thus
the party whose main 'raison d'être' had been its 'constituent
function' lost its claim to be the privileged defender of the presidential state.
    However, the Gaullist Party by the mid-1970s was a rather dif-
ferent organisation than it had been during its heyday in the
sixties. In the first place, its electoral base had shifted significantly. Its working-class support, which had been closely linked
with the personal appeal of General de Gaulle and which reached

its high point in the 1965 presidential election, declined significantly with the development of the left-wing coalition in the late 1960s and the early 1970s, especially following the Events of May 1968, which polarised party politics more closely along conventional ideological and class lines. Its support from voters who identified with the centrist parties reached its apogee in the subsequent elections of June 1968 – fought by the UDR on a strongly anti-Communist platform – but was rapidly eroded by the opposition of a number of centrist groups, including a large section of Giscard d'Estaing's Independent Republicans, to de Gaulle's regional and Senate reform proposals; centrist defections ensured the defeat of these proposals in the referendum of April 1969, after which de Gaulle himself resigned the presidency.

Pompidou, elected in June 1969, attempted to reconstruct the party as a coalition of the Right, placing industrial development more firmly at the centre of the government's policy concerns, granting a number of concessions to small business and to the agricultural sector, and bringing back Giscard d'Estaing, much favoured in the business and financial communities, as Minister of Finance. Thus by the time of Pompidou's death in April 1974, and Giscard's decision to stand for president against the official UDR candidate, Jacques Chaban-Delmas, the position of the Gaullist Party as having a unique claim to national legitimacy and cross-class appeal had already been seriously eroded.[27] The UDR had to compete, none too successfully at the time, with the regrouped 'old parties' of the Right and Centre under Giscard's umbrella, and, indeed, by the mid-seventies the social profile of the Gaullist electorate was virtually indistinguishable from that of the pro-Giscardian parties.

In the second place, the organisation and leadership of the party itself had changed. Even under Pompidou there had been a growing clash between UDR leaders concerned primarily with the more technocratic 'pompidoliste' policies of industrial development and those factions concerned either with social policy (like Chaban-Delmas, who was Prime Minister from 1969-72) or with foreign and defence policies (like Michel Debré, the Defence Minister, who had been de Gaulle's first Prime Minister from 1959-62). In replacing Chaban with the leader of the 'traditional' Gaullist faction, Pierre Messmer, in 1972 Pompidou was able to keep these quarrels under control for a time. But in the year before his death, following the relatively successful parliamentary elections of March 1973 (and during a time when his worsening illness was an increasingly ill-kept secret), these groups continued to jockey for position with Chaban-Delmas succeeding in taking control of the party apparatus – despite his lack of favour with Pompidou – in the summer of 1973.

The presidential election of 1974 split the UDR apart, with Messmer failing in his bid to become the compromise candidate (Chaban would not withdraw) and the aspiring new leader of the technocratic group, Agriculture Minister Jacques Chirac (one of a group of ambitious ex-civil servants who had developed a strong

local power base and had come to be called the 'young wolves')
tacitly supporting Giscard on the first ballot. Following Giscard's
election, Chirac, whose reward was the premiership, swiftly
asserted control of the UDR machine, ousting the 'barons' of the
1940s, 1950s and 1960s whose positions had derived from their
long political association with de Gaulle. Eventually, after Chirac's
growing clash with Giscard over economic policy had led to the
Prime Minister's resignation in August 1976, the Gaullist party
was itself reorganised along more hierarchical lines with Chirac
as president of the retitled RPR. Non-'chiraquien' Gaullist leaders
have been in an ambivalent position ever since, as we shall see
later (pp. 43-5).[28]

By the time that these changes were taking place, however, the
basic structures of economic modernisation had already been set
in place through the close collaboration between the Gaullist
leadership and the technocratically oriented bureaucracy. The
processes of advanced capitalism had become dominant within the
French business and financial communities themselves, as the
younger heirs of the old bourgeoisie pursued a new 'cursus
honorum' of high-level technical and managerial qualifications, as
marketing adapted to European and international horizons, and
as firms increased their rate of concentration and technological
innovation.[29] Structural adjustment came to depend far less upon
the active direction of the state - although French industry, like
industry in all advanced capitalist societies, was still integrally
dependent upon the state for support, perhaps even more so
than in other Western economies because of the integrated elite
structure of the private and public sectors. The specificity of
Gaullism in public and economic policy had been overtaken and
the presidency itself had been captured by coalition partners
with no love for planning and state control - as evidenced by the
accession to the premiership of the 'liberal' economist Raymond
Barre following Chirac's resignation.[30] The Gaullist movement,
shorn of its tasks of national unity and constitutional renovation,
became, at least in part, redundant.

While the state retained a gamut of ways to aid and to intervene
in the economy, state pressure was no longer required to ensure
that French society - especially French private capital - would
adhere to the norms and objectives of advanced capitalism. State
indicative planning, which had gradually declined in the prosper-
ous conditions of the late 1960s, had been further undermined
during Giscard's term as Pompidou's Finance Minister. And the
conditions of recession in France and the world precipitated by
the oil crisis of 1973-4, and lasting throughout the late 1970s and
into the 1980s, undermined the credibility of planning and 'fine
tuning' of advanced capitalist economies throughout the Western
world. Under Barre, while the planning process continued formally to function, its task of the overall co-ordination of French
economic development had been allowed to wither and it became
merely a set of state aid programmes for particular sectors of the
economy - although the overall weight of state intervention did

not decline significantly in the long term.[31]

The Gaullist Party under Chirac's leadership also lost credibility among the business community in the early years of the recession, when Chirac's policies as Prime Minister - more and more in conflict with Giscard's views, and based on reflating the economy and regaining the expansionist tempo of the Pompidou years - were blamed for creating inflation in a world climate which was seen to require austerity. The policy of creating 'national champions', although successful in the oil industry and at first in steel, was undermined by failure in electronics and computing (the leading French company was eventually merged with an American firm) and later in steel, as world demand for steel slumped and the entire European steel industry found itself in crisis. Furthermore - on a more mundane level - once Chirac had resigned, business and financial leaders no longer sought out the Gaullists for access to government support and bureaucratic influence; the most important channels to power ran through the Giscardian factions.[32]

In foreign policy, the Gaullists also lost the momentum they had gained in the 1960s when de Gaulle was seen to challenge American hegemony. France became closer to NATO, co-ordinating its military policies with the Western allies although never formally rejoining the military organisation. Giscard d'Estaing, especially in his African policies, tried to establish himself as the true bearer of the Gaullist tradition of independence, and the rhetoric of grandeur remained. But the specific stance of the Gaullists on these issues was only clear in two areas: that of European integration, on which the RPR was reduced to fighting the 1979 elections to the European Parliament on an anti-European platform, led not by Chirac but by a newly assertive Michel Debré, and in a tacit alliance with the equally anti-EEC Communist Party; and the demand that the government agree to the building of an additional nuclear submarine, thought to be necessary to the maintenance of an effective independent nuclear deterrent. (The basic issue of the existence of the independent deterrent itself had by this time been either accepted or shelved by all of the major parties).

In terms of its basic historical functions - an independent foreign policy, the 'dominant party' both of government and of the right-wing coalition, and the creation of the conditions for the successful transition to advanced capitalism - Gaullism had, by the late 1970s, lost its credibility and its legitimacy in the eyes of even the majority of right-wing voters. Yet its leverage is still strong, as the 1981 presidential and parliamentary election campaigns have demonstrated, a strength which owes much to its organisational dynamism and the growing dominance of Chirac's leadership. As French politics enters a new historical phase under the presidency of François Mitterrand, the Gaullist Party is also entering a new stage of development as it attempts to regain its position as the leading party of the Right.

GAULLISM: PROBLEMS AND PROSPECTS

This far we have been primarily concerned with describing the historical specificity of Gaullism during the crucial period covering the transformation of France into an advanced capitalist society, and the Gaullist contribution to the emergence of a form of liberal democratic state which played a leading role in that transformation. That this transition period is over, and that such a contribution is now history, does not alter the fact that political parties which grow up around particular issues often retain their 'esprit de corps' and residual features of their original 'raison d'être' long after those issues have been defused or settled. In adapting their organisation and ideology to new circumstances, they yet reflect their historical origins, whether in terms of rhetoric, or voter allegiance, or the persistence of control by an elite pursuing a 'reconversion' strategy: the example of religious parties in Western Europe is often commented upon.[33] In this section, we shall briefly survey the problems of adaptation which the RPR is facing, especially in the light of the Socialist Party's comprehensive victories in the 1981 presidential and legislative elections.

The problems of a 'successor' or 'inheritance' party - a type found mainly in the Third World and representing a broadly-based national movement which had previously played a dominant role in a period of national transformation such as a colonial independence movement - provides key clues to the current situation of Gaullism. The goals of such a party or movement, like those of historical Gaullism, are seen to be above not only the rivalries of factionalism, but also the self-restraint of pluralism; the task at hand is claimed to be one which requires efforts which go beyond the limits of party competition and require nationalitarian unity - the creation (or re-creation) of a 'general will' which gives the polity itself existence and cohesion.[34] Furthermore, support for such a movement - if it is successful at establishing its claims during the transformation period - must necessarily be heterogeneous; individuals, groups, fractions and classes which in 'normal' times would have competing and conflicting interests and ideologies coalesce around the goals of the movement (sometimes around a charismatic leader of such a movement who is seen to embody those goals) and either postpone or disguise their 'sectional' goals. And finally, linking the two levels already mentioned, lies the organisation and leadership of the movement/party itself; linked by the sense of common participation in an historic struggle, their 'gemeinschäftlisch' bonds - which, as in the ideal-type traditional family, are seen to reconcile hierarchical authority with the brotherhood of a common purpose[35] - allow leaders and cadres to escape the longer-term imperatives of bureaucratisation, routinisation, personal or factional rivalry, and intergenerational renewal which are the stuff of organisational life.

Of course, a standard way of reconciling the gap between the transformation period and a subsequent transition to 'normalcy'

might be to turn the rule of the movement into a form of dictator-
ship - possibly linked with attempts at populist renewal at the
base, as, for example, in Libya. Various kinds of 'personalism' -
attempts to renew charismatic bonds through a transmission of
powers analogous to that practised by the Roman Catholic Church
in the selection of a new Pope - have also been suggested and
tried.[36] But if the post-transformation regime is a liberal-
democratic one, in which competitive elections to the formal offices
of power in the state become the rule, then there are essentially
only three types of adaptation possible (although every real case
is something of a hybrid): first, there is continued dominance,
either as a dominant party in a pluralist system (i.e., the Indian
Congress Party until the mid-1970s) or as a single party with
effective internal pluralism (i.e., the Tanzanian CCM); secondly,
at the other end of the scale, there is fragmentation and disappearance, typified by the Federalist Party in the post-colonial
United States (although such disappearance is often followed by
instability and regime collapse, as witnessed by the number of
military coups which have followed liberal-democratic experiments
in post-colonial states); and thirdly, there is the possibility of
adaptation to a reduced role along several dimensions, with the
cultural memory of the heroic period becoming, in effect, a 'digni-
fied element' of the party's constitution. In the last case, resistance to and resentment of the movement's decline on the part of
its leaders, cadres and hard-core supporters can be great, and
the lack of well-established and strongly-internalised liberal-
democratic norms both in society and in the party itself can lead
to an authoritarian response. On the whole, Gaullism has avoided
the latter.[37] But its adaptation has not been a simple one, and
has involved changes on a number of levels: institutional power;
survival in a changing party system; economic and social perspectives; and the legitimation of authority. Let us examine these in
turn.

The RPR and Institutional Power
The starkest contrast between the ideological goals and self-image
of Gaullism, on the one hand, and the realities of the current
political situation, on the other, is to be found in the relationship
between the movement and the political institutions of the Fifth
Republic. Deprived of the presidency in 1974, the premiership in
1976, clear dominance of the National Assembly in 1978 (with the
relative growth of the UDF), participation in the government in
May 1981 (with Giscard's defeat), and membership of a parliamentary majority in June 1981, the 'raison d'être' of Gaullism could no
longer be the institutionalisation of a new regime with which it
was organically linked. The smooth functioning of the institutions
would benefit only the Socialist Party and its allies; were they to
be the eventual heirs of General de Gaulle? In fact, the Gaullists
had been slowly modifying their stance towards the institutions of
the Fifth Republic for some time.
    The strength of the UNR and the UDR in the sixties had lain in

its close links with de Gaulle and Pompidou: with the first, because the party was the creation of power, pliable to the General's
will for the most part, and dependent for its own electoral strength
on its role as a support for presidentialism, especially in the critical elections of November 1962; with the second, because Pompidou
had, as Prime Minister from 1962-8, made himself the leader of the
legislative majority, the creator of party organisation and strength,
and when de Gaulle left office after his referendum defeat in 1969,
the party's virtually unanimous choice for the presidency was
Pompidou. However, with Chaban-Delmas's struggle for control of
the party machine in 1972-3, and with Chirac's support for Giscard
in 1974, the bond between the party and the presidency was
broken. Giscard's view of the President's supervisory role over
the government forced Chirac, as Prime Minister, to fight a losing
battle to maintain and enlarge his own freedom of action; and the
RPR was created to combat presidential power, as shown in the
electoral campaign of 1978 and the parliamentary battles over
Barre's budgets in 1979-80 and 1980-1.[38] Chirac's decision to stand
for the presidency in 1981, to direct his campaign at Giscard
rather than Mitterrand, and to refuse to ask his supporters to
vote for Giscard on the second ballot, was the logical culmination
of this strategy.

   Thus despite the RPR's continuing rhetoric of defence of the
institutions of the Fifth Republic, the organisational interests of
the Gaullist Party no longer coincide with the way those institutions actually work. The most convincing demonstration of this
is to be found in the statements of Chirac during the parliamentary
election campaign, when, instead of arguing (as the Gaullists had
done since 1958), that the stability of the institutions depended
upon the continued congruence of the parliamentary majority with
the presidential majority, he called for the return of a right-wing
majority to 'co-habit' with a Socialist president to prevent him
from taking extreme measures - ironic when one remembers that
it was the RPR which blocked Giscard's proposals to permit the
left-wing opposition some token consultation, and the sharing of
control of parliamentary commissions, after the 1978 elections.[39]
Between the two rounds of voting in 1981, Chirac, having lost all
hope of an RPR-UDF victory, even called for the Senate - the old
bugbear of de Gaulle - to play a balancing role in the regime![40]
So despite the fact that Chirac's long-term strategy is aimed at
winning the presidency for himself, its effective outcome thus
far has been to sever the links of the RPR with the positions of
power which had turned Gaullism into a potent political party in
the first place.

Gaullism and the Party System
In 1962, the UNR-UDT eclipsed the other parties of the Right and
Centre-Right; by 1969, it was being hailed as a new 'dominant
party' (in a category with the Indian Congress, the Mexican
Institutional Revolutionary Party and the Swedish Social Demo-
crats) and the only 'catch-all' party in the French spectrum. In

1974, Chaban won only 15.9 per cent of the vote in the presidential election, and in May 1981 Chirac won only 18 per cent; and in June 1981, the RPR was reduced to a parliamentary group of only 88 members (79 RPR plus 9 'apparentés') from 155 in 1978, 183 in 1973, 296 in 1968 and 245 in 1967.(For 1981 figures see Appendix). Thus the RPR's current position is a complex one, for despite the fact that it is still the largest party of the opposition, the strategic possibilities of that role are both circumscribed and extremely tricky to manipulate.

The major French parties are required by the constraints implicit in the institutional system of the Fifth Republic to fight a battle on two fronts - not only against the opposing coalition, but also against the main coalition partner of each - and each party must fight this battle in different conditions at different times and on different levels - especially the presidential and the parliamentary.[41] Within this context, Gaullism has been on the defensive since 1974 at least. Having come to take for granted its dominant position, the loss of 'successor' status has left it with a number of quandaries which it has been unable to resolve. Much of its energy is wasted in resentment - a feeling of having its right and proper position in the state usurped by others - and the impossibility of a return to heroic status has led to disarray. When Roland Nungesser found that the new RPR parliamentary party contained only 16 fellow survivors from the 1958 National Assembly - which itself had been dominated by new faces (mainly UNR) - he observed wryly: 'Il y en a qui parlaient de recours. J'ai l'impression qu'il faut crier au secours!'[42]

Its strategic problems lie on five levels: long-run objectives, relations with the UDF, relations with the Mitterrand Administration, intra-party factional quarrels, and the strengthening of the organisational base. In the long term, Chirac has, since taking over the UDR in a 'coup de théâtre' in December 1974, tailored that organisation and its descendant the RPR to his own presidential ambitions, and its first test - the battle for the mayoralty of Paris between Chirac and Giscard's hand-picked candidate, Michel d'Ornano, in March 1977 - was successful in spite of huge left-wing gains at the expense of the broad Right in the country as a whole. But he has often been forced onto the defensive: attempting to minimise losses to the newly-formed UDF in 1978; taking on a strident and unpopular anti-European campaign (under pressure from Michel Debré - in order not to split the party leadership) alongside the Communists in the European Assembly elections of June 1979; conducting a guerrilla war against Barre in Parliament, while avoiding any confrontation which would actually bring the government down (and thus alienate the RPR ministers in that very government - such as Alain Peyrefitte - who distrusted Chirac in the first place); fighting off challenges to his own presidential candidacy from RPR leaders Michel Debré and Marie-France Garaud (formerly Chirac's 'eminence grise'), who received 1.66 and 1.33 per cent of the votes on the first ballot respectively; attempting to defeat Giscard while retaining his own personal credibility in the right-wing coalition, a virtually impossible task; formulating a strategy, based on agreed, single RPR-UDF candidacies in most constituencies in the June 1981 elections (a strategy which, arguably, led to larger losses than necessary); and attempting to formulate a strategy for opposition within Parliament which could include the rapidly fragmenting UDF.

Thus the badly-eroded RPR under Chirac lacks credibility. Its UDF 'allies' realise that they need to maintain links with the RPR but do not trust it after Chirac's 'premeditated treason' (Giscard's bitter parting comment on 10 May). Its rejection of the Socialist offer of the presidency of a parliamentary commission, and its strident and intransigent reaction to Prime Minister Mauroy's parliamentary programme, indicate that the role of a constructive opposition is still foreign to the RPR - despite Chaban-Delmas's guarded approval of parts of the Socialist programme.[43] Indeed, given the virulence of Gaullist opposition to Giscard (around one-sixth of Chirac's first-round voters switched to Mitterrand on the second ballot), Chirac and the RPR will have to face the problem of what to do about those Gaullist leaders who openly supported Mitterrand on the second ballot, such as Philippe Dechartre, Pierre Dabezies and Léo Hamon. A group calling itself 'Gaullism and Socialism', including a number of former Gaullists who declared that 'Gaullism and Socialism constitute two different strands of the same desire for effort and for progress', appealed to voters to support PS candidates in the parliamentary elections.[44] And the man who had, in 1974, been considered Chirac's main rival for the leadership of the UDR - Michel Jobert, Pompidou's Foreign Minister - led his small, independent Gaullist group (the Mouvement des Démocrates) into Mitterrand's camp well before the presidential election, and was rewarded by the Ministry of Foreign Trade - with the elevated status of Ministre d'État.

None the less, as the leader of the largest opposition party, and with a dynamic and (relatively) successful first-ballot campaign behind him, Chirac remains the only credible presidential candidate on the French Right with a view to 1988. Still under 50 years old, he can afford to wait. And it must be remembered that the Socialist 'landslide' of June 1981 in fact reflected a total Left vote which was down by 45,000 on March 1978. (The total right-wing vote, however, was down by 3.2 million.) Thus, if the RPR can mobilise potential right-wing voters who abstained in 1981, Chirac's long-term strategy might yet succeed should the Mitterrand presidency falter. As the 'Le Monde' journalist André Passeron has pointed out, the RPR intends to model itself on the highly successful transformation of the Socialist Party after its setback in 1968.

The first stage is to start at the bottom - trying to roll back the Socialist positions in local government (achieved in 1976-7) at the cantonal elections due in 1982 and the municipal elections in 1983. The recruitment of new, young candidates - to replace the 'notables' who had established themselves in the RPF and the

UNR and who still remain the backbone of RPR electoral strength
- is a key priority. Other plans include the slimming down of the
Parisian headquarters of the party, the establishment of links
with the local press, setting up a 'club de réflexion' to be a policy
think-tank, streamlining the party structure (bloated from years
of participation in power), a move away from Chirac's strategy
of attracting a mass membership to one of appealing to voters
through a move towards the Centre (especially at local level),
increasing co-ordination with other right-wing parties (including
links between the RPR and UDF parliamentary groups) and mar-
ginalising the more hard-core supporters of Giscard. But the gap
between these plans and strategic realities seems rather large.

Economic and Social Perspectives
The main weakness in Gaullist strategy is that it lacks a coherent
policy image - other than being vaguely right-wing and authoritarian - and that policy discussions within the leadership are as
likely to be disruptive as effective. With the period of capitalist
transformation over, the contradictions between the support for
the RPR in the business community and its voting strength among
shopkeepers, industrialists, professionals, farmers, etc., on the
one hand, and its interventionist history in the first 15 years of
the Fifth Republic, on the other, make it difficult to work out a
clear economic strategy targeted on key groups (as the PS has
done) without alienating leadership factions and specific groups
of voters. In a sense, the RPR has been shielded by being both
a part of the Giscardian coalition since 1974 - and therefore not
needing to define or apply an economic strategy at the governmental level themselves - and yet maintaining an oppositional
stance towards Giscard and Barre; thus they have had the best
of both governmental and oppositional worlds.

And yet this has not prevented splits on policy issues. Debré's
stridency on Europe, on economic nationalism, on the need to
raise the birth rate, among other things, gives him a strong
personal following in the party which has at times challenged
Chirac's supremacy. Alain Peyrefitte's repressive reputation as
Barre's Minister of Justice, especially in the introduction of last
year's Security and Liberty Law, provides him with a following
in the party on law and order issues - despite the fact that he
was the leader of the pro-Giscardian faction within the RPR. And
Chaban, whose economic policies as Prime Minister - represents
by Jacques Delors - now Mauroy's Finance Minister - represents
a continuing threat to Chirac on both personal and policy levels;
indeed, the striking parallels between Chaban's programme as
Prime Minister, set out in his 'new society' speech of July 1969,
and the programme announced in July 1981 by Mauroy, have been
closely examined by 'Le Monde' journalist Raymond Barrillon.[45]

Thus for the first time ever, the Gaullist Party must elaborate
coherent policies. Under de Gaulle and Pompidou, all that was
left to the executive; under Giscard, attacks on Barre 'tous
azimuts' allowed the RPR the luxury of demanding both a reflation

of the economy and a reduction in public expenditure.[46] What sort of policies emerge from the process of discussion which is about to get underway will be difficult to predict, as the various viewpoints and factions collide and attempt to compromise. What is more likely, however, is that, in order to keep the party together, the RPR's programme will remain vague on a number of key areas – such as anti-inflation policy, economic planning, employment policy, international trade policy and taxation policy – and that Chirac, in trying to broaden his public appeal, will employ general rhetoric and avoid specific commitments. Indeed, his view is that the economic conjuncture will do all of the work for him – in particular, that a flight of Arab, American and West German capital from France will leave Mitterrand with a choice between austerity and autarchy, both of which can be easily attacked, and which are not easily balanced.[47] Failing such providential events, however, it is likely that the RPR's main economic thrust will be traditional right-wing attacks on state interventionism, Socialist bureaucratisation, public expenditure and high taxes. The Gaullists can no longer simply claim to be above party politics or in favour of a strong state in the area of economic policy; they have become a right-wing party like the others.

Conclusion: The RPR and the Legitimation of Authority
Gaullism, at the height of its power in the 1960s, represented more than the economic management of the capitalist transformation or the stabilisation of political control – it symbolised a new legitimacy of the state itself, a blending of old and new ideological elements into what Almond and Verba have called a 'rain or shine' implicit cultural acceptance and support of the state and its norms.[48] But more recent events have shown that this embryonic legitimacy, or 'protolegitimacy', was attached not to the Gaullist Party, but to the 'gaullien' practice of the state; its true test was not which party was in power, but how each party in power used the opportunities provided by the institutional mechanisms of the Fifth Republic. Therefore, the transition from 'protolegitimacy' to real legitimacy would only come with the peaceful transfer of power to the opposition and the transmission of supportive attitudes about the state to a new generation, for whom it would be, in de Gaulle's phrase, 'second nature' – a cultural 'fait accompli'.[49]

It is here that the dissonance between the RPR's self-image and the strategic necessities of adaptation are most likely to conflict in the long run. Gaullism's ties with the legitimacy of the Fifth Republic came from the notion, again in de Gaulle's words, that 'Everyone is, has been, or will be, "gaulliste".' The notion that Gaullism was not really a party – for parties represented only a partisan or sectional interest – but a 'union' or 'rassemblement', depended upon its ability to retain its cross-class appeal and its efficacy in completing tasks that were beyond the capacity of previous regimes. And it depended upon the ideological centrality of the three 'pillars' of Gaullism – foreign policy, the presidential

institutions and the Gaullist Party - in an organic relationship
with each other and with the coming of the prosperity and modernisation of the advanced capitalist era.

Today the claims of the RPR to such status, as important as
they are for many of its longer-serving leaders, cadres and
supporters, have a kind of tacky air to them. Despite the fact
that formal links with the RPR were severed gradually during the
seventies, the seamier side of Gaullism - the Service d'Action
Civique - has emerged once again in a multiple murder near
Marseilles, said to have been carried out in order to protect
secret details of the extensive network left over from the clandestine war against the French Algerian Secret Army terrorists
(OAS), a network upon whose illegal activities the Socialist
government, unlike its predecessors, intends to clamp down.[50]
Chirac himself, a tireless politician with little of the cultural
depth of a de Gaulle, a Pompidou or a Mitterrand, is widely regarded as a tinpot authoritarian rather than as the great leader
of a new patriotic generation; he has neither the 'character' nor
the 'prestige' which de Gaulle described in 'The Edge of the
Sword' (1932) as the essential qualities of the true leader.[51]
However, this may merely reflect changing requirements.

He is regarded within his own party as the most efficient and
dynamic of the potential leaders of the RPR, although strident
and unimaginative. He is regarded by the Giscardians as a traitor
- but also as the only credible presidential candidate currently
on the right-wing scene. His strategies have often failed to get
to grips with short-term exigencies - although his long-term
prospects are taken seriously by many people from all parts of
the political spectrum. Indeed, his plans for the future - highly
sensible from a basic strategic perspective - may ultimately
succeed better than has been admitted here, given the kind of
alternation in power which is characteristic of stable liberal
democracies, the benefits of a period in opposition, and the
tendency for governments to lose elections rather than for oppo-
sitions to win them. But the constraints are real. Not the least of
these constraints is the fact that the mantle of 'gaullien' legitimacy
has fallen upon François Mitterrand - despite his long personal
opposition to de Gaulle - and on the Socialist Party.

Mitterrand's new image of 'gaullien' legitimacy has several
aspects. In terms of the institutions of the Fifth Republic itself,
the presidential strategy of Mitterrand - after his tireless quest
over three presidential elections, and the way that he, in office,
has re-established de Gaulle's style of 'arbitrage', circumscribed
presidential domain and sense of prestige - has confirmed the
significance of those institutions and shown them capable of
providing for both stability and change. In terms of the party
system, the Socialist Party has proved itself capable, on its own,
of creating that 'congruent majority' which is so crucial to the
functioning of the regime. Furthermore, if the Socialist economic
strategy succeeds, then the test of the successful economic
management of the advanced capitalist state (albeit in social-

democratic fashion) will have been passed. And in the sphere of foreign policy, Mitterrand's desire for a strong and independent policy, based on presidential dominance, is highly reminiscent of de Gaulle's - and a marked contrast to the vacillations and vanities of Giscardian foreign policy.[52] Indeed, one of his first actions in the area of defence policy has been to approve the construction of a seventh nuclear submarine - long a basic demand of the Gaullists - and to reorient French strategy away from the tactical nuclear weapons preferred by Giscard and back to deterrence based on submarine-based missiles.[53]

In a sense, then, Gaullism lives on independently of the RPR, and even in ways which reduce the party's credibility and scope for future development. But the right-wing opposition needs leadership, and Chirac not only wishes to fulfil that role, but also has the organisational resources to stake an effective claim. None the less, the 'Gaullism' which the RPR has come to represent bears little resemblance to the powerful, dominant party whose 15 years in control of the French state saw the transformation of French political institutions from instability to stability, of French foreign policy from vacillating and dominated by the United States to relatively strong and autonomous, and of French society from an unevenly developed and uncompetitive economy to advanced capitalism.

NOTES

1   For the concept of cadre parties, see Maurice Duverger, 'Political Parties', London, Methuen, 2nd edn, 1959, pp. 63-71.
2   Cf. Jean Charlot, 'The Gaullist Phenomenon: The Gaullist Movement in the Fifth Republic', London, Allen & Unwin, 1971; and P.G. Cerny, The New Rules of the Game in France, in P.G. Cerny and M.A. Schain (eds), 'French Politics and Public Policy', London and New York, Frances Pinter Ltd, St Martin's Press and Methuen University Paperbacks, 1980-1, ch. 2.
3   P.G. Cerny, 'The Politics of Grandeur: Ideological Aspects of de Gaulle's Foreign Policy', Cambridge, Cambridge University Press, 1980, chs. 5 and 10.
4   See Pierre Avril, 'UDR et gaullistes', Paris: Presses Universitaires de France, 1971, pp. 10-16, 52.
5   'The Politics of Grandeur', ch. 2.
6   See, e.g., Anthony Giddens, 'Capitalism and Modern Social Theory', Cambridge, Cambridge University Press, 1971.
7   Frank J. Sorauf, Political Parties and Political Analysis, in William N. Chambers and W. Dean Burnham (eds), 'The American Party Systems: Stages of Political Development', New York, Oxford University Press, 1967, p. 51.
8   For the concept of a 'modernising oligarchy', see David E. Apter, 'The Politics of Modernization', Chicago, Chicago University Press, 1965, pp. 138-144.

9 Stanley Hoffmann, Heroic Leadership: The Case of Modern France, in Lewis J. Edinger (ed.), 'Political Leadership in Industrialized Societies', New York, Wiley, 1967, pp. 108-54. And also, P.G. Cerny, The Problem of Legitimacy in the Fifth French Republic, paper presented to the Workshop on Normative and Empirical Dimensions of Legitimacy, European Consortium for Political Research, Joint Meetings of Workshops, University of Lancaster, 29 March-3 April 1981.

10 On the relationship between external and internal conflict, see Alfred Grosser, 'La IVe République et sa politique extérieure', Paris, Colin, 1961; and see Jacques Guyard 'Le miracle français', Paris, Seuil, 1965.

11 Discours prononcé à Bayeux, in Charles de Gaulle, 'Discours et messages', vol. II, Dans l'attente, 1946-1958, Paris, Plon, 1970, pp. 5-11.

12 See Jean-Marie Cotteret and René Moreau, 'Le vocabulaire du Général de Gaulle', Paris, Colin, 1969.

13 Charles de Gaulle, 'Mémoires d'espoir', vol. I, Le renouveau, 1958-1962, Paris, Plon, 1970, pp. 144-5 and 171.

14 Institut Français d'Opinion Publique, 'Les Français et de Gaulle', Paris, Plon, 1971. pp. 48-53, 89-100 and 111-22.

15 Martin A. Schain, Corporatism and Industrial Relations in France, in Cerny and Schain, op. cit., pp. 191-217.

16 'The Politics of Grandeur', ch. 10.

17 In suggesting the element of conscious design, there is little evidence about de Gaulle's objectives; however, by way of analogy, his arguments in the 1930s about the need for a professional army, centred on a highly trained and technically advanced elite officer corps, have a certain similarity to the Gaullist approach to economic management. See de Gaulle, 'Vers l'Armée de métier', Paris, Berger-Levrault, 1934.

18 Cf. Institut Français d'Opinion Publique; François Goguel, 'Modernisation économique et comportement politique', Paris, Colin, 1969; and Goguel, Combien a-t-il eu d'électeurs de gauche parmi ceux qui ont voté le 5 décembre 1965 pour le général de Gaulle?, 'Revue Française de Science Politique', XVII, 1, February, 1967, pp. 65-9.

19 Cf. Charlot, 'The Gaullist Phenomenon'; Otto Kirchheimer, The Transformation of the Western European Party Systems, in Joseph LaPalombara and Myron Weiner (eds), 'Political Parties and Political Development', Princeton, N.J., Princeton University Press, 1966, pp. 177-200.

20 P.G. Cerny, Cleavage, Aggregation and Change in French Politics, 'British Journal of Political Science', 2, 4, October, 1972, pp. 443-55; J.R. Frears, Conflict in France: The Decline and Fall of a Stereotype, 'Political Studies', XX, 1, March, 1972, pp. 31-41.

21 'The Politics of Grandeur'.

22 Ibid.; and Institut Français d'Opinion Publique, pp. 75-88.

23 Cf. Vincent Wright, 'The Government and Politics of France', London, Hutchinson, 1978; and Ezra N. Suleiman, Presidential

Government in France, in Richard Rose and E.N. Suleiman
(eds), 'Presidents and Prime Ministers', Washington, D.C.,
American Enterprise Institute for Public Policy Research, 1980,
pp. 94-138.

24 See Fred I. Greenstein and Sidney G. Tarrow, The Study of
French Political Socialization: Toward the Revocation of
Paradox, 'World Politics', XXII, 1, October, 1969, pp. 95-137.

25 Cerny, The New Rules of the Game; and J.R. Frears, Legitimacy, Democracy, and Consensus: A Presidential Analysis,
'West European Politics', 1, 3, October, 1978, pp. 11-23.

26 Hoffmann, Heroic Leadership, in L.J. Edinger, op. cit.

27 Jack Hayward and Vincent Wright, 'Les Deux France' and the
French Presidential Election of May 1974, 'Parliamentary
Affairs', 27, 3, Summer, 1974, pp. 203-36, and Presidential
Supremacy and the French General Elections of March 1973, in
ibid., 2 parts, 26, 3 and 4, Summer and Autumn, 1973, pp.
274-306 and 372-402.

28 Pierre Crisol and Jean-Yves Lhomeau, 'La machine RPR',
Paris, Fayolle, 1977.

29 Jane Marceau, 'Plus ça change, plus c'est la même chose':
Access to Elite Careers in French Business, in Jolyon Howorth
and P.G. Cerny (eds), 'Elites in France: Origins, Reproduc-
tion and Power', London, Frances Pinter Ltd, 1981, ch. 7;
Marceau, 'Class and Status in France: Economic Change and
Social Immobility', Oxford, Oxford University Press, 1977;
André de Lattre and Daniel Deguen, 'La politique économique
de la France', 5 vols, Paris, Les Cours de Droit, 1979; and
Diana M. Green, 'Managing Industrial Change: French Policies
to Promote Industrial Adjustment', London, HMSO, 1981.

30 Diana M. Green with P.G. Cerny, Economic Policy and the
Governing Coalition, in Cerny and Schain, op. cit., ch. 8.

31 Diana M. Green, The Budget and the Plan, in Cerny and
Schain, op. cit., ch. 5; also Green with Cerny, op. cit.

32 Pierre Birnbaum, 'Les sommets de l'État: essai sur l'élite du
pouvoir', Paris, Seuil, 1977; P. Birnbaum, The State in
Contemporary France, in Richard Scase (ed.), 'The State in
Western Europe', London, Croom Helm, 1980, pp. 94-114.

33 For the concept of a 'reconversion strategy', see Marceau,
'Class and Status', pp. 11-13 and on voter alignment see
Seymour M. Lipset and Stein Rokkan (eds), 'Party Systems
and Voter Alignments', New York, Free Press, 1967, Intro-
duction; Richard Rose and Derek Urwin, Social Cohesion,
Political Parties and Strains in Regimes, in Mattei Dogan and
R. Rose (eds), 'European Politics: A Reader', London, Mac-
millan, 1971, pp. 217-36; and Gordon Smith, 'Politics in
Western Europe', London, Heinemann, 2nd edn, 1976, pp. 17-24.

34 For a distinction between factionalism and pluralism, see
Giovanni Sartori, 'Parties and Party Systems: A Framework
for Analysis', Cambridge, Cambridge University Press, 1976,
pp. 3-17.

35 For the contrasting concepts of 'Gemeinschaft' and 'Gesellschaft',

see Ferdinand Tönnies, 'Community and Society', New York, Harper and Row, 1957, originally pub. 1887.

36 For a consideration of the impact of Emmanuel Mounier's 'personalist' doctrine on French elites in the 1930s and 1940s, see Jean-Pierre Rioux, A Changing of the Guard? Old and New Elites at the Liberation, in Howorth and Cerny, op. cit., ch. 5.

37 With certain notable exceptions: de Gaulle's flight to Baden-Baden and appeal for army support in May, 1968; the clandestine warfare against the OAS by the 'barbouzes'; the network centred on de Gaulle's aide Jacques Foccart; etc.

38 Cerny and Schain, op. cit., chs. 1 and 8.

39 Report in 'Le Monde', 28 May 1981; article by Jacques Chirac in 'Le Monde', 13 June 1981.

40 'Le Monde', 19 June 1981.

41 For a detailed analysis of these constraints, see Cerny, The New Rules of the Game.

42 'Le Monde', 4 July 1981; these 'bons mots' do not translate well: 'There are those who have talked of making a comeback. My impression is that all we can do is to shout "Help!".'

43 'Le Monde', 26 June, 5-6 July and 11 July 1981.

44 'Le Monde', 14-15 June 1981.

45 'Le Monde', 10 July 1981.

46 Green and Cerny, op. cit., pp. 168-72.

47 Passeron in 'Le Monde', 19-20 July 1981.

48 Gabriel A. Almond and Sidney Verba, 'The Civic Culture: Political Attitudes and Democracy in Five Nations', Princeton, N.J., Princeton University Press, 1963, ch. 3.

49 For an examination of these questions in some detail, see Cerny, The Problem of Legitimacy in the Fifth French Republic.

50 See articles on SAC, 'Le Monde', 23 July and 26-27 July 1981.

51 Charles de Gaulle, 'Le fil de l'épée', Paris, Berger-Levrault, 1932.

52 See article on European-US relations by André Fontaine, 'Le Monde', 5 June 1981.

53 'Le Monde', 26-27 July 1981.

3 'NOUVELLE DROITE': CULTURAL POWER AND

POLITICAL INFLUENCE

Michalina Vaughan

It is by no means obvious why the Nouvelle Droite (ND) should
be included in a study of French political parties. After all, it is
neither structured as a party nor concerned with the mundane
business of vote-catching. Without seeking power through the
ballot-box, its members have asserted their determination to
exercise influence by spreading their ideas within the political
elite. To acknowledge that they have done so, particularly over
the last two years, amounts only to endorsing the diagnosis of
'ideological contamination' formulated by the Left against the
majority parties. Even those who deny that the liberalism of
Giscardians and the populism of Gaullists would allow them to
accept wholly the ideology of the ND cannot dispute that the Club
de l'Horloge has effectively bridged the gap between the young
intellectuals of both parties and GRECE (Groupement de recherche
et d'études pour la civilisation européenne). Without indulging in
conspiracy theories, the objectives of the latter group, created
in January 1969, were distinctly elitarian, so that 'entryism'
into decision-making circles was advocated as an effective strategy.

In fact, the Nouvelle Droite did not infiltrate the milieux from
among which decision-makers are recruited, but suddenly spread
through them as the latest 'in-thing'. At first, this seemed a good
reason for not taking it too seriously, since it might have proved
no more than an intellectual fashion, launched by the press, sustained by the media, yet ultimately bound to run out of steam.
After all, Paris has always been a fertile ground for pseudo-
discoveries of a cultural kind. The intensity of the debates to
which they give rise is often no substitute for either depth or
durability. A mere ripple on the shallow waters of the Parisian
intelligentsia can hardly be expected to affect the political scene
– or could it?

In a way, appearances prompt one to dismiss the GRECE's claims
to pursuing long-term political objectives. The glossiness of the
publications it sponsors encourages the impression that they cannot be more than coffee-table magazines. The complacency with
which they record their own newsworthiness,[1] the coyness of the
inverted commas around the new right's name and the half-hearted
attempts to rename it 'new culture', the constant listing of contributors, sympathisers and mere authors of letters to the editor
– all these signs of frivolousness might be held sufficient to dismiss the whole enterprise as one more form of intellectual snobbery.
Undoubtedly, the up-market prettiness of these reviews and their
relentless name-dropping pander to a persistent, if regrettable,

52

French taste for 'la vulgarisation culturelle'. Nevertheless, it is also possible to detect much more serious undertones in the campaign conducted by the ND with a view to gaining 'le pouvoir culturel'. After all, power may derive from prestige rather than create it and this appears to be a case in point.

This elusive concept of 'cultural power' denotes a systematic attempt to launch new ideological tenets and undermine those which have been dominant since the Liberation. A new world-view 'transcending the Right and the Left'[2] is being formulated or reformulated to challenge all forms of traditionalism - Christian thought as an inspiration to the Right, as well as Marxism and Freudian reductionism. In the thirties, the radical philosopher Alain had pointed out that challenging accepted political outlooks as equally irrelevant is characteristic of the Right's approach: 'When I am asked whether the cleavage between right-wing and left-wing parties, right-wing and left-wing men, still has a meaning, the first idea that occurs to me is that the man who asks the question is certainly not a man of the Left.' Instead of the established dichotomy between optimism and pessimism, equality and freedom, collectivism and individualism, an alternative conception of order as the responsibility of a meritocratic elite, as equally antithetic to egalitarian postulates and to the practice of liberalism, is being propounded. Such ideas are not new, but link back with trends which belonged to a much earlier socio-political climate. In ideology, as in fiction, film and fashion, 'la mode rétro' is proving successful, perhaps because certain themes were considered taboo for a long time, as were certain uniforms or tunes.

Thus it is to the Germany of the twenties and the thirties that the ND turns for inspiration. Between the defeat of 1918 and the consolidation of Hitler's power in 1931, the protagonists of the so-called 'conservative revolution' were influential in cultural and political life. They denounced both liberal individualism and Marxist materialism. They asserted the creativeness of conservatism, aimed at reviving the past, by contrast with reactionary ideologies, which attempt to restore it. This particular tenet of the GRECE is traced back to the works of Moeller van den Bruck by Alain de Benoist. 'The reactionary imagines the world as it has always been. The conservative sees it as it will always be . . . Reactionary politics is no politics at all. Conservative politics is the great politics. Politics becomes great only by creating history.'[3] It is by reference to the same dichotomy that the French predecessors of the ND are condemned. 'The old Right in France has always been reactionary. The reactionary spirit may be the thing I detest most in the world. The old French Right always seems to want to resurrect something, as if it wanted to go back to an earlier stage, automatically assessed as better. Some want to go back to 1789, others to 1933 or to 1945. It depends on one's nostalgia. This type of attitude has always proved sterile.'[4] Willingness to learn from German conservatism in the inter-war period should, of course, not be confused with any 'nostalgia' for 1933. The article on Moeller van den Bruck stresses that, like Spengler,

he rejected racist theories in favour of the primacy of culture
and that he had 'nothing but contempt' for Hitler.[5] It is tempting
to ask whether the subtle distinctions drawn by the GRECE between German anti-democratic writers and national-socialism
amount to casuistry. They certainly have not stopped their critics
from invoking 'guilt by association' and denouncing as fascist
values which are by no means the prerogative of the extreme
Right.

The crucial issue is not so much one of origins as of repercussions. It is more important to reflect whether, as diagnosed
by the Socialist monthly 'Après-Demain', 'a radical change of the
French ideological landscape'[6] has really occurred than to debate
over the exact scope of the derivative and the innovative in the
thought of those to whom a responsibility for this transformation
is imputed.

Ideas which no one put forward since the war reemerge gradually. They can be summarized as one idea: social inequalities,
injustice, in short, the world as it is, stem directly and spontaneously from the nature of things; the existing social order
is therefore the necessary result of human nature in the present
stage of its development and the only possible progress consists
in letting the mechanisms of this 'nature' operate unconstrained.
Any step taken to hamper the free operation of the market, the
free play of natural selection, is a fetter upon social development, an unbearable constraint upon nature, a factor of regression . . . Certainly this ideological evolution fits the crisis
of capitalism like a glove.[7]

The anti-egalitarian emphasis of the GRECE has contributed in
no small measure to making elitism intellectually respectable. In
sharp contrast with the ideology which had been dominant since
the Liberation, it did not involve the use of either moralistic or
political argument, but harnessed somewhat indiscriminately the
findings of science, the lessons of history and the maxims of
common sense to the pursuit and advocacy of differences rather
than uniformity. From the outset, the ND 'identified their main
enemy, not as "communism" or "subversion", or "the left", but
as an egalitarian, regressive, negativist ideology'.[8] When first
mooted in 1968, such views had scarcity value; they would have
seemed provocative, had they enjoyed a wide audience.[9] Such was
clearly not the case. In accordance with its own elitist tenets, the
GRECE had from the outset a highly selective recruitment policy.
Being 'neither a party nor a movement . . . our strength is not
in the number, or the "electoral" weight of our members. This is
not to say that the influence we have is negligible - far from it.'[10]
While the actual membership is somewhat vaguely described as
'several thousands, organised on a regional basis',[11] the sphere
of influence is more accurately reflected by the readership of
periodicals issued by or associated with the GRECE. An indication
of their popularity may be found in the fact that the average

issue of 'Eléments' is approximately 1,600 copies and that of
'Nouvelle Ecole' about 1,200.[12] Their public has been increasing
of late, with the number of subscribers to 'Eléments' passing from
2,000 to 6,000.[13] It is also widened by the weekly 'Figaro-Magazine'
in whom the main exponents of the ND have found a regular, high-
prestige platform.[14]

This certainly does not amount, despite some shrill denunciations,
to anything like a take-over of French intellectual life by Rightists.
Still, the traditional monopoly of the progressive intelligentsia,
established firmly in post-war France and attacked by the GRECE
in the late sixties, was actually undermined in the late seventies.
This time-lag has been attributed by the ND to a conspiracy of
silence, whereby left-wing intellectuals refused to engage in
debate or even to acknowledge the existence of a challenge.
Eventually recognition came and soon paved the way for notoriety.
In a series of articles published in 'Le Monde' in March 1978 under
the title: Une nouvelle droite? (both the indefinite article and the
question mark were, no doubt, advisedly used), Gilbert Comte
explored the innovativeness of the new Right. A whole spate of
magazine and newspaper investigations and attacks followed.
Throughout the summer of 1979, the ND - as it was generally
called in print - received relentless publicity in the press and the
media: most of it was unfavourable, but contributed nevertheless
to turning a loose gathering of isolated intellectuals into acknowledged competitors for cultural leadership. While describing the
agitation of the press as hysterical (and its earlier silence as
conspiratorial - but then paranoia is not the prerogative of any
side in this particular controversy), Alain de Benoist admits that
its consequences were, on the whole, positive for the new Right.
'It is the first time *historically*, in thirty years at least, that in a
European country, a trend of thought classified as being "on the
right" reached such a level, both ideologically and in terms of
influence. A dynamic process has thus been initiated.'[15]

The level of attention was high in 1979-80,[16] perhaps excessively
so, since it is by no means obvious that the message of GRECE
was as novel as its spokesman held it to be. In retrospect, it now
seems that the level of influence gained was even higher, in other
words that the whole machinery of the media did not just create
a nine-day wonder. The degree of overlap between the ideology
of the ND and the official pronouncements of the Giscardian government ministers is striking. This is especially true in the sphere of
education, in which both Christian Beullac (Minister of Education)
and Alice Saunier-Sëité (Minister of Universities) have consistently
linked the future of training and research with a reliance on
selection. Contrary to the policy endorsed - though not always
very actively pursued - under the Fourth and the earlier stages
of the Fifth Republic (i.e., while the Fouchet, Faure and Haby
reforms were being introduced), elitism was acknowledged as a
national imperative. Somewhat unexpectedly, this theme of the
Giscardian government has been persistently presented as a mere
continuation of previous Gaullist policies. The view that the whole

educational policy of the Fifth Republic is fully consistent has
been put forward both by former minister René Haby ('It all began
with de Gaulle in 1958 when the entrance examination into second-
ary school was abolished') and by M. Beullac ('I feel in perfect
harmony with M. Haby; the law of 1975 is a great law').[17] The
contradiction between removing hurdles and defending the selection process does not appear to have worried anyone unduly, perhaps because a process of social discrimination was at work any-
way. Arguments about the continuity of policy, coloured by
electoral concerns, cannot conceal the change in style and rhetoric.
Significantly, the Club de l'Horloge will soon issue a new volume
to be entitled 'Un nouveau printemps pour l'Education'. The first
blossoms of this new spring have no doubt been exhibited by the
Club's member and ENA graduate, Philippe Baccou, in a recent
attack on the egalitarian taboo.[18] The advocacy of a differentiated
educational system, catering separately for problem children,
average pupils, good achievers and the gifted, reflects so accurately the postulates of the new Right as to exclude the hypothesis
that a mere coincidence exists in this case.

Indeed, Pierre Vial, General Secretary of the GRECE, has
recently expressed concern at the 'exploitation' of his organisation
by the then governing majority. 'We have been trapped by notoriety.
Our themes are now used to justify the unjustifiable. I do not
want the GRECE to become, to any extent, the ideological laboratory of a political majority.'[19] There is clearly a contradiction - as
Monsieur Vial admits - between the will to avoid any compromise
with politicians which would detract from the group's ideological
purity and the avowed intention to exert some influence in decision-
making circles. It is not possible to define the ends of the new
Right as purely cultural or 'meta-political' and at the same time
to engage in any form of militancy. The tension between these
approaches may well divide members of an organisation whose
structure has always been loosely knit and whose tenets are in
many respects ambiguous. Hence the possibility of a split is by
no means remote - there is no shortage of precendents for such a
happening on the French political and cultural scene. Attempts at
'recuperation' from the extreme Right, as well as 'exploitation'
by the Giscardians, threaten the integrity of the GRECE. Thus
the candidate of the extremist Parti des Forces Nouvelles (PFN)
to the presidential election, Pascal Gauchon, has adopted the
slogan: 'A new man for a new Right', despite strong repudiation
by Alain de Benoist and other ND leaders.[20] Mention should also
be made in passing of the Nouvelle Droite française (NDF) of
Michel-Georges Micberth, who claims to have inspired the ideas of
Alain de Benoist, and so be 'a born leader, . . . the archetype
of Protean man'.[21]

The real danger is not so much to be made ridiculous by the
efforts of the lunatic fringe to jump on the ND bandwagon, as to
be made odious by the accusations of belonging to the growing
number of neo-fascists. At first glance, this is too rough a company for the members of the GRECE, on the assumption that

intellectuals and bullyboys don't mix. 'One can hardly imagine
the philosophers and thinkers [of that group] . . . scribbling
swastikas on walls and posting threatening messages which end
with "Heil Hitler".[122] Yet the relationship between their ideology
and that of the Fédération d'action nationale et européenne (FANE),
an organisation which was involved in several violent incidents in
1980, then dissolved and renamed Faisceaux nationalistes européens (FNE) has proved somewhat controversial. While its leader,
Marc Frederiksen, claimed that the writings of Alain de Benoist
expressed the ideas of his movement, the latter strenuously
denied any such affinity. The bulletin of FANE, 'Notre Europe',
attributed any disclaimers to tactical considerations. 'The discourse of the GRECE is profoundly sound, the aim it pursues is
certainly commendable, even if a few differences . . . exist between us. The question revolves round the mask worn by the
GRECE.[123] Not unlike the Left, the extreme Right suspects the
ND of concealing its true convictions and of adopting a deliberately
bland, apparently apolitical approach in order to convey more
effectively a subversive message. Strenuous, though not altogether
successful, efforts have been made to differentiate the cultural
activities of the GRECE from any acts of violence, and particularly
from anti-semitism (after the bombing of a Paris synagogue in the
Autumn of 1980). In the words of Pierre Vial, 'the GRECE has
never ceased over the years to denounce all forms of extremism,
racism, intolerance and inducement to violence'.[24] Such statements
can be construed as 'protesting too much', even though the analo-
gies between Nouvelle Droite and neo-fascism are forced. There
are undeniable differences of approach, of style and, in all prob-
ability, of objectives between them. Yet the possibility of a slide
into extremism (at least, verbal) seems to threaten even high-
minded intellectuals. The sociologist Alain Touraine diagnoses this
risk of an evolution towards fascism.

> This new culture of the right is associated to a political and
> economic elitism which contrasts with national-socialism, since
> it was anti-aristocratic and wanted to be popular. However, if
> it is agreed that one may call fascism any authoritarian appeal
> to the cultural and institutional [étatique] unity of a nation, as
> a resort against popular movements that a ruling class can no
> longer contain, the new right is a [form of] fascism. While it is
> far from being able as yet to play the same part as [forms of]
> fascism which emerged in the wake of the First World War and
> of the Soviet revolution, it carries a logic of social repression
> which is fatal for democratic freedoms. Its ideologists may not
> all accept the use of political violence, but we remember the
> traditionalists who have become dedicated Nazis . . .[25]

The argument is that the inherent logic of any repressive ideology
leads to justifying repressive action and consequently that at
least some of its supporters, no matter how 'cultured', will ultimately be carried away by their own convictions into legitimating

the use of violence, or even engaging in it. The pressures of
world recession on the French economy and the attendant risks
of social unrest lend, according to Touraine, an added credibility
to this particular scenario. Without maintaining that history re-
peats itself, he draws a parallel with the evolution of Germany in
the thirties: similar causes might well bring about analogous
effects.

This is persuasive reasoning, though some weakness lies in the
implicit assumption that right-wing traditionalism alone is prone
to degenerating into fascist policies. Another lesson of the thirties,
and indeed of subsequent decades, is that ideologists classified
as left-wing are equally tempted to accept and even to advocate
repressive policies. The gradual transition from Marxism to
Stalinism is at least as well documented as that from traditionalism
to fascism. However, left-wingers have shown less proneness to
guilt feelings as a result of historical associations than their
counterparts on the right. 'The Right is ashamed to have been on
the right at the same time as Hitler. The Left is proud to be on
the left, even in the company of Stalin.'[26] At least, that is how
things used to be and, in this respect, the new Right is indeed
novel in exhibiting no such squeamishness. Its moral toughness,
or insensitivity, is largely due to the conviction that it is harness-
ing scientific findings, rather than outmoded prejudice, to the
defence of the social order.

This scientism is not unprecedented in the armoury of the Right,
since it can claim such eminent ancestors as Comte, Renan and
Taine, but it differs from any earlier version to the extent that
no overlap is necessarily assumed between the findings of research
and the dictates of morality. The encapsulation of ethics and
applied science under the concept of progress, characteristic of
nineteenth-century evolutionism, has given place to a realistic,
i.e., pessimistic, view of the natural, as well as the social, world.
One of the grounds on which the ND has been most frequently
and most intensely criticised has been its advocacy of sociobiology,
the latest version of Darwinism which emphasises the tendency for
the male to propagate his genes and thus to further the genetic
assertion of his kinship group. This is a criticism which appears
to have been violently resented and which Alain de Benoist sets
out to refute:

> To my knowledge, there has only been one text of the ND on
> sociobiology. It is the one I published in 'Le Figaro-Magazine'
> (30th June 1979), to introduce the French public to a debate
> which had for five years taken England and the United States
> by storm and about which, yet again, the intelligentsia had
> remained silent. In that article, after outlining the theories of
> the sociobiologists, I clearly pointed out their limits, which
> seem to me to be related to their reductionist tendency.[27]

Hence any attempt at genetic reductionism seems to have been rejected outright. Yet, in an article entitled L'heure de la socio-

biologie, published in 'Eléments' the following year,[28] the point is
made that the nature/culture dichotomy might be transcended, if
genetic engineering could ultimately produce a fit between innate
endowment, programmed by the genes, and cultural aspirations.
Meanwhile man remains free to choose, though the ability to make
decisions is unequally distributed between 'mass-men', incapable
of self-determination, and 'creative heroes', who generate 'new
cultural facts'.

This defensiveness towards any accusation of biologism is related to an overriding concern for the originality of culture, conceived as 'everything that is added to nature'.[30] In accordance
with Spengler's definition, culture 'delineates the stage at which
societies live by reference to *organic* principles, which conform
to their specific character. Obviously today, in Europe, cultures
have aged and have undergone the influence of materialist and
egalitarian tendencies. They tend therefore to become "petrified",
mechanistic or bureaucratised.[31] A double reservation is thus
made in response to biological determinists. First, the creativeness
of exceptional individuals is asserted, as a recurring historical
pattern and as a last resort in times of crises, hence possibly
(though this is never explicitly stated) as a future solution. 'In
periods of crises or extreme danger, no social, cultural or ideological category escapes this gregarious impulse, this quest for a
sword, symbol of a firm and strong authority.'[32] The egalitarian
assumptions which might be drawn from emphasising common
natural characteristics are thus discarded in favour of a culturally
rooted leadership principle. Secondly, the inequality of cultures
and their vulnerability to pressures, such as those of modernisation, which detract from their intrinsic originality, are put
forward. These appear to be abstract arguments of little relevance
to current political allegiances. Yet they have implications for the
respective attitudes of the ND and the neo-liberal Giscardians to
each other. The latter tend to favour any scientific theory favouring the reliance on nature rather than nurture and hence providing a justification for abandoning the pursuit of educational
equality. In this respect, they are indebted to the publications of
the GRECE and to its sympathisers for supplying them with what
appears to be corroborative evidence in support of elitist policies.
On the other hand, they also look to the new economists for arguments to vindicate monetarist policies and stress the inevitability
of market processes. It is partly because sociobiologists can be
interpreted as giving added credence to this school that their
writings have attracted attention. Yet it is precisely on this
ground that Alain de Benoist berates them.[33]

If a considerable degree of overlap between the policies advocated by the GRECE and those implemented by the Giscardians
can be found with regard to education, this convergence does not
exist in economic matters. Advanced liberalism draws its inspiration from the new economists and has lacked no official spokesmen even before 'the best economist in France' (as former Premier
Raymond Barre was described by President Giscard d'Estaing) came

to office. This approach is repudiated by the new Right as
materialistic, substituting quantity for quality and reducing moti-
vation to the pursuit of interests. In this respect, liberalism is
not held to be preferable to Marxism, which it generated (through
the influence of classical economists on Marx). Two major tenets
appear to be shared by liberal and Marxist economists, namely
that interests actuate human beings and that societies consequently
evolve towards ever more advanced stages of sophistication in
production. These two tenets are unacceptable to the ND. In the
first place, its supporters consider 'Homo oeconomicus' as the product of decadence, since his main concern is with owning rather
than with being. 'A very simple distinction: aristocrats attempt
to preserve what they are, bourgeois endeavour to preserve
what they have.'[34] Consequently, economic man cannot find fulfilment in being, and is for ever frustrated in his quest for expanding his material possessions, whether he lives under capitalism or
under any of the existing forms of socialism. '"Homo oeconomicus"
exists, but he is not a happy man. The satisfaction of his material
needs, of his needs centered on one sphere, does not slake his
desire, but stimulates it instead, rendering it insatiable and dis-
enchanted at once. Any concept of society based on welfare is
bound to fail to bring about happiness.'[35] Such supportive
examples as Huxley's 'Brave New World' are often quoted. The
underlying argument is that human beings are not primarily either
producers (as Marx believed) or consumers (as they are meant to
be under advanced capitalism). They have deep-rooted spiritual
needs, which the economy - despite the fact that it is necessary -
cannot fill.

Secondly, the assumption is challenged that societies are moving
along the same trajectory towards a level of economic advancement
defined as modernity. It is hardly original to equate this outcome
with the stage already exemplified by the United States. The rejection of American cultural patterns is almost as frequent in the
publications of the ND as their imitation was in Giscardian France.

> If the ruling class are to limit their ambitions to copying the
> manners of the United States, . . . if the mass media are to go
> on paying copyright for commercial shows to take over the radio,
> TV and show business, while French works are kept out, if the
> press and publishers are to continue drawing their inspiration
> from their senior colleagues, then 1984 has already become
> superseded. . . . Big Brother no longer has to watch over you
> in order to ensure that you conform, for today you are Big
> Brother.[36]

The idea that American behaviour patterns and life-styles have
taken over (or at least are taking over) is central to the analyses
of Europe conducted by the new Right. Despite their abhorrence
of Marxist collectivism, it is not there that the greatest threat to
Western European, and particularly to French, identity is found.
The invasion is economic and cultural rather than political and it

originates from the United States. Now this was totally incompatible
with the Giscardian emphasis on modernity, efficiency and 'keeping up with other Europeans' (which amounts to 'resembling the
Americans to the best of our ability'). It sounds like a difference
in cultural styles, but in practice it involves a total disagreement
about foreign policy. In so far as the Gaullists, or at least the
traditionalists among them, advocate a continuation of earlier
neutralist and pseudo-non-aligned (a free translation of 'Indépen-
dance tous azimuths') policies, there are receptive members of the
former majority who do not necessarily disapprove of such
attitudes. All the same, these are far too sharp to find many
supporters outside the ND fold. In order to endorse so dismissive
a diagnosis of both capitalism and Marxist socialism ('a plague on
both their houses'), some alternative views must be put forward.

In an attempt to utilise scientific research to buttress their condemnation of economism as a principle of social organisation, the
members of GRECE rely on the works of Georges Dumézil. A re-
nowned historian and linguist, he has specialised in the study of
Indo-European religions. His main finding is that in any society
a tripartite division exists between those acts which possess a
sacred character, those which are necessary to the conduct of war
and those which consist in productive work. However, he argues
that only the people who spoke Indo-European languages elaborated
an ideology whereby the religious, the military and the economic
were construed as different principles, from which a hierarchical
ranking of the corresponding specialisms was deduced. 'A treble
structure, corresponding to three functions . . . is the web of
the Indo-European conception of man and of the world, of nature
and of the universe.'[37] His theory provides arguments for down-
grading the 'third function' (production, wealth) to its proper
place, the lowest, and for advocating the values which were sup-
posedly shared, and should now be recaptured, by Indo-European
peoples in order to arrest the decadence of modern society.
Against the model of a mercantile civilisation, inspired by the
United States, that of a community linked by a common attachment
to the land, by ties of blood and tradition, and by the cult of
heroic deeds is asserted as indigenous rather than 'alien'. It
matters little that Dumézil himself should have expressed strong
reservations against the use to which his research is thus being
put.[38] Neither his reminder that his construct is theoretical rather
than descriptive, nor his warnings about the vulnerability of his
conclusions[39] appear to have been heeded by his unsought disciples. This is hardly surprising, since there is so much scope
for generalising from findings about the myths, rather than the
actual practices, of a remote past. Full advantage has certainly
been taken of this potential and bold generalisations are the new
Right's stock in trade.

The condemnation of Western materialism - as intrinsically no
better than its Marxist offspring - demarcates the new Right
from the new economists and their Giscardian followers. This may
not have always been clearly perceived by their Socialist critics,

but is nevertheless a genuine divide. Alain Touraine is perceptive
in stating that the ND is both influential within the ex-majority
and yet resisted by liberals within it. 'For the moment, while it
is fought by liberal Giscardism, the new right already weighs
somewhat upon the ideology of the majority and this weight may
increase as the crisis becomes more acute. . . .'[40] Meanwhile the
division is perpetuated mainly by a different conception of Europe,
not only in terms of its relationship with the United States,[41] but
also in the definition of the main European values. While the ND
might well attract some sympathies in repudiating materialism, it
antagonises many by rejecting also the whole Judeo-Christian
tradition. 'The monotheistic component of Western civilisation is
clearly recognisable in its intent, which is substantively identical
with that of Soviet society: to impose a universal civilisation based
on the dominance of the economy . . . and to depoliticise the
people in favour of world "management".'[42] Monotheism is blamed
for generating imperialist drives, legitimated by the conviction
of possessing the truth, and hence for the advent of colonialist
exploitation. Initiated under Christian auspices, this expansionism
established the domination of European powers and led to that of
the United States at present. The industrialisation of the world
is a logical and, alas, irreversible outcome of the belief that local
cultures not only could, but should be eliminated, because they
were inferior. Hence totalitarianism is a product of religious intolerance which, in turn, results from the conviction of possessing
the truth. It is the first monotheistic religion, Judaism, and its
offspring, Christianity and Islam, which are to blame for the per-
vasiveness of totalitarian policies and racial persecution. Conversely, their adherents, sharing in the possession of the only
religion conducive to salvation, were superior to unbelievers, but
equal to each other. Egalitarianism started among the chosen
people and was spread by the early Catholic Church, thus providing the seed-bed from which Marxism sprang.

This Nietzschean anti-Christianism is not exactly new, but it is
certainly unfamiliar in France. It is in sharp contrast with the
traditional commitment of right-wing parties to Catholicism,
whether from genuine fervour or from worldly-wise reliance on
religion to strengthen social control. It is also in contradistinction
to the view, popularised in the late seventies by the 'new philosophers' and particularly by Bernard-Henry Lévy,[43] that the only
genuine alternative to Marxist totalitarianism can be found in the
Judeo-Christian tradition. The debate between nouvelle droite and
nouveaux philosophes, when it does not sink to the level of
denouncing the formers' fascist leanings and the latters' (freely
admitted) former allegiance to Marxism, focuses on the claims of
Athens and those of Jerusalem as the cradle of 'our' civilisation.
Some of Lévy's arguments are reminiscent of Karl Popper denouncing Platonic philosophy as the source of totalitarianism.

Some of Alain de Benoist's arguments echo the philosophers of
the Enlightenment berating Catholic intolerance or exposing the
ethnic superiority asserted in the Bible. Both sides make occasional

valid points, and those of the ND are no doubt the more familiar,
to the extent that they have often been mooted by French anti-
clericals. Yet it is hardly possible to consider either contention
as anything but the product of systematic bias. It is equally a-
historical and untenable to attribute all the evils of totalitarianism
to the Judeo-Christian tradition as to maintain that none are
imputable to this value-system. The statement that 'the integration
of Christianity into the European mental system was the most
disastrous event in the whole of history'[44] is unlikely to persuade
dispassionate readers of anything but its author's partiality.
What may seem puzzling is the root cause of such extremism. Conflicting interpretations are possible and, among them, the assumption that monotheism is denounced on old-fashioned anti-Semitic
grounds cannot be discarded altogether. The multiple evils stemming from the adoption of monotheistic religions are, after all,
traceable to Jews. 'Historically it all started with Abraham. It is
not for nothing that the supporters of the three monotheist
religions, Judaism, Christianism and Islam, call themselves the
sons of Abraham.'[45] Not only are Jews responsible for all forms of
subversion in the past: the existence of the state of Israel is
shown to have prompted the oil crisis. 'It is Jewishness itself
which is at stake',[46] which is made the scapegoat in all ND analyses
of either the past or the present.

An alternative to this anti-semitic interpretation highlights the
anti-Christian bias of the new Right, and gives it its Nietzschean
ring. Christianity is denigrated as alien to the traditions of the
Indo-Europeans, as analysed by Dumézil, and as antithetic to
their aristocratic mode of organisation. Its advent precipitated
the fall of the Roman Empire, so that it proved to be 'the bol-
shevism of Antiquity',[47] undermining the structures of the family
and the polity. The achievements of medieval Europe perpetuated
the greatness of earlier, pre-Christian civilisations (Greco-Roman,
Celtic and Germanic). The main contributions of the West to
world civilisation in the sciences and the arts depended on the
emancipation of thought from dogma. Hence they were arrived at
'not *within* Christianity, but rather, in most cases *against* it'.[48]
The fourteenth round table of the GRECE, held on 9 December
1979, was dedicated to the investigation of totalitarianism in its
various forms - religious, cultural, political and economic. It was
during that meeting that the first public and violent protest
against the new right was made by the Organisation de defénse
juive (ODJ). Its supporters asserted that the definition of totalitarianism as 'monotheistic' amounted to an anti-Semitic slogan. In
the subsequent issue of 'Eléments', their version is unambiguously
repudiated. 'Jewish monotheism became truly totalitarian only
when it ceased being Jewish and claimed to submit to the law of a
single God peoples who held different religious views.'[49] Indeed
Jews have been prominent among the victims of Catholic intolerance from the days of the Inquisition onwards. 'The children of
Athens and of Jerusalem',[50] the pagan and Jewish victims of
religious intolerance suffered as a result of Christian persecutions.

The Church's claim to embody the truth paved the way to a similar assertion of spiritual power by secularised states. Political totalitarianism is thus a product of religious totalitarianism. So is economic totalitarianism, whose materialist concerns are merely a transposition of the ideal of salvation, whose secular counterpart, whether under capitalism or socialism, is prosperity. 'One may wonder . . . if Christianity, born in the Near-East, was not the carrier of a disintegrative germ which can be seen currently spreading everywhere.'[51] Even when the condemnation appears to be specific, it still hints at some inferiority derived from the geographical origin (or the genetic and cultural make-up of the founders) of the Christian creed. So some general inferiority of 'alien', non-European value-systems is posited.

While such systems have brought about and are accentuating the decadence of Europe, revival can only be achieved through a return to the myths of the Indo-European past. The assumption appears to be - despite all assertions to the contrary - that a hierarchy of cultures exists. Hence, by adopting unversalistic creeds, peoples who possessed a superior form of socio-political organisation, rooted in an original world-view, betrayed their own traditions. Critics have maintained that this stance is reminiscent of the Aryan myths on which Nazi Germany traded. This is strenuously denied, as is the gentler accusation of ethnocentricity. 'When it attempts to give back to Europeans the memory of their most remote past - not in order to return to it, but to link up with it - the new right does not undertake anything that it would not wish to see develop throughout the world.'[52]

However, even if it proved possible to reconstruct the remote past of all societies, including those now extinct, the outcome of such a search for 'roots' would in all likelihood provide additional fuel for ongoing controversies rather than afford illumination. The investigation of cultural differences would be but a preliminary to that of biological superiority. A contrast between the Judeo-Christian defence of the lower breeds and the weaker individuals may well be contrasted with the Nietzschean quest for superman and the master race. No matter how strenuously any connection between culture and genes is negated by the new Right, no matter how hard its spokesmen endeavour to impute racism to others,[53] the Indo-European aristocracies to which they look back are a racial, and not just a cultural entity.

> The appearance in history and the establishment of Indo-European aristocracies occurred by virtue of a double process: on the one hand, within Indo-European societies themselves, through functional division into three categories, on the other, as conquests and migrations took place, through the superimposition of an Indo-European layer on foreign populations. This aristocratic character of the first Indo-European civilisations is not doubted by anyone.[54]

Contrary to Pareto's terminology, an aristocracy is defined in this

context as characterised by merit, whereas an elite is only composed of those who - whether deservedly or not - occupy top-
ranking positions in a group. Thus both social inequalities and
racial supremacy are construed as meritocratically justified in the
remote past. One may well ask why they should not be so again
in the future.

There is no doubt that this heterogeneous mixture of popularised
science and historical myths can be harnessed to political ends.
In this version, culture is a kind of Pandora's box and those who
first delved in it may be dubious themselves about some of the
uses to which their findings are put. In his disclaimer of any
support for Giscardism, the General Secretary of the GRECE went
so far as to advocate a complete break away from any form of
militancy.

> I shall endeavour to persuade [the membership] that the calling
> of the GRECE is not temporal, that it must play the same part
> as the early Church, i.e. make a retreat in order to meditate
> about the future. To this end, we must condemn ourselves to
> political impotence, we must dig such trenches between poli-
> ticians and ourselves that they could not be filled.[55]

The wish to withdraw from the rough and tumble of politics
expressed through these somewhat mixed metaphors is, as Monsieur Vial himself admitted, unlikely to be shared by a majority
of members at the forthcoming yearly round table, to be held on
17 May 1981. Dissensions within the new Right appear to be inevitable. It seems unlikely that the 'contemplative' trend will
prevail. Even if it did, the impact of the publications issued by
or connected with this group has already been considerable,
especially given its comparatively modest resources.[56] The degree
of acceptance secured for its ideology during the last two years
among the reading public in France and the amount of interest
exhibited in other countries, especially in Italy, where a sister
review, 'Elementi', appears, cannot be written off as a mere fad.
An observer as acute as Raymond Aron notes that the new Right
is viewed as a response to the monopolisation of cultural debates
by the Left over a long period. Indeed he appears himself to
welcome the existence of a counter-ideology and to find some of
its components attractive.

> I have no anger against this new Right, because I think it is
> normal that there should be an ideology opposing the conformism
> of the Left. . . . Part of the ideas of the new Right, i.e. the
> liking for differentiation, for ethnic specificity, is not at all
> repugnant, there is no reason not to accept it.[57]

This assessment shows that the ND is 'acceptable' - at least in
part - to the Centre-Right, despite the extremism of some tenets
and the extravagance of some claims.

It seems surprising that moderates - who condemn the 'action

groups' of the extreme Right without qualification - should show
such lenience. After all, a number of the main tenets upheld by
the GRECE can be considered intellectually spurious and morally
unattractive. Is it really 'acceptable' that: 'Slaves are needed for
the emergence of a new aristocracy'? or that 'the evolution of
mankind is connected with racial differentiation'?[58] Either such
themes are becoming part of the ideology of the Right as a whole
rather than remaining the prerogative of a fringe or they are
merely treated as verbal excesses, word-games without real impact.
In the words of Trollope, 'it is so comfortable to have theories
one is not bound to carry out'. However, it is the kind of comfort
that twentieth-century intellectuals can no longer claim. Gramsci
has shown the extent of their 'cultural power' and attempted to
mobilise it. The new Right acknowledge their debt to him, while
they wage 'cultural war'.[59] The skirmishings of the French intelligentsia may be dismissed as a minor form of cultural warfare, but
the smallness of individuals does not entail the insignificance of
the species.

NOTES

1 The ideas of the 'new Right' continue to provide material for
  Parisian chroniclers, 'Eléments' - bi-monthly published by
  GRECE, 35, Summer 1980, p. 17.
2 P. Dommergues, in 'Le Monde diplomatique', December 1980, p. 2.
3 Quoted from A. Moeller van den Bruck, 'Das Dritte Reich',
  Berlin, 1923, quoted by A. de Benoist, Arthur Moeller van
  den Bruck: Une 'Question à la Destinée Allemande', 'Nouvelle
  Ecole', 35, Winter 1979-80, p. 65.
4 A. de Benoist, 'Les idées à l'endroit', Paris, Coperic, 1977,
  p. 74.
5 'Nouvelle Ecole', 35, p. 59 and p. 69.
6 P. Ducasset, in 'Après-Demain', February 1981.
7 Ibid.
8 A. de Benoist, 'Les idées à l'endroit', p. 18.
9 The first publication associated with the ND was 'Nouvelle
  Ecole' which appeared in March 1968 and of which A. de Benoist
  became editor in 1969.
10 P. Vial (ed.), 'Pour une Renaissance Culturelle', Paris, 1979,
  p. 25.
11 A. de Benoist, 'Les idées à l'endroit', p. 19.
12 Information supplied by P. Gibelin, Federal Secretary of
  GRECE, in a letter to the author dated 21 January, 1981.
13 'Le Monde', 24 March 1981, p. 14. These figures are given by
  the General Secretary of GRECE, P. Vial, who mentions a
  membership of 4,500 as against 1,000 three years ago.
14 This is the weekly supplement of the Parisian, Right-of-centre
  daily 'Le Figaro'. Four members of the GRECE, Alain de
  Benoist, J.C. Valla, P. de Plunkett and M. Marmin, are regular
  contributors. The editor, Louis Pauwels, is sympathetic to

the Nouvelle Droite.

15 A. de Benoist, 'Les idées à l'endroit', p. 25-6.

16 The title of an article published in 'Eléments', 32, November - December 1979, L'été de la nouvelle droite (by M. Montes, pp. 6-14) is no exaggeration.

17 'Le Monde', 20 January 1981, p. 14.

18 P. Baccou and Club de l'Horloge, 'Le grand Tabou', Paris, 1981.

19 'Le Monde', 24 March 1981, p. 14.

20 'Le Monde', 27-28 July 1980, p. 6.

21 A. Rollat, Un leader pour les surdoués, in 'Le Monde-Dimanche', 23 November 1980.

22 J.M. Tholleyre, Facettes françaises du néo-nazisme, in 'Le Monde', 7 November 1980.

23 F. de Vandamme, La nouvelle droite, in 'Notre Europe', quoted by Tholleyre, op. cit.

24 Letter to 'Le Monde', published on 13 March 1981.

25 A. Touraine, 'L'après-socialisme', Paris, 1981.

26 C. Legoux, Entre la jungle et la fourmilière in 'Le Monde', 27 October 1979, p. 2.

27 A. de Benoist, 'Les idées a l'endroit', p. 21.

28 Interview with Y. Christen, biologist and scientific contributor to 'Le Figaro-Magazine', published in 'Eléments', 35, Summer 1980, pp. 13-16.

29 G. Locchi, Ethologie et sciences humaines, in 'Nouvelle Ecole', 33, Summer 1979, p. 63.

30 P. Vial (ed.), 'Pour une renaissance culturelle', p. 36.

31 Ibid.

32 D. Venner, Le modèle napoléonien, in 'Eléments', 35, Summer 1980, p. 10.

33 A. de Benoist, 'Les idées à l'endroit', p. 22.

34 P. Vial (ed.), 'Pour une renaissance culturelle', p. 49.

35 Ibid.

36 Ibid., pp. 240-1.

37 J.-C. Rivière, Pour une lecture de Dumézil. Introduction à son oeuvre, in 'Nouvelle Ecole', 21-22, Winter 1972-3, p. 30. The whole issue is devoted to Dumézil's work and most contributions have been published by J.-C. Rivière (ed.), 'G. Dumézil à la decouverte des Indo-Européens', Paris, 1979.

38 In an interview with C. Jannoud, published in 'Le Figaro', 20 April 1979.

39 E.g. the almost complete lack of traces of any 'trifunctional ideology' in Greece and, by contrast, its presence in Japanese traditions challenge the basic assumptions of Dumézil. Cf. J.-P. Demoule, Les Indo-Européens ont-ils existé? in 'Historia', 28, November 1980.

40 A. Touraine, 'L'après-socialisme'.

41 The fifteenth round table of GRECE, held on 17 May 1981, focused on 'a defence of the peoples against the American-Western civilisation' and attacked 'multinational companies as more efficient [in destroying cultures] than the disciples of

Marx'. In the words of Alain de Benoist, 'there are two forms
of totalitarianism, whose nature and effects are very different.
The one, in the East, jails, persecutes, hurts the bodies, but,
at least, leaves hope intact. The other, in the West, results
in creating happy robots. It air-conditions hell. It kills the
souls.' ('Le Monde', 20 May 1981.)

42 G. Faye, Pour en finir avec la civilisation occidentale, in
    'Eléments', 34, April–May 1980, p. 5.
43 B.H. Lévi, 'Le Testament de Dieu', Paris, 1979.
44 A. de Benoist, La religion de l'Europe, in 'Eléments', 36,
    Autumn 1980, p.5.
45 Opening speech by P. Vial at GRECE round table of 9
    December 1979, 'Le Monde', 11 December 1979.
46 S. Trigano, C'est je Juif qui est en question, in 'Le Monde',
    1 September 1979.
47 P. Vial (ed.), 'Pour une renaissance culturelle', p. 208.
48 Ibid., p. 209. cf. also Aïde Benoist, 'Comment peut-on être
    païen?', Paris, 1981.
49 A. de Benoist, Le XIVe Colloque du GRECE, in 'Eléments',
    33, February–March 1980, p. 12.
50 M. Marmin, 'Les enfants d'Athènes et de Jérusalem', in 'Le
    Monde', 8 October 1980. Written after the bombing of a Paris
    synagogue, this article elicited angry responses from the
    Jewish community and the Anti-Racist League.
51 P. Vial (ed.), 'Pour une renaissance culturelle', p. 193.
52 A. de Benoist, Ce que nous disons, in 'Le Monde', 29
    September 1979.
53 A. de Benoist, Marx-Darwin: quel est le plus raciste des
    deux?, in 'Le Figaro-Magazine', 28 March 1981, pp. 100-1.
54 A. de Benoist, 'Les idées à l'endroit', p. 123.
55 'Le Monde', 24 March 1981, p. 14.
56 The number of contributors is small, with the same names
    recurring again and again. The financial resources are not
    known, but for the fact that 'Eléments' is published by a
    limited company with a capital of 70,000 francs. Yearly sub-
    scriptions to the GRECE are of 1,200 francs minimum and some
    members pay one tenth of their income every month. (P. Vial,
    'Pour une renaissance culturelle', pp. 27-8.)
57 B. Frappat and D. Wolton, L'optimisme glacé de Raymond
    Aron (interview with R. Aron), in 'Le Monde-Dimanche', 21
    September 1980.
58 Quotations from speeches by Y. Blot at the GRECE round
    table of 16 April 1972 and general assembly of 2 May 1974,
    quoted in 'Le Monde', 27 March 1981.
59 A. de Benoist, 'Les idées à l'endroit', pp. 250-9.

PART TWO: THE LEFT

4 THE STRATEGIES OF THE FRENCH LEFT:

FROM THE 1978 DEFEAT TO THE 1981 VICTORIES

Neill Nugent

THE AFTERMATH OF THE 1978 DEFEAT

Until François Mitterrand's election as President of the Republic
in May 1981, and the unprecedented victory of the Socialist Party
in the subsequent June parliamentary elections, the Left in the
Fifth Republic was establishing a reputation for having the potential to take control of the reins of government but always failing
when opportunities presented themselves. Levels of support in
opinion polls, parliamentary by-elections and local elections were
not sustained on the most important occasions of all: national
elections. As a result, the coalition of Centre-Right forces which
emerged after 1958 to provide General de Gaulle with a majority
in Parliament, and which gradually enlarged itself in the 1960s
and 1970s, won every national election after 1962: in all, five
parliamentary elections and three presidentials.

The defeat in the March 1978 elections was particularly traumatic
for the Left. First, because expectations of victory had been
raised to unprecedented levels. For almost three years all the
indications had been that victory and an overall majority in Parliament was likely. Secondly, because the defeat, when it came,
appeared to be self-inflicted. From mid-1972 when the Communists
(PCF), the Socialists (PS), and the small Left Wing Radicals
(MRG), had signed the Common Programme of Government, until
September 1977, when negotiations to update the 1972 document
broke down, the whole impetus of the Left had been focused on,
and directed towards, an election victory. Yet with that victory
in sight the credibility of the Left as a viable alternative government was severely undermined by the September breakdown. In
the words of so many observers, defeat was snatched from the
jaws of victory.

After March 1978 the erstwhile partners were seemingly concerned to confirm and consolidate their defeat. The election inquest
led to bitter recriminations with each of the two major parties
vehemently denying any responsibility for what had happened.
The PS were accused, by the PCF, of having 'veered to the right',
of standing in the opportunist tradition of their predecessors (the
SFIO), and of being content to come to power merely in order to
'manage the crisis'. In their turn, the PCF were accused by the
PS of having deliberately turned their backs on power in order to
safeguard narrow party interests and of engaging in an 'objective
complicity' with the Right.

Many opportunities presented themselves after the March defeat

71

for renewed co-operation. The deepening economic crisis, the widespread unpopularity of Prime Minister Raymond Barre's austerity policies, the whiff of scandal from the Élysée and elsewhere, and the increasing tensions within the governing majority, all held out the possibility of considerable political benefits for the Left. But far from its constituent units uniting to attempt to reap such benefits, the Left saw its credibility undermined even further by sharp internal divisions within each of the three parties. In the PCF an unprecedented debate took place in which criticisms were directed against various aspects of the party's policy, organisation and strategy. Similar, but more open and more personalised disputes within the PS resulted in it seeming to resemble more and more a confederation of tendencies. Even the MRG had its problems with its leader in the 1978 election campaign, Robert Fabre, leaving the party to sit as an independent in Parliament. The subsequent contest for the MRG leadership was marked by clear and open disagreements over the party's future role, strategy and identity.

ALTERNATIVE PATHWAYS TO POWER

The collapse of the Union de la Gauche and the disarray in which the Left found itself after the 1978 defeat inevitably raised again the much debated question as to how the governing majority might eventually be dislodged from power. There were only two possible alternative strategies to left-wing unity of some kind.

1. The construction of a third force: a great Centre alliance spreading itself across the political spectrum between the Communists on the Left and the Gaullists on the Right.

Such a possible realignment found favour in several quarters and, indeed, appeared to be the dream of President Giscard d'Estaing. In his book 'Démocratie Française', written in 1976, he claimed:

Contrary to glib assertions, France is not divided in two over major social problems. . . . If one had to trace lines of cleavage on the majority of important issues, none would go down the middle. Our country's sociological centre already possesses real unity and the figures suggest that it comprises much more than half the population.[1]

There was something to be said for this view of French society. The combined vote of the PS, the MRG and the 'Centrists' within the governing majority - the latter of whom since early 1978 had been loosely united in the Union pour la Démocratie Française (UDF) - was 46 per cent in March 1978 and 51 per cent in the European elections of June 1979 (27.5 per cent for the UDF, 23.6 per cent for the joint PS/MRG list). Public opinion polls suggested they could retain most of that support were they to come to an 'arrangement'. For example, a 'Sofres' poll in March 1979 found

that 27 per cent of UDF voters favoured a UDF-PS government
and a further 46 per cent favoured a government made up of the
coalition majority (i.e., UDF plus the Gaullist RPR) enlarged to
include the PS.[2] At the same time 29 per cent of Socialist voters
favoured a UDF-PS government and 13 per cent favoured the PS
entering government with the existing majority. Furthermore such
an alliance could even have hoped to attract support elsewhere,
for the same poll showed 56 per cent of RPR voters would have
liked to have seen the PS enter government with the UDF and
RPR.

Attractive though a third force strategy was to Giscard, however, it was ruled out on the part of the PS, for a number of
reasons:

First, opinion poll evidence always has to be interpreted with
caution and care. The same 'Sofres' survey showed 23 per cent of
PS voters favoured a Union of the Left government while 30 per
cent favoured a PS-only government, i.e., 53 per cent did not
express a preference for an accommodation with the Centre-Right
or any part of it. Furthermore, when options were restricted to
relations with the PCF, 43 per cent were still willing to negotiate
some sort of programmatic agreement and a further 23 per cent
believed the two parties should at least enter into second ballot
electoral arrangements. Only 22 per cent wanted no agreement of
any kind between the parties.

Secondly, the two main previous attempts during the Fifth
Republic to construct a third force had shown that there were too
many obstacles in the way. Gaston Defferre's proposed candidacy
for the 1965 presidential elections and Jean-Jacques Servan-
Schreiber's more modest attempt to re-group the Centre in the
early 1970s both foundered on the rocks of party loyalties, personal jealousies, policy divisions, and the seemingly irreversible
movement towards bi-polarisation between the Right and the Left.

Thirdly, there was no reason to suppose that there was any
significant support for such a development amongst PS members
(as opposed to voters) or leaders. Certainly Michel Rocard, who
is usually thought of as the leader of 'the Right' within the PS,
gave no hint that he seriously entertained the idea. Furthermore,
were he to have done so he would undoubtedly have split the party
and probably have found himself in a clear minority.

Fourthly, and this is related to points two and three, such an
alliance would have made little ideological sense. Though the PS
may have been 'to the Right' of the PCF and the UDF 'to the Left'
of the RPR (though much more arguably so) there was little,
other than a generally favourable attitude to Europe - and even
then the Socialists embraced a large dissident minority - that the
two shared. Individual politicians within each camp may have been
attracted to a Centrist grouping but a wholesale and fundamental
realignment seemed scarcely possible when the PS was committed
to extending significantly the interventionist powers of the state
in social and economic affairs whilst the UDF leant towards increased liberalism.

Indeed on the crucial issue of economic policy there was a marginally greater ideological affinity between the PS and the RPR than there was between the PS and the UDF. It was partly on this basis that the Gaullist leader, Jacques Chirac, for his own political purposes, referred in September 1980 to 'convergences' between his party and the Socialists. Not surprisingly - in view of past antagonisms, the ideological gulf between the PS and the RPR on most matters, and suspicions of Chirac's motives - Socialist leaders hastened to dismiss Chirac's musings as having any implications for the strategy of the PS.

2. The pursuance by the left-wing parties of totally independent courses of action.

The problem with this was that in the past it had been electorally disastrous. Most notably, in the 1958 elections to the first Parliament of the Fifth Republic a totally disunited Left had found itself grossly underrepresented in terms of the votes/seat ratio. The PCF had been the hardest hit: with 19 per cent of the vote on the first ballot it had won only 10 seats; the Gaullists with 19.5 per cent had gained 199. Similar effects of disunity had been demonstrated in the 1969 presidential election when the Left, unable to agree on a joint first ballot candidate because of the ill feeling generated by the 'events' of May 1968 and the Soviet invasion of Czechoslovakia, had found itself without any candidate at all on the second ballot.

Total independence, therefore, seemed only to make sense if the Left, or a part of it, did not really want national office. Some commentators in the late 1970s argued precisely this with regard to the PCF - believing that it feared the risks and compromises of government would threaten its organisational discipline and its ideological unity. However, the history of the Left during the Fifth Republic hardly supported this view. The PCF took much of the initiative in developing electoral agreements in the 1960s and then, when it became apparent that something more was needed if victory was to be attained, made programmatic 'concessions' by liberalising its policies and associating itself in the mid-1970s with 'Eurocommunism'. While the events of 1977-8 demonstrated that the party was only prepared to enter government on certain conditions and would not pay any price in the cause of unity and electoral success, they did not provide evidence of a fear of office. Furthermore, the 1978 legislatives demonstrated once again the party's concern to be well represented in Parliament, for although it failed to reach its publicly announced minimum percentage for an agreement on second ballot withdrawals, 21 per cent of the vote, it nevertheless in the event quickly agreed such a pact with the PS and the MRG. In so doing it dropped most of its demands of the previous six months and thereby earned the wrath of those members who were not prepared to accept such blatant electoralism.

In any case, quite apart from the fact that total independence - up to and including electoral isolation - would apparently condemn the constituent parties of the Left to continued opposition, the ability of the leadership of any of the parties actually to attempt and to maintain such a strategy was circumscribed by the internal problems such a course of action would have raised. This was because a majority of PS and MRG members and voters, a substantial number of PCF members, and possibly a majority of PCF voters, were opposed to the idea of complete independence. Indeed, in the PCF's case, the edging of the party towards increased - though by no means total - isolationism from the autumn of 1977 was a prime cause of the decline in membership and fall-off in active participation that was apparent from the spring of 1978. This movement, as many saw it, towards the political ghetto was also associated with challenges, unparalleled in the post-war era, to the omnipotence of central leadership control. These challenges included an internal debate which affected most sections of the party, 'indiscipline' of some local 'élus' in the September 1980 senatorial elections,[3] and a refusal of many Communist voters to follow official preferences in the November/December 1980 by-elections.[4]

As the 1981 presidential election approached it appeared therefore that the only realistic electoral challenge to the governing majority could come from a Left displaying some sort of unity, if only at the electoral level. To understand the way in which the parties of the Left approached the campaign and the legislative elections which followed, it is necessary first of all to consider the significance of important developments and debates within the two main parties themselves over strategy and tactics.

THE SOCIALISTS

After uncertainties and disagreements during the 1960s as to how their gradual decline in support might be arrested - a decline which reached its nadir in 1969 with Defferre's miserable 5 per cent in the presidential election - the Socialists increasingly during the 1970s put their faith in the alliance with the Communists. Although there was not complete agreement on exactly how this strategy should be pursued, because the differing tendencies which had come together in 1971 to reconstitute the Socialist Party at Epinay had different perspectives, the determined pursual by the party leader François Mitterrand of the Communist axis was on the whole accepted, particularly when it became clear that it offered considerable electoral benefits. In the 1973 parliamentary and 1974 presidential elections the left-wing alliance, made more credible following the signing of the Common Programme, only narrowly missed gaining overall majorities and the PS itself saw its vote reaching heights unknown since the early days of the Fourth Republic. These successes were repeated in the 1976 cantonal and 1977 municipal elections when the Left, for the first time in the Fifth Republic, succeeded in gaining more than 50 per cent of the popular vote.

Not surprisingly, the collapse of the agreement which had been so responsible for this success provoked not only the expected embitterment towards the PCF but a reappraisal of PS strategy too. There was no open movement towards the centre ground which the SFIO used periodically to occupy, but frustration at the continued exclusion from national office inevitably produced a search for strategic alternatives. This, in turn, brought Mitterrand's position as leader of the party into question since he had, in no uncertain manner, personally identified himself with the union of the Left and had worked assiduously for it. Furthermore, with electoral euphoria no longer a binding force, longer-standing grievances and resentments, such as those over Mitterand's rather haughty manner and personalised, not to say domineering, style, came to the fore. The fact that he was now in his sixties and was, despite his achievements, acquiring the reputation of being a loser, provided further ammunition for those who wished to change various aspects of party affairs.

Accordingly there was, from the autumn of 1977, an increasingly public debate within the PS, with four main currents, some would say factions, competing for attention and influence. Though the friction between them was sometimes presented as one of personality clashes and naked power struggles, important differences over policy, tactics and strategy were present. The four tendencies were grouped around:

1 François Mitterrand. The party's highly pragmatic leader expounded the view that there was no realistic alternative to the established PS policy of seeking a 'clean break' with capitalism or to the strategy of some sort of left-wing unity. Though the Communists were reluctant bedfellows Mitterrand publicly proclaimed that a new alliance of the Left must eventually be forged.
2 Michel Rocard. He called for a 'new language and renewed practical policies', designed to divest the PS of 'archaic' and 'outdated' policies. By reducing its commitment to statism and emphasising its own lack of dogmatism the PS would be strengthened and the PCF, for fear of further decline, might well be forced to move in a democratic direction. This would provide firmer ground for re-negotiating the alliance.
3 Pierre Mauroy. Though allied with Rocard, Mauroy presented himself as a potential peace-maker between the Mitterrand and Rocard groups. Standing on most issues somewhere between the two, he continually emphasised that internal reconciliation was not only possible but indispensable if the party was to grow.
4 The left-wing CERES group. A close relationship with the PCF was seen as the first priority and this was thought to be possible only if the PS adopted such CERES positions as its demands for extensive nationalisations and a major redistribution of income.

At the Party Congress at Metz in April 1979 the votes for the

motions presented by these currents were as follows: Mitterrand
47 per cent; Rocard 21 per cent; Mauroy 17 per cent; CERES 15
per cent. This meant that Mitterrand, to maintain an overall
majority, and thereby retain his post as First Secretary, had
either to seek a broad composite motion around which the party
could unite, or form an alliance with the supporters of one of the
three other tendencies. Tactical considerations won the day. With
the Congress overshadowed by the looming 1981 presidential
elections, and with Rocard increasingly making it clear that he
would like to be a candidate, it was in Mitterrand's interests to
push Rocard and Mauroy into a minority position. CERES were
sympathetic to this because they considered Rocard to be too close
to the 'technocratic right', and also because an alliance with
Mitterrand allowed them to take up posts in the Secretariat, from
which they had been excluded since 1975. (The important 16-
member Secretariat is reserved for those who are in the majority
at congresses.) Accordingly the Mitterrand and CERES currents
linked up to form a new majority.

After Metz, jockeying for position continued unabated. With
the power relationships between, and indeed within, the new
majority and minority currents being highly fluid - positions were
not always as clearly defined as they at first appeared to be -
manoeuvring was always possible. In terms of strategy, however,
the differences between the currents increasingly came to matter
less as continuing attacks on the party by the PCF made it clear
that the Communists were unlikely to change or temper their
hostile attitude to the PS before the presidential election. Whatever strategy preferences Socialists may have had, the fact of the
matter therefore was that the PS was increasingly in the position
of having to plough its own furrow and emphasise its own potential strength if it was not to appear to be wholly dependent for
possible electoral success on the PCF.

It was in this context that Mitterrand began to adopt a stiffer
and more independent stance vis-à-vis the Communists. In February 1980 he floated the idea of a homogeneous and independent
Socialist government although he added that, in prevailing circumstances, it could, at best, only be established on a temporary
basis. In September 1980 he made it clear that whatever the outcome of the first ballot of the presidential elections the Socialists
would not negotiate with the Communists between the two ballots.
In moving towards this harder line he was thus in effect, because
of circumstances, also moving some way towards the Rocard position on strategy: emphasising the independence of the PS whilst
hoping (and probably expecting) that, in the presidential elections, Communist support on the second ballot would ultimately
be forthcoming. Thus by January 1981, when Mitterrand was
formally designated Socialist candidate for the elections (a designation which became virtually automatic after Rocard withdrew
his candidature in November 1980) something approaching a
consensus on strategy had emerged in the PS.

THE COMMUNISTS

From the mid-1960s the Communists committed themselves to the task of bringing into office a left-wing government united on an agreed programme. Their good faith appeared to be confirmed by a number of developments: a 'liberalisation' of policy and ideology; a decline in influence of Stalinist hardliners; a great influx of new members, apparently attracted by the more democratic image; and the decision to support Mitterrand as the common candidate of the Left in the 1974 presidential elections.

Though there were always doubts about the depth of the PCF's conversion to democratic and reformist ways, the suddenness of their 'stiffened' demands in 1977, which culminated in the September breakdown, came as a general surprise. Explanations for it have since been rife and have ranged from an alleged change in the balance of power within the Politbureau, between 'hardliners' and 'softliners', to the hand of Moscow once again making itself felt. The most plausible and generally accepted view, however, is that the relative weakening of the party's position within the Left was the decisive factor. For while the Left as a whole had expanded its electorate during the 1970s it was the PS within the Left which had reaped most benefits.

The PCF, at no little risk to its own internal unity, had made many ideological 'concessions' in its movement towards 'la voie démocratique', even to the extent that some of its leaders feared the party's very identity was being threatened. Yet there was little to show for this electorally. The PS, on the other hand, was rapidly gaining in popularity and was benefitting disproportionately from electoral pacts. This brought about a complete change in the balance of power within the Left. During the 1960s the PCF had been the senior partner and most stable element. The Socialists and Radicals, the two main constituent units of the non-Communist Left, had been in decline and had been hopelessly divided, both between and within themselves. They had presented little threat – of an ideological, organisational or electoral kind – to the PCF, which had thus felt able to take much of the initiative in the tentative steps of the Left towards unity. But the situation changed with the growth of the PS, all the more so when it appeared that some of their new support was at Communist expense. The increasing support for the Socialists even included inroads into what the PCF regards as its 'special reserve': the working class.

By the mid-1970s the PS had overtaken the PCF in electoral popularity and had become, for the first time since 1936, the largest party of the Left. Opinion polls in 1977 were suggesting that whilst the PCF would be restricted to its usual 20 per cent or so of the vote in 1978, the PS might win as much as 30 per cent. When the PS made it clear that it would not 'compensate' the Communists for its relative weakening – by, for example, acceding to a request to divide key ministries into two – the PCF decided the disadvantages of continuing with the Union de la Gauche had become too great.

Just as Mitterrand, in the early 1970s, had warned of the
dangers of a weak PS resulting in an unbalanced union, so PCF
leaders from September 1977 warned of a strong PS producing the
same situation in the other direction. So, for example, André-
Lajoinie, a member of the Politbureau, openly stated in 'L'Humanité'
in April 1979 that the 'Union around a programme' had not facilitated PCF growth, but, on the contrary, had worked to 'the sole
benefit of the Socialists'.[5] But if a consequence of this was that a
rebalancing of the union was a condition for renewal, as PCF
spokesmen suggested, it was difficult to see how that might be
achieved other than by undermining PS credibility and therefore
support. For whilst there was evidence of more goodwill, on the
part of the electorate, towards the PCF than there had been before
its 'liberalisation' began, the long-standing static nature of the
party's vote, at around 20-21 per cent, suggested that, in prevailing circumstances at least, an equilibrium could not be created
at the electoral level by moving the PCF 'up' to meet the PS. It
could only be created by bringing the latter 'down' to the PCF's
level.[6]

As well as calling for a 'rebalancing of the union' the PCF after
the September breakdown became preoccupied with its own unity,
strength and distinctiveness. The revolutionary nature of the
party was brought once more to the fore in public statements.
Members were urged to engage in 'social struggles', to remember
that their mission was 'revolutionary', that their party was 'the
only true representative of the working class', and to spare no
efforts to reconstitute the union 'from the base'; all phrases which
in the past had heralded periods of isolationism. Further indications of the party drawing in on itself were seen in the firm
reaction of the leadership to the much publicised internal criticisms
that were voiced after March 1978. There may not have been, as
there were in former times, wholesale exclusions, but there were
'purges' of party functionaries who were associated with dissent,
and, in classic Communist style, attempts were made to marginalise
and isolate critics by suggesting that, consciously or not, they
were doing the enemies' work. The clearest indication of all of an
apparent return to roots was seen in the renewed emphasis that
was given to the merits of the Soviet system. Previous criticisms
of Soviet 'deficiencies' became muted, the balance sheet of Eastern
European socialism was constantly portrayed from late 1978 as
'globalement positif', and the invasion of Afghanistan was applauded
(even though the PCI and PCE condemned it). Amidst great publicity Georges Marchais even visited the Soviet Union, for the
first time in six years, only two weeks after the invasion.

But whether these various developments really indicated a
complete change of strategy and return to the political ghetto was
always doubtful since the change in direction was far from being
complete. Whilst the Common Programme was now viewed as having
been based on over-optimistic and mistaken assumptions, the new
emphasis on union at the base, rebalancing the Left, and building
Socialism through struggle was portrayed by party leaders not as

a substitute for union at the top but as a precondition for its
future resumption. Most of the municipal councils which were
jointly run by the Left - and since 1977 they had constituted a
majority of the largest towns in France - were still functioning
relatively smoothly. Moreover, there was no 'reversal' on those
issues which led to descriptions of the PCF as 'taking the Italian
road' and becoming 'Eurocommunist': the commitments to civil
liberties, multi-partyism and a 'French road to Socialism' all remained.

Clearly a strong measure of anti-Socialism is an important part
of the PCF's make-up, perhaps even, as Jean Daniel has argued,
a condition for its survival.[7] But although open hostility towards
the PS grew as the balance of strength within the union changed
and as the distinct identity of the PCF became threatened, the
events from September 1977 did not set in motion an irreversible
backward movement within the PCF. Indeed the continuing dominance of the essentially pragmatic Georges Marchais, and his careful ambiguity on many points, suggested that the party, having
consolidated its renewed autonomy, might once again change its
approach.[8] Moreover it always seemed likely that, at a minimum,
a measure of second ballot mutual support would continue with the
Socialists in those elections where it was encouraged by the electoral system. For while the PCF, as part of its post-1977 strategy,
had been increasingly anxious to make it clear that 'désistement'
was no longer automatic, the party in practice had little to gain
from maintaining an across-the-board electoral isolation, except
perhaps in the case of an indisputable movement of the PS towards
the Right. The fact that the PCF after 1977 did, in the last analysis, continue to participate in left-wing electoral arrangements,
indicated that the party itself recognised that complete independence made little sense.

THE PRESIDENTIAL ELECTIONS

Although public opinion polls from late 1980 suggested that
Mitterrand and Giscard would be very close in the event of a
second ballot contest between them, it would be fair to say that
until a relatively late stage in the presidential campaign most
observers and commentators doubted whether, in the last analysis, Mitterrand could win. This was partly because of the electoral
ploys Giscard could hope to utilise as a result of his incumbency
in office, partly because opinion polls had flattered the Left on
previous occasions only to deceive on the day as floating 'Centrist'
voters had opted for the status quo, but in large part too it was
because the Left just seemed to be too divided to be a credible
option.

The arithmetic of political life might have been such that the
PS and the PCF needed each other if the Left was to win a national
election but their deep mutual mistrust was, as we have seen,
open and each was extremely wary of what it saw, with good

reason, to be the design of the other for dominance. Left-wing unity thus appeared to be a delicate balance and that balance had become upset with the growth of the PS in the 1970s. The consequences of this unbalancing had been as follows:

1. As the PS had become strong the PCF, as well as pondering on its future influence and role in the political system, had resurrected its long-held scepticism with Socialist intentions: like its SFIO predecessor the PS was believed to be always potentially open, especially in office, to approaches from its right.
2. At the same time, so as to avoid the possibility of merely becoming a 'supportive force' to the PS, the PCF had taken steps to strengthen its identity and to extend its extra-electoral strength in the unions and elsewhere. This had led it to reconfirm its traditional features and to become intransigent in its attitude to the non-Communist Left.
3. An intransigent PCF had put the PS in the position of either making major concessions in negotiations - without any guarantee that the Communists would be willing to come to agreements, but with a strong risk that moderate Socialist supporters would be scared away - or standing firm and thus undermining the ability of the Left to present itself as a united, coherent, and viable political force.

The two main parties of the Left thus found themselves entering the presidential contest not only competing for votes, but with different aims.

For the PCF a good vote for their candidate Georges Marchais - which meant at least 20 per cent - was vital. This was not because it was thought Marchais could win through to the second ballot, but because it would help to re-balance the Left, it would demonstrate that a substantial section of the electorate accepted the party's claim that a strong PCF was necessary to guarantee real change, and it would help to silence those internal critics who were still attacking the leadership for its post-1977 policies and strategy.

In addition to mobilising a reasonable PCF vote, Communist leaders were also anxious, though they could not publicly say so, that Mitterrand should not win on the second ballot. Such an eventuality could open the way to a big advance on the part of the PS and a possible marginalisation of the PCF: exactly what the Communists had fought against since the autumn of 1977. Accordingly a campaign was fought in which almost as much attention was devoted to attacking Mitterrand - claiming he really wanted to govern with the Right and continue with present policies - as attacking Giscard. Clear suggestions from the PCF that in the event of a Mitterrand victory it would be firm in its demands on policies and for Communist ministers, and strong hints that social turmoil would ensue as part of a campaign to ensure these demands were granted, were aspects of a strategy to gain votes from left-wing Socialists and the assorted extreme Left parties whilst, at the same time, scaring moderate Mitterrand supporters. In this way, it was hoped, the PCF would be either strong enough to exact concessions from a successful Mitterrand or, a more likely outcome, it would be able to bring about his defeat without actually withholding an endorsement of his candidacy on the second ballot. (Such a withholding could have been very damaging since public opinion polls and the November 1980 by-elections had shown that a refusal to back Mitterrand on the second ballot would be widely ignored by Communist voters.[9]

For Mitterrand and the Socialists a difficult balancing act was required. On the one hand a leftist stance had to be maintained in order to keep the party together and to ensure that the first ballot votes for the other left-wing candidates came his way on the second ballot. On the other hand, if support was to be gained in the Centre and amongst disillusioned voters of the Right it was necessary for Mitterrand to demonstrate that in the event of his election he would not be a Communist hostage, constitutional and social chaos would not ensue, and policies would be pursued which would not simply benefit one section of the population. Accordingly his campaign, to which all Socialist currents rallied, was marked by constant attempts to reassure, which meant glossing over those sections of his and the Socialists' programme which were most likely to disturb moderate voters. On the central question of relations with the PCF Mitterrand insisted that his policies remained faithful to the union of the Left, but he also made it clear that the composition of the government under his presidency would depend on the outcome of the legislative elections which he would immediately call. Moreover, it was stressed that there could be no question of the PCF being part of a government of the Left as long as it attacked the PS and until it modified its policies on such questions as Afghanistan, Soviet SS20 missiles, and the range and pace of domestic social and economic reform.

The combined Left vote on the first ballot - 46.9 per cent - was similar to the first ballot vote in previous elections: 45.8 per cent in 1973, 46.2 per cent in 1974, 48.6 per cent in 1978, and 47.5 per cent in the 1979 European elections which were held on a system of proportional representation. The 46.9 per cent, however, contained a major shift within the Left - the PCF lost one quarter of its electorate - to poll its lowest figure in a national election since 1936 - whilst the PS advanced to poll its highest figure since 1936. This change in the balance of power very much conditioned attitudes for the second ballot and, ultimately, played a crucial role in determining the outcome of the election itself. For whereas Mitterrand was confirmed in his strategy, the Communists were forced to reappraise their approach in order to try to minimise the effects of the major setback they had clearly experienced. With anything other than an endorsement of Mitterrand likely to be ignored by Communist voters the party's Central Committee, after a meeting which was marked by recriminations and disillusionment, unconditionally called on supporters to vote for Mitterrand

on the second ballot. With the vast majority of Communist voters
responding to this call, and with the supporters of the other left-
wing candidates doing likewise, the Left was thus almost com-
pletely mobilised on the second ballot. The first ballot gap between
Right and Left was then closed by indiscipline on the Right –
about one quarter of Chirac's supporters either abstained or
voted for Mitterrand – and by the transfer of most of Lalonde's
Ecologist votes to Mitterrand.[10]

Table 4.1: Presidential Elections 1981

	First ballot % vote		Second ballot % vote
Mitterrand (PS)	25.8		
Marchais (PCF)	15.3	Combined	Mitterrand 51.7
Laguiller (LO)	2.3	Left 46.7%	
Crépeau (MRG)	2.2		
Bouchardeau (PSU)	1.1		
Giscard d'Estaing	28.3		
Chirac	18.0	Combined	Giscard
Debré	1.7	Right 49.3%	d'Estaing 48.2
Garaud	1.3		
Lalonde (Ecologist)	3.9		

   The Ecologists were doubtless attracted by certain specific
overtures made in their direction by Mitterrand, notably a promise
to put a brake on the nuclear power programme. But they were
also clearly affected, and the Chiracians who were disillusioned
with Giscard were even more so, by the transformed nature of the
Left since 1978. The break up of the Union de la Gauche, which
has generally been seen as the main reason why the Left lost in
1978, was in 1981 thus a principal reason for Mitterrand's victory:
it had forced him to be more – and to be seen to be more – independent, and this, along with the low vote for Marchais in the
first ballot, considerably reduced the force of the charge that in
office he would be a Communist hostage. Mitterrand thus became
less of a risk to those voters who in the past had not normally
supported the Left but who now wanted change or, for one reason
or another, simply wanted to rid themselves of Giscard.[11]

THE LEGISLATIVE ELECTIONS

For the legislative elections which followed his victory Mitterrand
asked the electorate to confirm the choice of May and give him
the means of implementing his policies. To bring this about the
Socialists naturally continued with the strategy which had brought

them success in the presidential elections. They appealed to the
centre-ground - or, more specifically, to disillusioned supporters
of the majority - by attempting to counterbalance the prospect
of change with the promise of continuity and responsibility. At
the same time, the Socialists sought to appeal to Communist and
far-Left voters by presenting themselves as the party which was
now potentially in a position to bring about change. Finally, they
sought to ensure that although nothing much was given away to
the PCF in promises, the Left would be united on the second
ballot at the polls. The attempt to bring these apparently conflicting aspects of the strategy together took place on two levels.

The first level was the presidential and governmental. Mitterrand
appointed the cautious and conciliatory Pierre Mauroy as Prime
Minister and together they appointed a government which balanced
the various currents within the PS. They also brought in the
'Centre-Left' in the form of prominent figures from the MRG and
made an appeal to the Centre and the Right by appointing as one
of the five Ministers of State, Michel Jobert, who had been Foreign
Minister under Pompidou and who had rallied to Mitterrand during
the presidential campaign. The actions of the new government displayed a similar considered balance. 'Respectability' and moder-
ation were demonstrated in a series of measures to bolster the
falling franc and restore confidence on the stock exchange, in the
reference to a commission of the PS proposals to nationalise eleven
large companies, and in the assertion that France's legal commitments overseas would be fulfilled - the new Foreign Minister,
Claude Cheysson, said France's word was 'sacred'. Change and
reform were equally demonstrated in various ways: the minimum
wage, pensions, family and disability and lodging allowances,
were all raised; 200,000 jobs, it was announced, would be created
in the public sector; plans for a controversial nuclear power plant
in Brittany and the extension of an army firing range at Lazac
were abandoned; a number of assorted measures, such as the
decision to drop Giscard d'Estaing's proposed prosecution of
'Le Monde' for daring to question the independence of the judiciary,
signified a liberalisation in the civil liberties field; finally, in
foreign affairs it was made clear that there would be a new interest
in third world problems.

At the second level, the party political, the PS quickly and easily
negotiated agreements with the MRG and Huguette Bouchardeau's
PSU. In both cases the agreements covered common policy positions, a general second ballot withdrawal in favour of the leading
first ballot candidate, and PS 'presents' - in the form of its agreement not to enter candidates on the first ballot against 13 MRG
candidates (including all of its 10 deputies) and one PSU candidate (Bouchardeau). The major problem, however, was the relationship which should be established with the PCF.

The Communists had three interrelated aims in the elections:
to recapture the votes they had lost on the first ballot of the presidential elections; at least to preserve the seats they already
held in Parliament; and to get a share of the political momentum

created by Mitterrand's victory. To achieve these aims they maintained the muted stance they had adopted since the first ballot
of the presidentials: greatly moderating their earlier demands,
virtually dropping their previous attacks on Mitterrand and the PS,
and making it clear that the PCF was 'ready at any moment' to
begin negotiations for a role in government. It presented itself
as a key part of the new presidential majority and as the close
partner of the Socialists.

The Socialists' response was to welcome what Jospin called 'the
change of tone' in the PCF but to treat it with great caution.
After almost four years of vilification Socialists were not prepared,
especially when things were going so much in their favour and
the balance between the PS and the PCF was so radically altered,
to act as if nothing had happened. They wanted to exact maximum
guarantees and be sure that the policy differences which still
so clearly existed between the two parties were sorted out before
they could contemplate governing together. As a result, what
emerged after negotiations led by Jospin for the PS and Marchais
for the PCF, was a joint declaration which partly patched up the
Union de la Gauche but stopped short of what the Communists
wanted. In the delcaration the parties sought to pave the way 'for
a great victory in the elections' and to bring about the conditions
which would create 'a coherent and lasting majority'. More specifically they set out a list of agreements in specific policy areas
(which were mainly on domestic institutional and socio-economic
issues); they acknowledged that disagreements remained; they
agreed to 'confirm and reinforce' Mitterrand's victory by 'developing their co-operation'; and they made a second ballot electoral
agreement. But there was no commitment by the PS to accept
Communist ministers after the election. That would be left to a
meeting after the second ballot when the situation would be reviewed.

Table 4.2: Parliamentary Elections 1981

	First ballot % vote	Number of seats
PS/MRG	37.5	284
PCF	16.2	44
Extreme Left	1.3	–
Other Left	0.7	6
RPR	20.8	84
UDF	19.2	62
Other Right	3.2	11
Ecologists	1.1	–

In the legislative elections the Socialists gained a larger proportion of the vote than any other single party had done since modern
political parties first began to emerge in the early years of the
century. In terms of parliamentary representation the Left - or

the new 'majorité presidentielle' as it was soon being called – won a greater proportion of the seats, 67 per cent, than it had done even at the times of the Popular Front or the Liberation. The Socialists became only the second party in the history of the Fifth Republic to enjoy an overall majority in their own right.

As well as signifying an historic triumph for the Left the elections also witnessed what could prove to be an historic rebalancing of the Left. After the presidential elections PCF leaders had claimed the poor vote for Marchais was explained by 'special' circumstances: the mechanics of the electoral system, the absence of a PCF candidate in 1974, the fear that there might be no candidate of the Left on the second ballot. The parliamentary elections, however, far from 'rectifying' the situation within the Left in the way the Communists had initially hoped, merely exacerbated it further. Whilst the PS/MRG greatly increased their vote and more than doubled their representation in Parliament, the PCF did not recover the votes it had lost in the presidential elections and saw its number of seats halved. This weakening of the PCF was then further confirmed when, anxious to have something to show and to offer to its supporters, it elected to enter government with the Socialists but was able to do so only after being forced to sign a declaration in which it gave way to the PS on virtually every issue where the two parties were at variance.[12]

CONCLUDING REMARKS

Many factors combined to explain the events which in 1981 totally transformed the face of French politics. Some of these have not been discussed, or have only been touched on here since the focus of this chapter has been the problems and dilemmas of strategy for the Left. So, for example, no attention has been given to the demographic changes in France which have for some time favoured the Left. Similarly little has been said of the effects of the world recession, of the consequences of Giscard d'Estaing's economic policies, or of the intense competition between the parties and personalities of the majority which from 1976-7 in some ways mirrored the rivalries on the Left.[13] Undoubtedly, however, a major determining factor in 1981 – and arguably the single most important factor – was the changed circumstances in which the Left found itself as compared with those elections in which it had been narrowly defeated in the 1970s. The rupture of the Union de la Gauche, which had seemingly condemned the Left to continuing opposition, forced a strategy on Mitterrand for the presidential elections which enabled him, in circumstances which were propitious, to appear less disturbing than formerly to sections of the Centre-Right electorate. Once the psychological 'breakthrough' of a left-wing victory had been achieved, and the PCF as a result of their presidential vote were less of a 'threat' than ever, Mitterrand's presidential campaign prediction came true and 'a huge popular movement [shattered] the established political framework'.

NOTES

1   Published in English as 'Towards a New Democracy', London, Collins, 1977. This quote pp. 46-7.
2   'Le Nouvel Observateur', 9 April 1979.
3   In seven départements the PCF broke from traditional 'republican discipline' and maintained candidates against Socialists on the second ballot. Not all PCF electors - and in senatorial elections electors are principally made up of local councillors - voted for their own candidate on the second ballot.
4   The clearest example of this was at Aveyron where the leadership of the fedération had recommended its electorate to abstain on the second ballot rather than vote for the MRG. (Though one section - Villefranche de Rouergue - did advise Communist voters to support the MRG). The greater part of the Communist electorate ignored the fédération's recommendation and cast their vote for the MRG candidate. In those constituencies where the Socialists were the leading party of the Left the PCF gave only a half-hearted recommendation to vote for them on the second ballot; again PCF electors proved to be much more enthusiastic in their support.
5   'L'Humanité', 10 May 1979.
6   In 1979-80 there were indications that the PCF was even having difficulty holding onto its 20-21 per cent. Some opinion polls suggested a PCF presidential candidate might only be able to poll 15-16 per cent on the first ballot.
7   J. Daniel, 'L'ère des ruptures', Paris, Grasset, 1979, p. 278.
8   His ambiguity was no more clearly seen than in the different interpretations which could be - and were - given to his addresses to the Twenty-Third Party Congress in May 1979. For the speeches see 'L'Humanité', 10 and 14 May 1979.
9   See note 4 above. For a fuller account of the elections see G. le Gall, Senatoriales: la fin de la 'discipline republicaine'?, 'Revue Politique et Parlementaire', Sept.-Oct. 1980, pp. 9-14.
10 According to a 'Sofres' poll conducted just after the presidential elections the transfer of votes on the second ballot was as follows: 92 per cent of PCF voters supported Mitterrand; 73 per cent of Chirac voters supported Giscard d'Estaing, 16 per cent supported Mitterrand, and the rest abstained or did not reply; 53 per cent of Lalonde's voters supported Mitterrand, 26 per cent supported Giscard d'Estaing, and 21 per cent abstained or did not reply. The poll is published in 'Le Nouvel Observateur', 1-7 June 1981.
11 According to the 'Sofres' poll the major single source of disillusionment with Giscard was his insufficient effort to combat unemployment. Conversely the most important single reason for Mitterrand's success was said by voters to be his wish to bring about major changes in French society.
12 The PS-PCF declaration is printed in 'Le Monde', 25 June 1981. The major PCF concessions were on Afghanistan (where the parties declared themselves to be 'in favour of the with-

drawal of Soviet troops'), Poland, and the range and pace of socio-economic reforms.

13   The 'Sofres' survey (see above) gives some indication of the relative importance of these factors in the presidential election.

5 THE FRENCH COMMUNIST PARTY AND 'CLASS ALLIANCES':

INTELLECTUALS, WORKERS AND THE CRISIS OF

SOCIAL IDEOLOGY

Jolyon Howorth

> Of all classes that stand face to face with the bourgeoisie to-
> day, the prolétariat alone is a really revolutionary class.
> Karl Marx, 'The Communist Manifesto', 1848.

> Our definition of the proletariat is based on the same scientific
> criteria as those first elaborated by Karl Marx.
> Georges Marchais, '23rd Congress of the PCF', 1979

Ever since the dawn of organised Socialism in France, the theory
and the practice of the Left have been bedevilled by the ideological problem of how to interpret Marx's celebrated dictum.
What, exactly, is 'the proletariat'? If the 'proletariat alone is a
really revolutionary class', what role can be played in that revo-
lutionary-historical movement by non-proletarian social groups?
If an 'alliance strategy' linking the struggles of proletarians and
non-proletarians is to be adopted, under what conditions should
this be done and what are the advantages and disadvantages of
such an alliance? In the course of its history, the French Left
in general and the PCF in particular have, at different moments,
produced very different responses to these questions. But the
responses have never proved satisfactory and the questions themselves have become more and more acute. Today, as the ranks of
white-collar workers (scientists, technologists, researchers,
teachers and engineers) continue to double approximately every
15 years, the question of class alliances has become, in many ways,
the most serious ideological problem which faces the PCF. This
chapter will examine the ways in which the party has attempted
to respond to the important sociological mutations which have
accompanied the development in France of an advanced technological society. ('Intellectual workers' is a translation of 'travailleurs
intellectuels' and covers such categories as engineers, technicians,
cadres and other white-collar groups. 'Ouvriérisme' and 'ouvriériste'
(literally 'workerism' and 'workerist') were first used in the 1860s
to designate the revolutionary self-sufficiency of the proletariat
which, for its emancipation, had to avoid all contact with non-
workers.)
Even prior to the First World War, the old SFIO grappled (unsuccessfully) with the question of the role which could be played
in the party by 'intellectual workers'.[1] In the 1920s, the PCF
developed a highly polarised 'ouvriériste' ideology which rejected
in absolute terms as objective class enemies anybody from outside
the ranks of the industrial proletariat.[2] This notion was accom-

panied by the first concerted attack on 'bourgeois' art and culture and gave rise to the first hesitant attempts to define and
create a specific 'proletarian' art form.[3] In this analysis class
alliances were neither ideologically desirable nor politically
feasible.

During the Popular Front era, however, this line was abandoned
in favour of another one (equally polarised) calling for an extremely broad political alliance extending to the confines of the
commercial bourgeoisie.[4] At the same time, Communist writers like
Paul Vaillant-Couturier began to argue that 'culture' was neither
bourgeois nor proletarian but French. From the mid-1930s until
the late 1950s the social ideology of the PCF tended to oscillate
between these two basic lines. Since the Second World War, there
has been a profusion of party publications dealing with the general
problems of culture, class alliances and intellectual workers.[5]
Within these variegated writings, three rather separate problems
have often been confused. First, the essentially politico-aesthetic
problem of the relationship between art and culture on the one
hand, and class and hegemony on the other. Second, the somewhat esoteric, 'in-house' problem of the 'special relationship' between the PCF and generations of artists and writers. Third, the
fundamentally sociological-ideological problem of class structure,
class consciousness and class alliances. Without neglecting altogether the first two problems, this chapter will nevertheless concentrate almost exclusively on the third.

CLASS AND POLITICAL STRATEGY UNDER THE FIFTH REPUBLIC

It was the polarisation of French politics engendered by the Fifth
Republic which forced the party to face up squarely to the political need for a coherent approach to the question of class alliances.
This political necessity was enhanced by the ideological imperative
of responding to the recent innovatory sociological theories of
the 'new working class'. Since 1958, growing numbers of industrial
sociologists had been arguing that the old blue-collar proletariat
had, under the influence of the consumer society, exchanged its
revolutionary aspirations for mortgages and motor cars. The 'revolutionary class', it was now asserted, was composed of those
intellectual workers (cadres, engineers and technicians) for whom
the designation 'new working class' was being coined. These new
theories generated an intense ideological debate, some sociologists
insisting on calling these new strata the 'new middle class', others
accepting the label 'new working class' and others again (including the PCF) refusing to see them as a class at all.[6] For the
purposes of this chapter, we shall refer to these groups either as
the 'new working class' or as intellectual workers.

Despite its overall hostility to these new theories, the PCF, in
a series of milestone statements, gradually began to pay cautious
court to the rising engineers. But a more systematic analysis was

necessary, and in 1966 a special session of the Central Committee, meeting in Argenteuil, drew up a resolution on 'Ideological and Cultural Problems'.[7] This resolution which dealt essentially with the role of intellectual workers in contemporary society, appeared to represent something of a turning point in PCF ideology. It was stated unequivocally that the party's need for intellectual workers (to contribute to the theorisation of revolutionary change) was as great as their need for the party (to bring about the political implementation of that change). Although it was made clear that the direction of the alliance would be one in which the intellectuals would come over towards the 'party of the working class' in order to 'share the workers' experience',[9] it was nevertheless obvious that the PCF had understood the vital necessity of attracting into its ranks the growing numbers of intellectual workers being secreted by what some sociologists were already calling 'post-industrial society'.

However, it was also evident that, despite a number of randomly chosen quotations from Marx and Engels (which effectively proved nothing), the Argenteuil resolution broke no new ideological ground. The motive force behind it was not sociological theory but political reality, in particular the need to forge an 'alliance of all democratic forces' through 'the policy of unity between the PCF and the Socialist Party'. Through Left-unity, the party hoped not only to galvanise the political aspirations of these new intellectual workers but also, thereby, to emerge as the dominant force in a credible opposition with a viable governmental programme. Six years later, in 1972, the Common Programme of the Left had been duly signed and the strategy seemed to be paying off. The new Socialist Party, which had emerged at Epinay in 1971 out of the shambles of the SFIO, was something of a political infant and the PCF, with its new democratic image, had reason to suppose that it would be the Communists (rather than the Socialists) who would reap the harvest of left-wing support sown by the seeds of social change occasioned by the advent of the technological era.

But this was only possible if the party succeeded in addressing the new intellectual workers in terms which were appropriate to their own experiences and aspirations. It was not sufficient to appeal to them politically ('Come to us for we are the strongest and the best'). What was desperately needed was an objective analysis of the place of the 'new working class' in the evolving economy and society of contemporary France. By the end of the 1960s, the debate about the 'new working class' had been raging in fits and starts for the better part of a decade. At first, the party avoided any major involvement in the controversy, leaving it to individual party theoreticians to defend 'Marxist orthodoxy'.[9] But those who were quietly pronouncing the funeral oration of the PCF's traditional constituency - the industrial proletariat - and noisily the vanguard role of the 'new working class' became more and more vociferous and even, in the person of Roger Garaudy,[10] and in the wake of May 1968, introduced the heresy into the party's Central Committee. Clearly, the time had come for a major new ideological statement.

STATE MONOPOLY CAPITALISM AND INTELLECTUAL WORKERS

This took the form of the publication, in 1971, of the two-volume 'Traité Marxiste d'Economie Politique: le Capitalisme Monopoliste d'Etat.'[111] In this long treatise, the party addresses two important questions: first, the overall trend of capitalist concentration and its relationship with the state; second, and of vital importance for our purpose, the effect of these developments on social structure and class relationships. Space does not allow more than the briefest analysis of these important new ideas. Basically, the PCF believes that under state monopoly capitalism, there are no intermediary classes ('new working class', 'new middle class', 'old' middle class or 'petite-bourgeoisie') between the two principal antagonistic social forces of the capitalist era. These intermediary groups (which do figure as a class in Marx's scheme of things[12]) are christened by the PCF 'intermediary social strata' and are examined severally in terms of their potential for eventual fusion with either the proletariat or the bourgeoisie proper. There are many theoretical factors, in the PCF's view, which govern the way in which each of these separate 'social strata' will eventually move. But already, the PCF marshalls two major ideological arguments (which are to be used constantly throughout the 1970s and up to this day) to justify the overall hypothesis which holds that most intellectual workers can come to identify with the programme and policies of the PCF. The first is that, as these workers are increasingly subjected to the uncertainties and tensions of all salaried personnel (wage-bargaining, job tenure, fulfilment, status), they will arrive at a spontaneous but growing awareness of the conditions of existence of the working class. Eventually, they will identify with proletarian struggle. The second theoretical argument concerns the notion of the 'collective labourer'. This notion is to be found in Marx but in a highly embryonic and very ambiguous form. It suggests, in brief, that, as the division of labour becomes more specialised and intricate, with the development of advanced technology, so the producers of a given commodity (and of the surplus value thereby secreted) must be seen as an industrial community, the 'collective labourer'. This therefore furnishes the PCF with an ideological justification for broadening the definition of the industrial proletariat to include growing numbers of technicians, draughtsmen and engineers. The dividing line between those strata capable of 'joining' the proletariat and those whose destiny lies with the bourgeoisie is still very largely drawn in terms of their relationship to the ownership of the means of production. But the general conclusion is that there are only a tiny number of Frenchmen with class interests inexorably opposed to the programme of the PCF.

   This essentially 'optimistic' ideology, which constituted the party's major response to theoreticians of the 'new working class',

was soon subjected to a number of theoretical attacks from Marxists
close to the PCF who urged caution against the dangers of alliance
with what, in their view, remained the class enemy.[13] More ominously, however, the optimism implicit in the new line was soon
subjected to its first practical test in the general elections of 1973.
While the PCF's share of the national vote remained steady, the
PS share (which had stood at only 5 per cent in the presidential
elections of 1969) rose spectacularly to 21 per cent.[14] The PS was
further catapulted to national prominence by François Mitterrand's
narrow defeat in the presidential elections of 1974. Under these
circumstances, faced with the possibility of the Socialist Party
not only dominating the Left, but also exercising an appeal to the
'new working class', the PCF attempted to render more generally
digestible the dry esoterism of the two-volume treatise on state
monopoly capitalism by giving birth, in 1974, to a new socio-
political infant.

UNION DU PEUPLE DE FRANCE

Union du Peuple de France (Union of the French People - UPF) is
one of those theoretical bastards born of the uncertain (and in
some ways unnatural) union between ideological impasse and
political imperative. There is little doubt that it was political
necessity (rather than sociological analysis) which acted as mid-
wife. The concept was launched at the hastily convened extraordinary 21st Congress of the PCF in October 1974.[15] In their
introductory speeches, both Paul Laurent and Georges Marchais
stressed the dramatic new political situation which had arisen in
France since the presidential elections. That situation, which
justified the calling of the Congress, was symbolised in general
terms by the near-majority of left-wing voters who had backed
Mitterrand earlier in the year. But more specifically, what worried
the PCF were the recent developments in the Socialist Party. These
developments were spelled out - significantly - in the section of
Marchais' speech in which he explains the meaning of UPF. The
preoccupations of the PCF at the time of launching the slogan are
obvious: the PS seemed to be beginning to renege on the revolutionary dimension of the Common Programme; and the Socialists
were clearly attempting to overtake the Communists in electoral
support. In short, how was the PCF to cope with the Socialists'
undoubted electoral success among those very 'intermediary social
strata' the Communists had been wooing - with little success -
for ten years?

The answer was Union du Peuple de France. If, argued Marchais,
'almost half of all Frenchmen could approve of [the Left] last May'
there was no reason why 'millions more can not be won over to our
cause'. However, such a statement is no more than a political
wager and rests on very shaky ideological foundations. For the
ideological bases of UPF are no more solidly grounded than those
originally expressed in the treatise on state monopoly capitalism.[16]

Pursuing the two main arguments launched in that treatise, the
PCF continued to hold that, owing to the 'mass salarisation of
the working population' and to the generalisation of 'collective
labour', and given the traumatic consequences of the economic
crisis, the growing ranks of intellectual workers would increasingly be capable of gravitating towards, and eventually identifying
with, the historical struggle of the working class, as expressed
by the PCF. Moreover, the party claimed for good measure that,
in addition to intellectual workers, there was no reason why
'Christians, patriotic Gaullists, reformists and democratic centrists' could not also, eventually, join the ranks of Communist
voters. Indeed, a close reading of the sociological breakdown of
those who, in this view, are irrevocably committed to the fortunes
of the 'monopoly caste' suggests that all but several tens of
thousands of Frenchmen can be accommodated under the generous
umbrella of UPF.[17]

It must nevertheless be stressed that the core component of
UPF remains the industrial proletariat. All the other classes will
'gravitate towards' and gradually come to identify with this 'inexorably revolutionary' class. And, in order to refute those sociologists and statisticians who had been arguing for years that,
numerically, blue-collar workers were on the decline, the PCF
began re-examining the figures with a view to including in the
category of 'industrial worker' several million technicians and
employees who had hitherto been classed as 'white collar'. The
difference in interpretation between the PCF statistics and those
furnished by INSEE is instructive in this regard.[18]

In the two years following the birth of UPF, the notion was
projected to the forefront of PCF campaigning. It became the
main slogan at the seminal 22nd Congress in February 1976, it was
reinforced by an updated version of 'the overture to Christians',
it presided over the quasi-official launching of Eurocommunism
in June 1976 and underlay Marchais' major speech to 2,000 intellectuals in June 1977. But the main obstacle to the dissemination of
this new line was that it was competing for the same social support
with two other ideological concepts, which were very closely linked
to each other. The first were the theories of the 'new working
class' which posited two main arguments running directly counter
to the main propositions of UPF: first, that intellectual workers
did not need the experience of the proletariat in order to join the
revolution, since their own position at the heart of the contradictions of post-industrial society had already shaped them into
the revolutionary vanguard; and secondly that the type of political
solution they envisaged was poles apart from that traditionally
exemplified by the PCF (they favoured politics rather than
economics, were concerned about control rather than property,
advocated autogestion rather than nationalisation, flirted with
ecology rather than promoting productivism). The second competing ideology was the Socialist Party's own response to the rise of
the intellectual worker: the 'front de classe'. Rejecting utterly
the concept of UPF which they regarded as an ideological nonsense

devoid of any socio-political reality, the socialists posited a
historical alliance between manual and intellectual workers, based
on equality of role and function and excluding most of the more
sociologically dubious petty-bourgeois elements which the PCF
was trying to embrace within the confines of UPF.[19]

The acid test of these various ideologies came during the cantonal elections of 1976. Once again, the PCF made little headway
nationally whereas the PS, with 30 per cent of the vote, shot to
the prized position of 'the first party in France'. Consequently,
in November 1976, the PCF reached a turning point. In an apparent
reversal of the spirit (if not the letter) of UPF, the Communists
launched the slogans which were to be used for both the municipal
elections of 1977 and the general elections of 1977: 'make the rich
pay' and 'priority to the poor'. Union of the French People, having failed to capture the imagination (still less the votes) of those
millions of intellectual workers for whom it had been designed,
was being quietly discarded. For the vital general elections of
1978, the PCF returned to a scarcely veiled and somewhat aggressive 'ouvriérisme'.

POST MARCH 1978: THE CRISIS OF THE INTELLECTUALS

It is not my intention to present or analyse the general internal
crisis which rocked the PCF in the wake of the elections. This has
been dealt with elsewhere.[20] What I wish to do in this section, is
to examine the way in which the party attempted to resolve its
apparently volatile or at least inconsistent attitude towards the
question of class alliances. It was of course the intellectuals in
the party who raised a storm of protest about the changing line
on class alliances and the electoral consequences of that change.
As a result, they also found themselves excluded from the columns
of the party press, and this constituted a second area of grievance
and a second source of revolt, with which we cannot be concerned
here.

In the wake of March 1978, dozens of articles and letters, peti-
tions and manifestos flowed into the non-Communist press from
Communists protesting the 'abandonment' of the party's appeal to
intellectual workers and criticising the crude 'ouvriérisme' of the
electoral campaign. At this stage nobody questioned the correct-
ness of the party's decision to pay urgent attention to the situation of 'the poor', although several writers regretted the use of
the term, arguing that its psychological impact may well have
been counterproductive. But all the 'dissidents' of 1978 lamented
the alienating effect which the electoral campaign had had on
intellectual workers. In response, the party leaders, alternating
crocodile tears with crocodile teeth, defended the slogan 'priority
to the poor' in highly emotional terms and accused those same
intellectual workers to whom UPF had been addressed of having
sabotaged the left-wing victory because they were afraid of the
slogan 'make the rich pay'. François Hincker stated bluntly that

UPF would only have been viable as long as the proletariat (i.e., the PCF) remained the motive force behind it and as long as those intellectual workers who joined the Communist movement did not expect any reward for their political loyalty other than the hope of a general social revolution from which they would benefit along with everybody else.[21] And Georges Marchais prefigured the imminent demise of UPF by discovering that there was, after all, social and political incoherence in what he called 'a heterogeneous gathering of the discontented, an accumulation of disparate and sometimes contradictory demands'.[22] It took 15 long years of evolution to develop the genus UPF. It took less than a few months in 1978 to render it extinct. By the time of the party's 23rd Congress in May 1979, the expression and the concept had disappeared totally from the Communist lexicon (without death certificate, burial or funeral oration).

The criticisms which were levelled from within at the party leaders did not confine themselves to expressions of regret about the party line on class alliances. They were also directed at the notions which the PCF leadership held concerning the appropriateness of various types of action and political commitment. Since May 1968, intellectual workers had increasingly been attracted by the new 'causes' of the 1960s: ecology, libertarianism, feminism, urban renewal, soldiers rights, anti-nuclear power. The PCF's appeal to intellectual workers had, on the contrary, always been couched in terms of an invitation to step forward into a glorious technological future of increased production and consumption. But, in the wake of March, many a voice was raised, like that of Jean Elleinstein, calling on the party to keep up with the political times and to pay serious attention to 'the struggle against the bureaucracy and the increased role of the State, autogestion, feminism, hierarchical relations in the firm, the problems of urban society'.[23]

As we saw, the dissidents did not, at first, call into question the party's notion of 'priority to the poor'. They merely regretted the practical corollary of that slogan: the abandonment of other social categories. But little by little, one began to see the expression of serious doubts about the 'vanguard role' of the industrial proletariat. Jean Elleinstein acted as trail-blazer in October 1978 when he suggested that 'there exists today a new disposition of social forces in France, in which the salaried middle strata have increasing new importance. The symbol of this alliance ought to be less the hammer and sickle than the hammer, the ball-point and the computer.' And he added, for good measure, that 'the Communist Party . . . has not understood the extent to which Marx's sentence about the proletariat alone being truly revolutionary is now obsolete. There are equally, in 'The Communist Manifesto', a whole series of notions which are irrelevant today'.[24] But Elleinstein, ever the maverick in the party, had become such a controversial figure that other dissidents were beginning to find him an embarrassment.[25]

Nevertheless, other party intellectuals have now begun to ques-

tion the 'historical primacy' of the proletariat. Bernard Edelmann
has repudiated one of the fundamental tenets of Marxism: that
the working class exists as a permanent oppositional force with a
revolutionary will. He argues, on the contrary, that the workers
have been progressively integrated into the juridical structure
of French labour law and are now firmly embedded in 'the system'.
Yvonne Quilès and Jean Tornikian, in their study of the contemporary working class, have revealed a depoliticised, dejected
social group obsessed with sexuality and down-payments. And in
a more sophisticated empirical study, Jacques Frémontier has
recently implied that the proletariat, far from representing the
Leninist vanguard, is now riddled with petty-bourgeois morality
and values.[26]

How has the party leadership responded to this concerted on-
slaught on its ideological positions? The first concern was to reassert, in unequivocal tones, the fact that the PCF was the 'party
of the working class'. On the eve of the 23rd Congress, the
Political Bureau published the findings of the party's own internal
sociological survey which showed that 80 per cent of party members
were drawn from the ranks of the working class. And at the Congress itself, Georges Marchais mixed indignation with assuredness
in asserting that: 'Yes, we are the Party of the poor. . . . If
there is still any question about this, it is not because of an
excess of Party activity on behalf of the poor but because of the
inadequacies and insufficiencies of that activity'.[27] And a succession of orators, addressing the question of class alliances, did
little more than reassert the need for intellectual workers to step
in line behind the proletariat.

Yet the problem of the intellectual workers was not about to disappear. If the party was to make any national headway at all, it
had to try once again to produce an ideological appeal to the 'new
working class'. The experience of Left-unity and UPF had been
largely negative and a more cautious approach was called for.
Consequently, at the same time as they reasserted in ringing tones
the primacy of the proletariat, the party leaders, in true Janus
fashion, took several major decisions aimed at recruiting among
intellectual workers. First, they elected René Le Guen, leader of
the CGT's federation of managers, engineers and technicians
(UGICT), to the Political Bureau. Second, they decided to hold a
special session of the National Council to discuss the whole question of class alliances. Third, they decided to scrap two party
publications: 'France Nouvelle', the official weekly, which had
become a hot-bed of dissidence; and 'La Nouvelle Critique', the
'intellectual' monthly, which was accused of esoterism (and had
also lapsed into dissidence). These publications were replaced in
March 1980 by a new glossy weekly aimed precisely at 'intellectual
workers'. The title chosen - 'Révolution' - indicated that the party
was not offering any hostages to fortune. Finally, a decision was
taken to reorganise the party's two research institutes (Institut
Maurice Thorez and Centre d'Etudes et des Recherches Marxistes)
and to form a new body, the Institut des Recherches Marxistes.

All of this new activity in favour of recruitment among the 'new working class' temporarily calmed the dissidents and debate within the party went into a six-month lull.

During that time, the European elections provided a further test of the party's 'social appeal'. A preliminary analysis suggests that, in many of its more traditional 'proletarian' bastions, the influence of new technology, by significantly modifying the professional and social structure of the constituency, had shifted electoral support away from the PCF and towards the PS. This trend had been noted as a cause for concern by Jean Garcia, Communist Senator for Seine St Denis, in his speech to the 23rd Congress.[28] The European elections revealed erosion of the party's support in some 60 departments, among them some of the most urban in France (Bouches du Rhône, Isère, Loire, Moselle, Nord, Pas de Calais and Seine), and, more ominously, in some of the party's long-standing municipalities (St Quentin, Aubagne, Firmini, Calais, Le Havre, Dieppe, Colombes, Levallois-Perret). The party only managed to maintain its 'standard' national score of 20 per cent owing to its nationalistic campaign in the wine-growing south, where, with tactical support from the Catholic wine-growers' leader, Emmanuel Maffre-Baugé, spectacular headway was made in departments like the Hérault, Lot, Aveyron, Tarn and Lozère.[29] Alas, wine-growers, unlike technicians, hardly count as a rising class. The problems of political sociology seemed to be growing daily.

They exploded with a vengeance in October 1979 when the 'Fiszbin Affair' entered the public domaine.[30] Henri Fiszbin, a lathe-operator, had risen to be the first secretary of the Party's Paris Federation, Deputy for the 18th arrondissement (1973-8), candidate of the united Left for mayor of Paris (1977) and head of the Communist caucus at the Hôtel de Ville. In January, he resigned the first of these positions reportedly on grounds of ill-health. But in October it became clear that not only he but his entire eight-man secretariat had been forced to resign. Their 'crime' was an over-zealous promotion of UPF in the Paris area.

For many years, the Paris Federation of the PCF had been concerned about the 'deproletarisation' of the capital and had been making special efforts to reach out to the intellectual workers who had long been the dominant social group in the city. These efforts had ranged from the establishment of study groups to examine the specific problems of technical and managerial personnel, to 'open house' meetings at which members of the public were invited to sit in on the deliberations of the party and open up discussion. The results of these activities, which had been consecrated and encouraged by UPF, were seen in the municipal elections of 1977 when, despite the erosion of the working-class population of the capital, the PCF had won two extra seats on the council.[31] But the wholesale reversal of the party line in 1977 and the overtly 'ouvriériste' slogans of 1978 had a devastating effect on the party's fortunes in Paris and two parliamentary seats were actually lost (including Fiszbin's). The party leaders decided to

make a scapegoat out of the Paris Federation and the eight federal
secretaries were summoned to give account of themselves at a
special meeting of the Political Bureau on 11 January 1979. There,
they were accused of right-wing deviationism, political opportun-
ism, excessive zeal in appealing to the 'new working class', neglect
of the 'old' working class (one member of the Political Bureau had
noted the absence of council house tenants at a party meeting),
too conciliatory an attitude towards the Socialist Party and other
similar misdemeanours.[32]

Eventually, after much heart-seaching, and having resigned
most of his party offices - including membership of the Central
Committee (the first man in the history of the party to do so) -
Fiszbin decided to break with a 60-year-old tradition and speak
out by publishing his account of the affair in 'Les Bouches
S'Ouvrent'. In this book, he makes an impassioned plea in favour
of a serious effort to open up real dialogue with intellectual
workers. He argues cogently that the party can appeal to these
strata provided it does so in a way which takes account of their
experiences and requirements. Alas, he concluded, the party had
decided to go in the opposite direction. In a bitter article in
'L'Humanité' in January 1980, he accused the PCF of having
abandoned any attempt to appeal to intellectuals and of having
reverted to a narrow-minded and politically disastrous 'ouvriérisme'.[33] This article was in fact written as Fiszbin's contribution
to the preparation of the National Council session on 'Intellectuals,
Culture and Revolution'. It is from these deliberations, which
took place at Bobigny in February 1980, that we see the current
state of PCF ideology on the question of intellectual workers.[34]

The Bobigny resolution estimates that there are now $4\frac{1}{2}$ million
such intellectual workers in France, a figure which has doubled
since the Argenteuil meeting in 1966. However, it insists on the
enormous disparity within their ranks, both in 'material' terms
(salaries and objective relationship to the means of production)
and in 'ideal' terms (life-style, class consciousness and social
aspiration). There is, as yet, no firm agreement on how to classify
these strata but there is unanimity in concluding that they do
not and cannot represent a 'class'.[35]

Nevertheless, despite the failure of UPF, the party still maintains that they can be persuaded to join the revolutionary ranks.
Again and again, during the speeches at Bobigny, the two arguments first adduced in the treatise on state monopoly capitalism
are marshalled in defence of this proposition. Owing to their status
as wage-earners, they will eventually understand what struggle
is all about; and owing to the generalisation of collective labour,
they can be classed, objectively, as producers of surplus value.
Some theoretical work has now been produced to abolish the old
distinction between manual and intellectual labour in favour of a
new one between 'productive' and 'non-productive' labour. The
former is broadly defined to include many areas of the tertiary
sector, but the latter remains extremely vague.

However, despite the reassertion that these intellectual workers can be won over, the Bobigny resolution (noting that, in recent years, their vote has tended to be Socialist or 'Giscardian'), stresses that this will be an extremely arduous and lengthy task. It is this emphasis on the difficulties involved which constitutes the main break with the theory of UPF. Echoing the spirit of the resolution, many speakers stressed that most intellectual workers were unreceptive to the ideas of the PCF and had a far greater propensity to vote for right-wing candidates. But all was not deemed hopeless since the 23rd Congress had secreted the ideo-logical instrument which would allow the party to reverse that trend and win the intellectuals over: 'la guerre idéologique' (ideological warfare). The notion of ideological warfare posits that the forces of imperialism are on the defensive and are resort-ing to an ideological version of Custer's last stand by trying to persuade intellectual workers to accept the logic of the economic crisis, concur in the restructuring of industries and agree to the need for national 'consensus'. In this ideological warfare, the Socialist Party has revealed itself to be the objective ally of the forces of imperialism. (This point is stressed by virtually every single speaker.) Under these conditions, the PCF believes, intellectual workers will eventually understand that only the party can offer them the possibility of overcoming the contradiction of their situation.

That contradiction is well presented and clearly analysed both in the resolution and in many individual speeches: the intellectual aspirations of the 'new working class' in favour of the unbridling of creative research, the harmonisation of man and nature, of science and society, the generalisation of culture and education, the widespread development of the fine arts, all these are seen to be directly threatened by the implacable logic of the economic crisis, industrial redeployment, monetary disequilibrium, profit imperatives, career uncertainties and the ever-present threat of unemployment. However, there is nothing new about any of this. It has all been said before a hundred times, by Mallet and Touraine, by Naville and Gorz, and even by Marcuse. Moreover, the reasons offered as to why the intellectual workers should flock to the PCF remain somewhat less than convincing.

To argue that intellectual workers must join the party of the working class because change can only come about by struggle and only the working class knows how to struggle is merely to assert, in circular fashion, precisely that which needs to be proved. To argue that, since intellectuals are directly interested in culture, they must wish to defend the national culture; and that since the national culture involves social justice, scientific progress, democratic advance, national independence and a new morality; and that only the PCF really stands for all these things, is to produce a multifaceted sophistry which, in the opinion of the present author, is unlikely to convince those who are not already true believers.[36]

The problems with the Bobigny sessions are manifold. The basic contradiction between the political need to cope with the rise of

intellectual workers, and the ideological need to reaffirm the
vanguard role of the working class, remains unresolved.[37]
Intellectual workers are apparently of no interest to the PCF
other than to the extent to which their class consciousness can be
brought into line with that of the proletariat. Never are they considered to have any historically valid specificity of their own.
Moreover, the concept of ideological warfare is crude and ill-
defined (there is not a single reference to Gramsci throughout
the book) and amounts to little more than the hope that if certain
basic slogans ('the PS is reactionary', 'the PC is democratic') are
repeated often enough, people will begin to believe them. Finally,
perhaps most important of all, is the fact that the most significant
intellectuals in the party - the dissidents - were totally absent
from the 'debates'. Where were those who, since March 1978, had
attempted to produce a dialogue with the leaders, who had tried
to re-think the question of class alliances in terms of the specifics
of the 'new working class'? Where were Elleinstein, Althusser,
Goldring, Parmelin, Raymond Jean, Quilès, Rony, Buci-Glucksmann,
Balibar, Moissonnier, Adler, Kehayan and a host of others?
Absent. In their place, one finds a profusion of party faithfuls,
many of whom began their speech by expressing their total and
utter agreement with the Political Bureau's resolution. One isolated
and courageous individual, Jean-Pierre Marchand, flew the flag
of revolt.

He protested against the PCF's tendency to consider anyone who
voiced criticism of the leadership as an enemy of the party. He
protested against the way in which democratic centralism was interpreted as leadership infallibility. He agreed that the alliance between intellectuals and workers was vital but suggested that this
needed to be understood by workers as well as by the intellectuals.
He asserted that intellectual workers were no more subject to the
electoral promises of Giscard d'Estaing than some sections of the
working class. And he offered the view that the party line on
Afghanistan would turn off more intellectuals than would ever be
seduced by the Bobigny resolution.[38] A whole phalanx of speakers
then hastened to disavow him, to ridicule him and to suggest
that he simply had not understood the complexity of the situation.
The 'debates' at Bobigny amount to a slavish approval of a pre-
ordained line. The ideology remains in crisis. Since Argenteuil,
there appears to have been no progress whatsoever.

There are even indications that the party is reverting to a
pre-Argenteuil sectarianism on the specific question of the 'class
dimension' of culture. These indications have emerged in the
party's new 'intellectual' journal, 'Révolution'. The short history
of 'Révolution' has been one of ongoing crisis. The original editorial board had drawn its net as widely as possible and included
representatives from the entire spectrum of intellectual opinion
within the party. But although the members of the board were
appointed in June 1979, it only met twice before the appearance of
the first number on 7 March 1980, and then more than half the
members were not invited. As early as April 1980, there were

murmurs of discontent about the lack of open debate within the journal. But in May and June, two articles by Lucien Marest, a member of the cultural section of the Central Committee, caused a major storm. Marest's articles have been subjected to various interpretations, but they were widely believed to have represented a regression from the Argenteuil line which had proclaimed the 'autonomous', neutral, essentially humanistic nature of all cultural creativity. Now Marest argued, among other things, that artists and writers ought to interest themselves more closely in problems affecting the world of labour; that the organisers of party fêtes should refuse to engage entertainers who were in disagreement with Communist policies; and that certain works of art and litera- ture were more appropriate to working-class readers than others.[39]

Incensed by these articles, one of the sub-editors of 'Révol- ution', François Hincker, wrote a hard-hitting reply, accusing Marest of having gone back on the promises of Argenteuil. His article was refused by the editor and he resigned from the board. His resignation was soon followed by that of several others, Serge Goffard, Gilles Perrault and a second sub-editor (out of four), Michel Cardoze. Jean Elleinstein, who had been placed 'outside the party' in the autumn, was also removed from the editorial team. On 21 June 1980, a major confrontation took place when the full editorial board met. Outspoken criticism of the policy of the paper, of the party line on intellectuals and of the recent Marest articles was expressed by a wide range of opinion. The party line was defended by Claude Mazauric and Jack Ralite.[40] But nothing was resolved. The paper is having great difficulty in achieving its subscription target of 50,000 (it is currently believed to be in the region of 15,000). In short, the publication whose function was to 'break through' to intellectuals in general seems to be having some difficulty in pleasing its own editorial board (composed ex- clusively of PCF intellectuals) and is having even less success with the intellectual in the street.

In conclusion, several fundamental points need to be stressed. The first, and most obvious, is that the question of the political support of intellectual workers is the major political issue facing the Left in the years to come. The PCF cannot avoid facing up to this question. Secondly, the question of intellectual workers raises that of the overall objectives of the PCF. Is the party attempting to act as a force for social transformation which em- braces all the various aspirations towards social change which manifest themselves? Or is it merely content to act as an opposi- tional pressure group which expresses, in political terms, the demands of the single social group it represents? The party does not seem able really to decide on the answer to these questions and tends to alternate between them. However, and this is the third point, if it does decide on the former strategy, then the need becomes urgent for a serious ideological line on intellectual workers. So far, this line has simply not been forthcoming. The PCF's entire strategy has been political rather than ideological (and in this sense one could argue that it has no strategy at all,

merely tactics). Fourthly, one cannot help observing that, in its
attempt to find a political appeal to the 'new working class', it has
been forced, more and more, to adopt some of the language of the
extreme Left ('les gauchistes'). It has recently paid lip service
to the problems of feminism, the youth movement and autogestion
(while steadfastly resisting in the most reactionary manner the
siren sounds of ecology, racial integration, gay liberation and
drug-taking). But in so doing, it has only rendered itself incred-
ible, not so much on account of the ideological U-turns this has
involved as because of the disparity between these new causes
and its own internal practice, hierarchy and structure.

Fifthly, and finally, one must assess the reasons for the PCF's
failure to attract the intellectual workers. There are three over-
riding reasons. First, the profound mistrust with which the
party is viewed by the 'new working class'. Only time - and con-
sistency - can eliminate that mistrust. Second, the existence of
the Socialist Party as a viable and serious political force on the
Left. Not until the PCF recognises this fact can there be any hope
of ideological progress (France is the only major country in the
world with two equally powerful, historically-rooted and political
valid parties of the Left). Third, the PS strategy of 'Front de
classe' appears to be more in tune with the reality of French
society today than do the more ambitious projects of the PCF.
But now that the PS has staked out its claims on the ideological
new frontier, the PCF will have difficulty in occupying that particular piece of territory. Meanwhile, its electoral support continues to be subject to sociological and political erosion. In the
first round of the presidential elections on April 26 1981, Georges
Marchais lost heavily in some of the most traditional industrial
areas of France.[41] In the areas where modern high technological
plant has been replacing the older forms of heavy productive
industry, the party's failure to get across to the incoming ranks
of intellectual workers seems to have been clearly reflected in the
vote. In Paris itself, Marchais scored only 9 per cent (as against
15 per cent for the PCF as a whole in the general elections of
1978 and 19 per cent for its presidential candidate Jacques Duclos
in 1969). In the general elections of June 1981, the party was
totally eliminated from the capital. Where it had boasted seven
Parisian deputies in 1973 and three in 1978, it lost all of these
before a heavy Socialist advance in 1981. In the industrial suburbs
of Paris which, as Jean Garcia had warned in 1979, have recently
been subject to rapid industrial transformation in favour of offices
and advanced technology, the result was probably even more tell-
ing. Marchais' share of the vote was 10 per cent down on the
party's 1978 score in traditional Communist bastions like Seine
Saint-Denis, Essonne, Hauts de Seine and Val de Marne. This
negative trend was accentuated by the general elections in June.
Whereas in 1978 the PCF had held 27 seats in the eight departments of the Ile de France (Paris and its so-called 'Red Belt'),
it emerged from the June 1981 contest with only 13 of them intact.
Three of its four seats in the Essonne were lost as were its remain-

ing seats in Seine-et-Marne and Val d'Oise. Most revealing of all, in Seine Saint-Denis, which has been an unflinching party stronghold since 1920, it lost four of its nine deputies. Nationwide, the PCF lost exactly half of its parliamentary seats. It is, of course, impossible to say with any accuracy how this decline should be analysed or explained. But even a cursory glance at the sectors just referred to suggests both a failure to get through to the intellectual workers and a falling off of support among the traditional blue-collar constituency. This has to some extent been exacerbated by the 'knock-on' effect of the Socialist landslide and may be mitigated in the future. But all the signs suggest that the long-term structural changes being brought about in France's social geology will render the task of appealing to a new class more rather than less urgent.

The PCF seems nowadays, despite having ministers in the government (or even, some would argue, because of it), in a state of uncertainty similar to that of Colombus. When he set out, he did not know where he was going (Argenteuil). When he arrived, he did not know where he was (CME, UPF) and when he returned, he did not know where he had been (Bobigny). It would be a fool or a knave who would presume to predict which way the party will turn its sails next on the increasingly vital issue of intellectual workers.

NOTES

1   Cited in Maurice Moissonnier, Le Mouvement ouvrier français et les intellectuels avant la Première Guerre Mondiale, in 'Cahiers d'Histoire de l'Institut Maurice Thorez', 15, 1976, pp. 32-3. There was also a major debate on this issue at the annual Congress of the SFIO at Nancy in 1907.

2   See Nicole Racine and Louis Bodin, 'Le Parti Communiste Français pendant l'entre-deux guerres', Paris, Colin (FNSP), 1972, 169-73.

3   Susan Bachrach, Pour un art prolétarien, pour un art républicain: changing French left-wing perspectives on culture (1928-1938), unpublished dissertation, University of Wisconsin, Madison, 1975; Jean-Pierre Bernard, 'Le Parti Communiste Français et la question littéraire, 1921-29', Grenoble, 1972; Pierre Loffler, 'Chronique de la littérature prolétarienne française de 1930 à 1939', Paris, 1967.

4   See Daniel Brower, 'The New Jacobins, the French Communist Party and the Popular Front', Ithaca, Cornell UP, 1968, III, IV.

5   Roger Garaudy, 'Le Communisme et la Renaissance de la Culture Française', Paris, Editions Sociales, 1945; Laurent Casanova, 'Le Parti Communiste, les Intellectuels et la Nation', Paris, Editions Sociales, 1950; (Comité Central), Débats sur les Problèmes idéologiques et culturels, in 'Cahiers du Communisme', 5-6, 1966; Léo Figuères, 'Le Parti Communiste

Français, la Culture et les Intellectuels', Paris, 1972;
Georges Marchais, Roland Leroy, 'Pour la Culture avec les
Intellectuels', Paris, Editions Sociales, 1973; Les Intellectuels
et le Parti Communiste Français: l'alliance dans l'histoire,
'Cahiers d'Histoire de l'Institut Maurice Thorez', special no.
15, 1976; (Conseil National du PCF), 'Les Intellectuels, la
Culture et la Révolution', Paris, Editions Sociales, 1980.

6   First given any theoretical sustenance in a special issue of
'Arguments' in 1958, the debate was fuelled by the publication
of two books in 1963: Serge Mallet, 'La Nouvelle Classe
Ouvriere', Paris, Seuil, and Pierre Belleville, 'Une Nouvelle
Classe Ouvrière', Paris, Julliard. For an excellent overview
of the 'state of play', see Gerard Adam, Où en est le débat
sur la nouvelle classe ouvrière?, 'Revue Française de Science
Politique', 1968, pp. 1003-23.

7   (Comité Central du PCF) Débats sur les Problèmes idéologiques et culturels, in 'Cahiers du Communisme', 5-6, mai-
juin 1966.

8   Ibid., pp. 276-7.

9   Gilbert Mury, A Propos de la Nouvelle Classe Ourvrière,
'Economie et Politique', Janvier 1965, pp. 90-110; André
Barjonet, Réalité de la classe ouvrière, in 'Nouvelle Critique',
110, 1959, pp. 24-39.

10   Garaudy was expelled from the Political Bureau, the Central
Committee and the party itself in 1970 for, among other things,
advocating a version of the new working-class theory. See
his 'Le Grand Tournant du Socialisme', Paris, Gallimard,
1969 and 'Toute la Vérité', Paris, Grasset, 1970.

11   Paris, Editions Sociales, 1971, 2 volumes.

12   See Tom Bottomore, 'Karl Marx', Oxford, Blackwell, 1979, pp.
19-27 (Bottomore's Introduction) and pp. 79-91.

13   Nicos Poulantzas, 'Les Classes sociales dans le capitalisme
d'aujoud'hui', Paris, Seuil, 1974; Christian Baudelot, Roger
Establet et Jacques Malemort, 'La Petite Bourgeoisie en
France', Paris, Maspéro, 1975. For an excellent overview
both of the PCF line and of its critics, see George Ross,
Marxism and the New Middle Classes: French Critiques,
'Theory and Society', 1978, vol. 5, part 2.

14   The PCF share of the electorate since 1958 has been as follows
(the PS share is indicated in brackets): 1958: 19% (15.7%);
1962: 21.7% (12.6%); 1967: 22.5% (18.8%); 1968: 20% (16.5%);
1973: 21.3% (20.7%).

15   'XXIe Congrès', p. 41.

16   For a brief summary, see G. Marchais, Union du Peuple de
France, qu'est-ce que cela veut dire? In 'Cahiers du Communisme', 11, novembre 1974, pp. 39-51. For a more complete
exposé, Claude Quin, 'Classes sociales et Union du Peuple de
France', Paris, Editions Sociales, 1976.

17   Quin, ibid., pp. 74-83.

18   According to the PCF, the industrial working-class in 1974
contained 10 million members, represented 44.5% of the working

population and had been on the increase ever since 1954 (Quin, ibid., pp. 33-5). According to INSEE, the 7.8 million industrial workers in 1974 represented 36.9% of the working population and had been falling steadily since 1970. See on this, Alain Duhamel, L'Evolution des Classes sociales vue par le PCF, in 'Le Monde', 9-10 mai 1976, p. 6. Also, Guy Pelachaud, Un Salarié sur Deux se dit Ouvrier in 'Cahiers du Communisme', octobre 1977, pp. 14-25 and Laurent Thévenot, Les Catégories sociales en 1975: l'extension du salariat in 'Economie et Statistique', juillet-août 1977.

19   For an explanation of 'front de classe', see Paul Bacot, Le Front de Classe in 'Revue Française de Science Politique', vol. 28, no. 2, 1978, pp. 277-95.

20   Jean Baudouin, Les Phénomènes de contestation au sein du Parti Communiste Français (avril 1978 - mai 1979), in 'Revue Française de Science Politique', vol. 30, 1980, pp. 78-111; Jolyon Howorth, The French Communist Party: return to the ghetto? in 'The World Today', vol. 36, 1980, pp. 139-47.

21   François Hincker, Parti Socialiste, Union du Peuple de France, Union de la Gauche, 'L'Humanité', 18 avril 1978, p. 4. He has now passed over into the ranks of the 'moderate' dissidents. Other 'party line' articles by Henri Fiszbin, 'L'Humanité', 11 avril 1978 and Louis Le Roux, ibid., 13 avril 1978.

22   'L'Humanité', 28 avril 1978, p. 9.

23   La Mutation nécessaire, 'Le Monde', 14 avril 1978. These problems were also raised in two special issues of the party's intellectual journal 'Nouvelle Critique', avril & octobre 1978 and in a remarkable statement by the Union of Communist Students calling for the summoning of a special party conference on these problems ('Le Monde', 10 mai 1978, p. 10).

24   'L'Unité', no. 310, 13 octobre 1978, p. 12. In May 1978, at a conference organised by UACES, at Sussex University, Elleinstein, in response to a question from the present author, stated that, in his view, intellectual workers had as important a role to play in the historic movement as the traditional proletariat.

25   Since his continued collaboration with 'Figaro-Magazine' and 'Paris Match', Elleinstein has been totally 'marginalised' by the other dissidents and on 6 October 1980 was deemed by the Central Committee to have 'placed himself outside the Party its organisation and its policies' - 'Le Monde', 8 novembre 1980.

26   Bernard Edelman, 'La Légalisation de la Classe Ouvrière', Paris, Christian Bourgois, 1978; Yvonne Quilès and Jean Tornikian, 'Sous le PC, les communistes', Paris, Seuil, 1980; Jacques Frémontier, 'La Vie en Bleu: Voyage en Culture Ouvrière', Paris, Fayard, 1980.

27   23e Congrès du Parti Communiste Français, Cahiers du Communisme', juin-juillet 1979, p. 66.

28   '23e Congrès', pp. 143-6.

29   Thierry Pfister, L'Evolution de l'électorat du Parti Communiste
     in 'Le Monde', 20 juin 1979.
30   The Fiszbin affair is explained in Henri Fiszbin, 'Les Bouches
     S'Ouvrent', Paris Grasset, 1980.
31   Fiszbin's own analysis of voting trends in the capital is in
     ibid., p. 30; Paul Laurent's reply, on behalf of the Political
     Bureau, is in 'France Nouvelle', 12-18 janvier 1980. For an
     overview, see F. Platone and F. Subileau, Les Militants com-
     munistes à Paris: quelques données sociologiques in 'Revue
     Française de Science Politique', vol. 25 (5), octobre 1975 and
     Les Militants communistes à Paris in ibid., vol. 26 (2), avril
     1976. Also, Françoise Subileau, Les Communistes parisiens en
     1977 in ibid., vol. 29, août-octobre 1979. Note that the Com-
     munist share of the vote in the presidential elections of 1981
     in Paris was reduced to just over 9%.
32   Details of the meeting between the Paris federation secretaries
     and the Political Bureau in 'Les Bouches S'Ouvrent', pp. 20-4
     and 88-110.
33   H. Fiszbin, Nous n'avons pas encore tiré toutes les leçons . . .
     in 'L'Humanité', 7 janvier 1980. This article drew an official
     reply/disclaimer in the following day's issue of the party
     newspaper.
34   (Conseil National du PCF) 'Les Intellectuels, la Culture et
     la Révolution', Paris, Editions Sociales, 1980.
35   The Resolution itself states that the vast majority of techni-
     cians and some engineers are now objectively part of the pro-
     letariat, a minority of engineers and cadres (managers) are
     the creatures of the monopolies and that, between these two
     groups, the overall majority of intellectual workers are in a
     'contradictory position', ibid., p. 347.
36   These arguments are deployed in 'Les Intellectuels, la Cul-
     ture et la Révolution', pp. 359-66.
37   Marchais contented himself with stating that there was no con-
     tradiction between 'the recognition of the rights and needs
     of intellectuals and the recognition of this fundamental theo-
     retical and political fact: the historic role of the working-
     class'. Ibid., p. 405.
38   Ibid., pp. 121-5.
39   The 'offending' articles were published in 'Révolution', 9-15
     mai and 6-12 juin 1980.
40   See the account of this meeting in 'Le Monde', 24 juin 1980.
     Ralite is now Minister of Health.
41   Patrick Jarreau, Le Recul de PCF est net dans ses bastions
     mais aussi dans ses 'terres de mission', 'Le Monde', 28 avril
     1981, p. 6. In fact, the PCF only improved on its 1978 score
     in two departments (Haute-Corse and Lozère) both of which
     are totally marginal to its activities in any case. More seriously,
     it lost very heavily in some of its most traditional working-
     class departments (Cher -12%; Seine-Saint-Denis -10.7%;
     Allier -8%; Pas-de-Calais -6.8%; Bouches-du-Rhône -6.6%;
     Nord -4.9%, etc.).

6 THE UNIFIED SOCIALIST PARTY (PSU) SINCE 1968

Vladimir Claude Fišera and Peter Jenkins

We could perhaps start this survey by briefly mentioning the main reasons why an analysis of the Unified Socialist Party (PSU) is a useful exercise. There seem to be three valid reasons for so doing; to begin with, the PSU celebrated its twentieth anniversary in 1980, offering a convenient milestone for observers to take stock of its position on the left wing of the French political spectrum.[1] Furthermore, the PSU has been actively involved in the 1981 presidential and legislative election campaigns represented by Huguette Bouchardeau and by 183 candidates. Finally, there is the actual and potential role in French politics represented by the figure of Michel Rocard, former leader of the PSU, presidential candidate in 1969, and a powerful rival to François Mitterrand's control of the Socialist Party since 1974. A discussion of the recent history of the PSU can perhaps offer some insight into Rocard's political trajectory since entering the Socialist Party in 1974.

Linking Rocard's name with the PSU may be a widespread and almost automatic reaction on the part of political commentators, or by way of introducing him at Socialist Party gatherings, but it is nevertheless necessary to point out that Rocard and the PSU are not synonymous, however much they may tend to be identified in the public eye. Not surprisingly, the PSU itself is very sensitive on this particular point, and reserves its rare displays of sectarianism for its fallen leader, as, for example, when it omitted Rocard's article from the issue of its paper, 'Tribune Socialists', celebrating the tenth anniversary of the May events.[2]

This question of the party's (now unwelcome) association with Rocard broaches the problem of the contradictory images which this small party has presented during the twenty years of its existence. There is the PSU active in the street demonstrations against the Algerian War, the PSU as the articulate spokesman of the 'new working class', arguing the case for the counter-plan and the need for structural reforms. Ironically, the early PSU was probably as much tied to the image of Pierre Mendès France, as it was later tied to that of Rocard, with his programme for 'decolonising the provinces', publicised at gatherings such as the one at Grenoble in 1966. Or, as a definite counter-weight to the image of the PSU as a radical, modernising, technocratic elite, there is the total immersion of the party in the events of May 1968, 'like a fish in water', to use Mao's phrase, symbolised by the massive rally at Charléty stadium. From 1968, a line of continuity can be traced to the PSU's active participation in the Lip factory occupation, and the developing struggle for 'autogestion', or self management.

The legacy of the Unified Socialist Party, that is, from the counter-plan of the 1960s to autogestion in the 1970s, is a contradictory one, and suggests some of the difficulty in assessing the contribution made by the PSU to the French Left. The problem has been highlighted by the caustic remark once made in 'Le Canard Enchaîné' to the effect that in the forthcoming election, all the established political parties would be presenting their programme to the voters, except, of course, the PSU, which would present two![3]

The origins of the PSU lie with the growth of opposition to the Algerian War, and to the politics of the SFIO under the leadership of Guy Mollet. The three political currents constituting the PSU each brought a distinctive contribution to the new party: the Autonomous Socialist Party led by Edouard Depreux, with 8,000 members and 2I SFIO deputies;[4] the Union de la Gauche Socialiste, composed of 4,000 members of the radical Catholic Mouvement de ('Liberation du Peuple', plus 2,000 from the 'Nouvelle Gauche'.[5] The UGS thus regrouped former Communists such as Gilles Martinet, Claude Bourdet from 'France-Observateure', and former Trotskyists such as Yvan Craipeau, once Trotsky's secretary, and Pierre Naville). Thirdly, there was the group of dissidents from the French Communist Party (PCF) grouped around the journal 'Tribune du Communisme', notably Serge Mallet, theorist of the 'new working class', and Jean Poperen.

The origins of the PSU gave it that quality most highly prized by new political organisations, then and now - visibility - given the degree of media interest in its activities.[6] Over and above this, the PSU also inherited an open, decentralised democratic structure, a certain libertarian style, and a healthy distrust of party bureaucracy. A sense of the élan of the new party is suggested by Michel Rocard's claim that the PSU possessed 'the militant courage and the creative questioning characteristic of the revolutionary movement: the Communist Party's organisational ability: and the handling of the legal apparatus which social democracy did well . . .'[7] Or, as suggested in the recent book by Hervé Hamon and Patrick Rotman on the French Left and the Algerian War, the setting up of the PSU represented an ambitious attempt to achieve the political equivalent of 'squaring the circle', i.e., reconstituting left-wing politics on a new basis, that of the 'socialist front', a non-hierarchical union of the labour movement and political parties.[8]

The evolution of the PSU during its first ten years has been described in detail elsewhere.[9] Looking at the PSU in the decade after 1968, it is possible to analyse its development along three main axes, in terms of its relationship to ideology, to political institutions (in particular social democracy), and finally to other social movements.

The PSU was very deeply affected by the events of May-June 1968 - during that year its membership grew by a third to 15,500 moving back towards its original peak held during the Algerian War.[10] The party's student base increased (40 per cent of members were now students),[11] but at the same time its working-class base increased, reflected in the rapid growth of factory branches.

The effect of the May events shifted the PSU firmly away from its earlier role of wooing the 'new working class'. Its new concerns were revolutionary, if not Leninist, with a touch of workerism common to groups on the far Left at that time. During the period 1968-71, the PSU flirted heavily with 'gauchisme', seeking closer relationships with Trotskyist groups such as the Ligue Communiste and Lutte Ouvrière.

The resultant factionalism at the party's Sixth Congress, Dijon, 1969, was strangely reminiscent of the divisions evident at its second congress at Alfortville in 1963, with the difference that the whole tenor of political debate was now firmly shifted towards the ultra-Left. The main focus of debate was the form of relationship that the party should have with the groups of the far left. The old SFIO was dismissed as a purely electoralist organisation. The PCF still had to be taken seriously, however, as a working-class party, despite its reformist policies. The PSU accordingly negotiated with it, unsuccessfully as it happened, with a view to arranging joint activity for the 1971 municipal elections.

During the years 1968-71, the PSU was energetically and wholeheartedly involved in refighting the battles of May 1968. This was not without some measure of success, as for example, with the 816,471 votes obtained by Rocard in the 1969 presidential election, and his subsequent victory over Couve de Murville in the by-election in October of the same year, which marked a high point of success for the party.

However, in political terms, the PSU was firmly locked into the project of developing itself as the revolutionary party. Returning to the question of imagery, Rocard has been quoted as claiming that the PSU would become the European equivalent of the Chilean MIR (Movement of the Revolutionary Left).[12] After prolonged and bitter internal debates, this project was finally abandoned by 1971, when various factions left the party, such as the Trotskyist faction which joined the Ligue Communiste. As had been the case with the period during the early sixties, this internal debate proved costly in terms of membership, and by 1972, the PSU was down to 9,000 members after its 1968 level of 15,500.[13]

On the positive side, the PSU had clarified its ideological position during this testing period, and 1972 saw the appearance of its main contribution to the political debates of the 1970s, in the form of the perspective of autogestion or workers' self-management. Its manifesto, 'Contrôler aujourd'hui pour décider demain', theorised the actual experiences of the factory occupations of May-June 1968. Autogestion offered itself as 'a realistic utopia', as a key preparatory experience for the working class in achieving the transition towards a socialist, self-managed society.[14]

The perspective of autogestion in industry owed something both to the Yugoslav experience of self-management, and to the limited attempts at establishing workers' control of production in 1968. In relation to local government, it also drew upon the experience of Nantes, where the town was briefly controlled by a strike committee during May 1968, with some degree of support from the local peasants. The theme of autogestion also testified to the PSU's attempt to develop a working-class base through the medium of factory branches. The relative success of the PSU in popularising the perspective of autogestion was perhaps indicated to some extent by the CFDT taking up this theme.[15] However, the key experience in this respect was undoubtedly that of the occupation and self-management of the Lip watch factory at Besançon, led by PSU member Charles Piaget. The banner outside the Lip factory, occupied in 1973, expressed the message with succint directness: 'It is possible. We produce, we sell, we pay ourselves.'

In terms of its ideology, the PSU became caught in a detour, building the revolutionary party, but succeeded in clarifying its programme as that of autogestion. Yet these immediate concerns led to the party being overtaken by events elsewhere. Its concern with ideology, rather than with political institutions, and in particular, social democracy, meant that it missed the crucial significance of the emergence of the Parti Socialiste out of the old, discredited SFIO.

Rocard's critique of the PSU, which appeared in the issue of 'Libération' on the tenth anniversary of the May events (the article earlier refused by 'Tribune Socialiste') admittedly had the advantage of hindsight.[16] He argued that the PSU had missed two significant developments – the Epinay Congress of the Socialist Party in 1971, and the adoption of the Common Programme by the PS, PCF and Left Radicals in 1972.

The PSU's initial reaction to the adoption of the Common Programme and the formation of the Union of the Left was fairly guarded – the Programme was criticised on the basis that it did not go far enough, and offered no perspective for autogestion, a rather purist approach, limited to its ideological content rather than the political effect that it was to have on French politics during the seventies.

For sections of the PSU leadership, the prospect of a new and dynamic Socialist Party placed in question the very need for the PSU as an autonomous political force. The PSU had always been at its most effective when social democracy was in disarray, as for example, in 1960-2, and in 1968-9. For many, there remained a basic ambiguity about whether the role of the PSU was to modernise social democracy, or to outflank it. Thus, when social democracy began to revive, then the temptation to fuse with it, and become its left wing, became almost overpowering, as in 1967 with the Fédération de la Gauche Démocratique et Socialiste, and again in 1974, with the Parti Socialiste.

Rocard's political project was initially developed cautiously, in terms considered acceptable to PSU members, who were traditionally wary of social democracy. Closer liaison with the Parti Socialiste, through the proposed Assises du Socialisme in 1974, was, it was claimed, intended to lead to a new, revamped 'Parti des Socialistes' (PDS) to include the PSU and CFDT trade unionists.

The Assises were heavily publicised in the PSU's weekly, 'Tribune Socialiste', to a somewhat sceptical membership.[17] The production team of the weekly were sympathetic to Rocard; the post of party National Secretary was now held by his co-thinker, Robert Chapuis, leaving Rocard a free hand to prepare the entry of the PSU into the Socialist Party.

However, just as in 1967, when Rocard himself had become Party Secretary, this drift towards accommodation with social democracy was vigorously rejected by the rank-and-file at the party's National Council of October 1974. Rocard and his followers, including much of the party's experienced cadre, and almost the whole of the Loiret and a few other departmental federations, then left to join the Socialist Party.

The central problem of the PSU's political role was once again graphically underlined. How could the PSU be most effective - as an independent force, a 'laboratory of ideas', without becoming either a satellite of the PCF, or more probably, being re-absorbed by social democracy? The PSU's original answer had been the policy of the 'socialist front' of all labour and working-class organisations. In the 1970s, it had renewed this approach with the call for 'popular unity' on the Chilean model, at its 9th Congress at Amiens, in 1974, as a more militant and class-conscious version of the Union of the Left. Yet it is possible to identify a certain softening of the PSU's attitude towards the union from its early, rather maximalist criticisms of it. Hence, in 1974, the PSU decided not to run Charles Piaget, the Lip strike leader, as presidential candidate, although this would appear to be the logical conclusion of its own policies on autogestion. Instead, the PSU supported Mitterrand's campaign. In 1977, the PSU joined with the parties of the Union of the Left in putting forward joint slates in many towns for the municipal elections, which, to some critics, provided the evidence that the party was abandoning its political principles to tuck in behind the Union of the Left.[18] Michel Mousel, now National Secretary of the PSU, even broached the possibility of the PSU taking office under a government of the Union of the Left, in an interview published in 'La Croix'.[19] Debating this change of tack with Alain Krivine of the Trotskyist Ligue Communiste Revolutionnaire, Gilbert Hercet of the PSU's Bureau National justified this approach with reference to the paramount need 'to get in position for the hour of reckoning in 1978'.[20] For the PSU, a participation in government would facilitate the creation of a mass, popular autonomous force which would exert pressure on the reformist united Left.

During the mid-1970s, the PSU described itself as 'the party of socialist self-management',[21] and saw itself as the political expression of the current for autogestion within the labour movement, and as a necessary counter-weight to the statist conceptions of reform held by the PCF and the PS. As the decade progressed, the PSU began to respond to other social movements, and to attempt to broaden the base of its appeal. Since 1971, the PSU had taken a position of active support for the emerging women's movement, and for the ecology and anti-nuclear movements from the Amiens congress of December 1974.[22]

This approach was evident in the PSU's participation in the local elections of March 1977 (half of its thousand councillors being elected on PSU or PSU-ecologists slates) and in the legislative elections of March 1978, following the break-up of the Union of the Left. The electoral results obtained by the party, ten years after the May events, provide a convenient point for assessing the party's performance, before going on to outline the present contours of the party, and its role in the 1981 elections.

In 1978, the PSU stood as the 'front Autogestionnaire' under the slogan 'Ecology, Socialism, Women's Rights', with some degree of support from women's groups, ecology groups, the Movement pour une alternative non-violente (MAN), and left-wing ethnic groups. The party's aim, as the main organised force in the Front Autogestionnaire, was to act as a rallying and regrouping point to those movements in critical support of the Union of the Left. The Front stood a total of 230 candidates, and collected 2.3 per cent of the vote in the first round. Even considering the context of the defeat of the Union of the Left, and the resulting demoralisation of the Left, this constituted a definite setback for the PSU. The contours of this situation were analysed in detail in a key article which appeared in the party's theoretical journal, 'Critique Socialiste', written by Pascal Gollet, who is, with G. Hercet, one of the party's few remaining Rocardians. The article is crucial to developing an understanding of the relative failure (at least in electoral terms) of the PSU's political project of the 1970s.[23]

The PSU's vote was 2.3 per cent, compared with the 4.2 per cent it had received in the 1973 legislative elections. In a closely documented comparison, Gollet argued that half of this decline in the vote was attributable to the Socialist Party, which had succeeded in 'nationalising' its vote in the intervening five-year period, i.e., it was less subject to those marked regional fluctuations in its vote which favoured the PSU in certain areas. The overall ratio of PSU votes to PS votes had been 1 to 2 in 1973, but was now in the order of 1 to 10. Rocard's defection to the PS in 1974 had contributed in part to this relative decline.

Since 1978 we have seen a confirmation of this trend, the PSU faring badly in national elections when big parties (the four major parties subsumed in the two blocks), personalities and the media tended to push to the margins the 'small ones' ('les petits'). As far as the PSU was concerned, there was one added cause for its decline: the PS gradually 'nationalised' its role, that is to say it increased its following in regions traditionally unresponsive to the old-style anti-clerical republican centrist SF10. These regions largely overlap with Catholic areas which were industrialised of late, in the wave of the fifties and the sixties. These were PSU strongholds both electorally and as regards presence at grass roots level. These are: Brittany, including Loire-Atlantique and excluding Ille et Vilaine; the Paris region (Paris itself, Essonne, Hauts de Seine, Yvelines); the Rhône-Alpes region; and the Doubs department. With Rocard's departure, the PSU lost part of its traditional appeal among modernist intellectuals, employees and technicians, teachers and trade union full-timers, many of them of Catholic origin. This meant the loss of crucial 'relays' at the institutional level such as the CFDT, the 'Nouvel Observateur' and some of its local notables both in councils and in clubs and associations. This in turn explains the 1.1 per cent result achieved by Huguette Bouchardeau on 26 April 1981, at the first ballot of the presidential elections, despite a successful campaign highly praised in 'Le Monde', 'Le Matin' and public opinion too: according to opinion polls by the end of the penultimate week of the campaign, the PSU candidate had trebled her score, reaching 3 per cent of the 'intentions de vote'. The PSU paid also for its lack of visibility and thus of credibility since 1973 as it did not field a candidate at the previous presidential elections in 1974, lost its sole spokesman ('figure de proue') in the same year and was absent in the 1979 European elections. There were some other reasons for this, such as strategic ones - people voted against the incumbent rather than for socialist ideas, for a break with 23 years of uninterrupted right-wing rule - and tactical ones too, such as the 'Chirac effect' when one of the last polls before the first ballot put Chirac at only 2.5 per cent behind Mitterrand who was thus under the threat of being eliminated from the final contest. This led PS spokesmen and allies, from Jean Poperen to Jean Daniel - the editor of 'Le Nouvel Observateur' - and finally Mitterrand himself to warn, nay to blackmail those who might 'scatter their votes for candidates unable to be present on the second ballot' because 'if the left is dispersed ('s'éparpille') it will be defeated',[24] despite the fact the Huguette Bouchardeau 'enjoys, however, our most evident human sympathies'.[25]

However one should not write off the PSU even as an electoral force. True, the PS seems to have 'stabilised' a part of the old PSU electorate (e.g., in Isère and in Doubs) and to have attracted PSU voters in constituencies where it trailed behind the Communist Party in 1978, as for instance in the Paris suburbs. However the PSU, which fielded 183 candidates (they were 230 in 1978 under the lable Front Autogestionnaire) under the name PSU or PSU - Alternative 81, increased its vote at the legislative elections by 0.8 per cent compared to the presidential elections, which is down only by 0.4 per cent on the 1978 score. In 130 constituencies out of 183 it did better than on 25 April 1981. This contrasts with a general reduction by half of the extreme Left vote in general with Lutte Ouvrière and especially the ecologists being decimated. The PSU did well in Britanny where it was allied with the regionalist Union Démocratique Bretonne.[26] Elsewhere, its best results went to candidates who had the additional support of radical ecologists.[27] These had split from the 'Aujourd'hui l'écologie' alliance which had been in existence under various names since the municipal elections of 1977. Even if one sets aside the few cases where the PSU faced a Left Gaullist or a Left Radical (left of centre MRG), which helped it to retain its old electorate, it appears that the

Unified Socialists scored more than 3 per cent of the vote in a
variety of scattered geographical areas, which are not always
traditional PSU or even left-wing zones. These are areas where
the PSU has an organisation on the ground, unlike Lutte Ouvrière
and the ecologists, a trade union or 'associative' activity - although
these were often swept over by the 'pink wave' - but first and
foremost where it possesses a network of local councillors.[28] This
corroborates the results of the municipal elections of 1977 when
the PSU obtained 7 per cent of the vote for its autonomous slates
in small localities - where proportional representation applies -
and obtained 1,000 'autogestionnaires' councillors overall, half of
them being elected in larger cities (of 30,000 inhabitants and
above) on Union of the Left slates as junior partners of the PCF
and PS.[29] This resilience was confirmed at the March 1979 district
elections (cantonales) when the PSU attracted 3.90 per cent of
the vote fielding 104 candidates. Despite the nature of these
elections, which should by nature present insuperable obstacles
to small parties, the PSU was up on its 1976 results and in places
up on its score of 1973.[30]

   This seems to indicate that this party, although battered by
bipolarisation, could have overcome its lowest ebb. It can now
survive without a charismatic figure and with no organic link with
a larger political (e.g., social democracy) or ideological (e.g.,
Catholicism) 'famille-mère'. Its Breton vote is now a regionalist
vote not a left Catholic vote and its electorate is now closest to
the ecological electorate not to the PS, PCF or Lutte Ouvrière
vote. It is strongest in departments which are shifting to the Left
but where the balance between Left and Right - if one looks at
the 10 May results - is still 50-50, such as Rhône, Loire, Hauts
de Seine, Finistère and Loire Atlantique. It certainly offers an
electoral outlet to radical dissent in right-wing ('bourgeois' or
traditionally Catholic) departments where the Left is in a minority
such as Paris, Yvelines and the West of France. The Socialist
Party promised the PSU in their electoral agreement, not without
hesitation, proportional representation at municipal, legislative
as well as regional elections.[31] Even its 1.93 per cent on 14 June
1981 would have given the PSU five MPs given proportional representation and five to the ecologists (which the PSU may in part
win over in the future),[32] whilst there seem to be no other independent competitors on the extreme Left as was the case in the
seventies and as the left-wing trends in the PS and PCF are either
assimilated or rejected in the wilderness.

   For the first time since 1974, the overall membership of the party
stopped falling, showing in 1980 an influx of new members (12
per cent more than in the previous year). After the electoral
campaigns of 1981 this trend has accelerated while radical trade
unions such as the CFDT get more votes at works councils'
elections but as yet no boost in membership. According to the
PSU registers, regions which have increased their numbers most
significantly are again Brittany, Paris as well as Midi-Pyrénées.
This 'other Left' which the PSU Congress at Colombes in February

1981 set itself as a goal will probably mean a further federalisation
and regionalisation of the organisation, clearly symbolised by the
twenty 'Plans Alter' already drafted between the Autumn of 1979
and 1981 by local activists as an alternative for regional development based on an increase in local jobs, agricultural equilibrium
and the search for sources of energy which could be recycled.
The central slogan is 'to live and to work locally'.

The gap between, on the one hand, the production of new
radical ideas which are later accepted by the whole Left and which
are the source of the PSU's prestige and, on the other hand, the
'institutional means' for putting them into practice forces the PSU
to stay inside the Left, which means in the present circumstances
a certain presence in or around government and Parliament.[33] It
means also and at the same time a quest for legitimacy at the local
level where the PSU must be perceived as different from the PS
and PCF. Paradoxically, the greater the organisational difference
and polarisation at the local level between the PSU and the reformist parties, the greater its chances will be of being accepted as
a bona fide partner at the central level. Conversely, Pierre
Mauroy's letter of 3 July 1981 offering the PSU participation in
government[34] and Michel Mousel's participation in the staff of the
Communist Minister for the Civil Service, Anicet Le Pors,[35] will
strengthen the hand of PSU local councillors and trade unionist
leaders. While Huguette Bouchardeau, Claude Bourdet and their
supporters see themselves as being part of the majority extended
to the CFDT, Gabriel Granier and the 'basist' tendency are very
reluctant to enter into any sort of agreement at the top and rely
more on a growing social movement for radical change. As tendencies – not as individuals – they cannot hope to join the 'governmental' Socialist Party[36] because of the emancipation of their
present voters and members from the 'classical' Left and of the
identification of the PS with the state and the establishment. This
runs against the 'immediate data' – i.e., instincts and deep seated
principles – of an electorate and a membership which are more
anti-capitalist, more libertarian, more egalitarian, more permissive,
more politicised, more revolutionary than the PCF, PS and ecologists' electorate and membership.[37] At the same time the PSU
electorate and to a lesser degree its membership is younger and its
membership (not its voters) has the highest proportion of women
of all French parties. While its members are much more in favour
of unity with the Communists than the PS voters, they are more
linked with Catholicism. Many of them come from working-class
Catholic right-wing families.[38]

Moreover, the PS may need the PSU's prestige and its intellectuals and 'shadow statesmen' but it can do without its members
and votes now that it has swollen its ranks so much. Similarly, the
PCF needs more than the PSU's institutional weight to catch up
with the PS, unlike in 1974-7 when it was busy wooing the PSU.
The PSU cannot any more attract or immobilise modernist Socialist
votes; those which it does attract are motivated by ideological
reasons not economic and social aspirations. The new PSU members

are mostly young people from the larger towns employed in the
social services and education but at their lower echelons: low
grade civil servants and young educated unemployed people.
They are often active in the non-violent, ecological and/or feminist
movements. If unionised they are in their great majority in the
CFDT[39] This produces a Left which is ready to vote for the PS
and the PCF as a vote against the Right and, until now, against
the status quo. Its 'utopian anticipation', to use Michel Mousel's
words, requires both autonomy and the opportunity to experiment
with new ideas inside the institutions. That is why the introduction of proportional representation, if and when it happens,
might bridge the gap between prophetic and practical politics as
far as the PSU is concerned and simply ensure its survival. It
remains to be seen whether the PS will offer to its old 'gadfly'[40]
this key to the future, now that it is no longer under electoral/
political pressure and, so far, under no social pressure. If one
compares the manifesto 'C'est l'heure' with the PS-PSU agreement
of 2 June 1981 one can see that most points which were left out
of the latter text are those which imply a weakening of Parliament,
of the state, of the Western Bloc, of the industrial system itself.
These themes may not be very popular among average voters but
among 'le peuple de gauche' and among young people they do find
- as the lapsed PSU leader Michel Rocard confessed recently -
'un immense resonance'.[41]

NOTES

1 See François Dalbert, 'Archives d'espoir: 20 ans de PSU
   1960-1980', Paris, Syros, 1980, p. 208, which is a compilation
   of articles and documents on the history of the PSU. 'Tribune
   Socialiste' (new series) 11, March 1980, contains a useful
   bibliography and chronology of the party (pages 38-9). See
   also the special issue of the PSU's theoretical journal, 'Critique
   Socialiste', 38-9, Paris, Syros, 1980.
2 See editorial comment by Jean-Marie Demaldent, political
   director of the paper, in 'Tribune Socialiste', 788, 15 June
   1978.
3 Quoted in Tony Cliff and Ian Birchall, France: the struggle
   goes on, 'International Socialism' Special, 1968, p. 54.
4 Charles Hauss, 'The New Left in France: the Unified Socialist
   Party', Westport, Conn. USA, Greenwood Press, 1978, ch. 2.
   This book is a detailed survey of PSU membership during
   1972-3.
5 Dalbert, 'Archives d'espoir'.
6 Hauss, 'The New Left', p. 227.
7 'Michel Rocard Speaks: An Interview with Andrée Hoyles',
   Spokesman Offprints, no. 13, 1971, p. 30.
8 Hervé Hamon and Patrick Rotman, 'Les Porteurs de valises:
   La résistance française à la guerre d'Algérie', Paris, Albin
   Michel, 1979, p. 226.

9   Byron Criddle, The PSU: an appraisal after 10 years, 'Parliamentary Affairs', 24, 1971, pp. 140-65. On the PSU in May 1968 see V. Fišera (ed.), 'The Writing on the Wall, May 1968', a documentary anthology, London, Allison and Busby, 1978, p. 327.
10   Hauss, 'The New Left', p. 215.
11   Criddle, The PSU, 'Parliamentary Affairs', p. 151.
12   Robert Bresler, A la Commission des Conflits, in 'Critique Socialiste', 38-9, p. 31.
13   Dalbert, 'Archives d'espoir'.
14   See Michel Mousel and the PSU's Economic Commission, 'L'Utopie réaliste', Bourgois, 1977.
15   See the article by Yvan Craipeau, in 'Tribune Socialiste', 739, 28 April 1977, on the CFDT's communiqué on the May events.
16   Michel Rocard, L'avenir de mai 67, 'Libération', 13 June 1978.
17   See articles by Robert Chapuis in 'Tribune Socialiste', 627-629, for July-September 1974.
18   Tony Thomas, PSU sets course for French Municipal Elections, 'InterContinental Press', 8 November 1976.
19   'La Croix', 10 July 1976.
20   Debate between Hercet (PSU) and Krivine (LCR) in 'Inter-Continental Press', 4 October 1976, freely translated from 'Politique-Hebdo', 10 June 1976, pp. 18-21.
21   Title of the 'dossier of welcome' given to new members: 'PSU Documentation', 106-7, March 1976.
22   A special issue of 'Tribune Socialiste' on women's liberation appeared in 1972. Prior to 1975, nuclear power had been defended, albeit cautiously, by Rocard and the PSU's Economic Commission, in 'Propositions pour sortir de la crise', Cerf, 1974.
23   Pascal Gollet, Le Front Autogestionnaire dans les élections legislatives de mars 1978, 'Critique Socialiste', 32, Juin 1978, pp. 18-46. Gollet's comments can be compared with an earlier analysis of the 1973 election results by Alain Richard, in Eléments de réflexion sur les législatives de mars 1973, 'Critique Socialiste', 13-14, mai-sept 1973, pp. 31-45.
24   'Le Monde', 22 and 23 April 1981.
25   J. Daniel, Why one must vote for Mitterrand, in 'Le Matin', 25 April 1981, p. 10.
26   See text of political agreement between PSU-Bretagne and UDB covering the five Breton departments in 'Tribune Socialiste Hebdo', 891, 20 June 1981, p. 7.
27   See complete results in ibid., 892, 27 June 1981, pp. 1-2 and electoral manifesto entitled The time has come (C'est l'heure) published in 'Le Monde', 20 May 1981 and signed by the PSU. 70 per cent of The Friends of the Earth, pacifists, some Left Radicals (MRG), trade unionists and assorted militants of the 1968 generation. See also 'Libération', 18, 20 and 25 May 1981.
28   'Libération', 16 June 1981; 'Tribune Socialiste Mensuel', July-August 1981, p. 10.

29   See Charte Communale du PSU, PSU, 1976, p. 25.
30   See 'Tribune Socialiste Hebdo', 818, 22 March 1979.
31   See text in ibid., 890, 13 June 1981, p. 2 and report of the PSU delegation in ibid., 891, 20 June 1981, internal supplement, p. II.
32   'Libération', 15 June 1981.
33   Re Michel Mousel's report to the PSU enlarged executive committee on 16-17 May 1981 in 'Tribune Socialiste Mensuel', June 1981, pp. 8-9.
34   'Libération', 5 July 1981, p. 7.
35   Ibid, 2 July 1981, p. 6.
36   See interviews of H. Bouchardeau in ASM&CF 'Newsletter', 5, April 1981, pp. 7-9; of C. Bourdet in 'Journal of Area Studies', Portsmouth Polytechnic, 4, Autumn 1981 and 'ASM-&CF Newsletter', 6, July-August 1981, pp. 5-8; and of G. Granier in 'Labour Leader', June and July 1981, all conducted by V.C. Fišera.
37   'Sondage Harris-France' in 'Tribune Socialiste', 759, 27 October 1977, and B. Rochebrune, '20 ans de luttes et de recherches', Supplement, PSU-Touraine, 12, 1979, pp. 34-6.
38   Roland Cayrol and Colette Ysmal, Une gauche originale, in 'Le Matin', 6 February 1981.
39   Tenir les deux bouts de la chaîne by H. Bouchardeau in 'Courrier du PSU', 27, June 1979, pp. 9-11.
40   See W. Schwarz, Madame Gadfly (on H. Bouchardeau) in the 'Guardian', 7 April 1981.
41   'Le Figaro', 17 April 1981.

PART THREE: DETAILED STUDIES

7   THE CERES IN TWO DEPARTMENTS - POLITICAL COMPROMISE ON AUDE AND VILAINE?

David Hanley

CERES is traditionally presented, by opponents and supporters, in quasi-mythical terms. For its enemies, it is the ideal antithesis of what good Socialists should be. Thus the Rocardian A. Salomon, in a recent polemic, suggests that its members are really Communists reluctant to admit the fact: not really feeling at home in a party which they at heart despise and which they see as a mere instrument for the propagation of their variety of Socialism, they have created their own machine, parallel to the official party.[1] Thus, 'like a proper Leninist assault-squad', led by a ruthlessly centralised Paris oligarchy, they have embarked upon the take-over of the party, federation by federation.[2] The motives for such behaviour are to be sought in a mixture of political naïvety (many CERES actually believe their own ideology) and more sordid questions of careerism. Poperen dwells similarly on the CERES obsession with 'capturing' the PS, compared with the more noble attempts of others (like himself) to 'win it over'.[3] Such views are, with slight variations, typical of what many followers of rival tendencies in today's PS think and - without much provocation - will say about CERES.

Needless to say, CERES has its own counter-myth in reply. The typical militant sees him or herself as the vital force of renewal (indeed the only such force) inside a party which, 'social-democratic' by nature, is constantly tempted to slide back towards the malpractices of its previous existence, when it used to be called the SFIO. The essence of social-democratic decay is ideological sterility and opportunistic political practice (alliances with the Right at all levels, and a style of running the party which was marked by 'notabilisme', clientelism and sometimes plain dishonesty). CERES sees itself as the only bulwark against such a tide: the rigour of its Marxist analyses and the exemplary actions of its militants inside and outside the party drag the party back towards Socialist practices by force of will (not for nothing is 'volontarisme' - the belief that sheer will-power is the major factor of political change - Chevènement's favourite word).

These myths are equally caricatural, though necessary and probably inevitable in a party which works largely by ideology. For purposes of mobilisation in intra-party competition, it is vital to portray self and rivals in bright ideological hue, if the correct reflexes are to be touched upon and activists encouraged to organise for the next meeting. Nevertheless, it might seem to outsiders that CERES is perhaps a more complex phenomenon than either of the above stereotypes suggests. Perhaps the origins of a CERES

varies from one département to another? Are its geographical and
sociological bases always the same? Are the links between Paris
and federation x or y always so tight and so one-way as opponents
believe and perhaps the Parisian oligarchs would wish? If these
postulates are true, then surely the political practice of the tendency must vary considerably according to local circumstances?

Many such questions spring to mind as soon as one goes beneath the ideological posturings of the different tendencies. My
research of late has involved visits to a number of federations,
selected in function of certain geographical, socio-economic, political and cultural variables, in an attempt to find evidence to
confirm or invalidate the thesis that CERES does indeed mean
different things in different places. This chapter will take two
départements, Ille-et-Vilaine and Aude. Though superficially
similar on the level of socio-economic structure, the two 'départements' have profoundly different political and cultural traditions
(see Tables 7.1 and 7.2).[4] Yet in both, during the seventies,
CERES has done well, rallying in its best days the support of
hundreds of militants as well as obtaining success for its supporters in local and national elections. It seems then that comparison of these two cases might show up possible diversities
inside the CERES and also, more generally, shed light on why
such groups succeed or fail.

*Table 7.1 CERES Strength (%) as shown in Indicative Votes
for Party Congresses - 1971-9*

	Aude	Ille-et Vilaine	national average
Epinay 1971	16.8	71.1	8.5
Grenoble 1973	12.3	66.7	21
Pau 1975[a]	18.9	53.3	25.4
Nantes 1978	13.3	17.2 (+72 for own motion)	24
Metz 1979	16	17.4 (+18.7 for motion F)	14.5

[a]The Pau figures reflect the final vote at the end of the congress,
i.e., the moment when CERES split from the majority.

The method followed is to take each département separately and
consider a number of variables, all of them potentially relevant to
CERES performance. First, one should clearly look at the long-
standing political and cultural tradition of the departement. Then
more particularly, it is necessary to examine the state of the local
Socialist Party at the time of its Epinay Congress (1971) in the
light of that tradition: this involves looking at the degree of
electoral implantation of the party, nationally and locally, and
linked to this, strength of membership and the vigour of party
machinery at federal level or below. In practice this means asking

Table 7.2: *First-ballot Performance of Left and Centre in Selected Legislative Elections, 1936-78, for Aude and Ille-et-Vilaine (% of Registered Voters).*

Year	1978		1973		1967		1958		1945		1936	
Department number	(11)	(35)	(11)	(35)	(11)	(35)	(11)	(35)	(11)	(35)	(11)	(35)
Radicals or Allies	1.6[a]	–	–	–	b	b	14.3	3.1	12.2	4.0	35.3	14.3
MRP	–	–	–	–	8.2[c]	24.9[c]	5.7	22.9	13.4	32.9	–	–
SFIO/PS	26.6	20.6	29.0	13.6	33.7	13.0	23.6	3.8	30.6	15.1	30.8	12.8
PCF	21.7	7.8	19.9	8.7	18.4	8.1	13.2	7.9	20.3	9.8	4.9	2.8
PSU	–	0.8	0.7	1.8	–	2.9	–	–	–	–	–	–
Other Left	1.7	2.1	0.9	1	1.2	–	–	–	–	–	–	–

a MRG votes (in 'primary' against PS).
b Counted with SFIO as part of FGDS alliance.
c In alliance with right-wing 'independents'.

if there was an SFIO apparatus worthy of the name which the
nascent CERES had to confront. This problem cannot be divorced
from a further one, namely, the state of other popular forces in
the département at the time of Epinay: what were the strength
and potential of the PCF, or the CGT? Was there a vigorous PSU
or a recognisable tradition of popular Catholicism, previously expressed, perhaps, in an MRP vote? What was the CFDT potential?
Finally, inside the PS itself, was there any trace of that strange
and implacable rival for the key place on the party's left, Poperenism? (Despite its relative eclipse of late, the motion 'M' of this
tendency scored 12 per cent at Epinay, compared with a mere
8.5 per cent for CERES.)[5] Having assessed briefly the presence
of such variables, I shall attempt to sketch the origin and development of CERES groups and then examine their political practice
within their federation, especially with regard to other tendencies.
This should, it is hoped, allow us some modest conclusion as to
the reasons for the groups' recent success or, where appropriate,
decline.

The endemic weakness of the Left in Western France has long
been a commonplace of political analysis and it was nowhere more
true than in Ille-et-Vilaine. A high agricultural population, scattered mainly in small farms, with the two large towns Rennes and
St Malo based less on industry (until quite recently) than on
tertiary activities, an omnipresent Catholic Church and a tradition
of resistance to Paris and its centralising republics – all these
elements meant slight prospects for the implantation of a Left
tradition. Overwhelmingly the département's sympathies went to
the Right, either to the independents or, more ambiguously to
the MRP. Fréville, senator-mayor of Rennes, who voted regularly
against the government till 1974, was a good example of what used
to be called 'opposition centrism', i.e., a culture that retained
enough of its Catholic and popular origins to think twice about
unconditional support for Gaullism. Clearly such hesitation was
partly due to awareness that part of the centrist electorate was a
popular one, hence in theory winnable by the Left. But the Left
in the late sixties in Ille-et-Vilaine amounted to precious little: a
small PCF presence in Rennes, unlikely to progress for want of a
CGT base in the few factories, and some SFIO residue at St Malo,
where a handful of Socialists sat in a centrist municipality, in one
of those arrangements which so outraged CERES elsewhere in
France (and which it usually exploited cunningly). In 1935 St
Malo had had a Popular Front mayor (a Radical) but that was long
ago.

It is hardly surprising, then, that by the peak of the Gaullist
Republic (c. 1967) the Socialists were in a parlous state. J.-P.
Michel (first Federal Secretary 1971-4) recalls some 35 members
of SFIO at the time, in four or five branches;[6] E. Hervé, mayor of
Rennes and himself first Federal Secretary 1974-7, puts the figure
nearer to 15.[7] Obviously there were no Socialists (mayors, etc.)
elected in their own right; the first came only in 1973. The PSU,
which R. Cayrol credits with 231 members in 1969, seemed much

better placed with its strong base among the Rennes intelligentsia,
and a more working-class, CFDT nucleus at Fougères, in the
east of the département.[8] Even the club 'Bretagne et Démocratie',
founded by the geographer M. Philipponneau, with its regionalist
bias and its links with the emergent CIR of Mitterrand might seem
to have had a better future. Thus anyone within SFIO wishing to
rejuvenate the party could at least feel that they were starting
from rock-bottom: and such were the feelings of the group who
within a few years would have contributed decisively to building
a Socialist political base in the département. I refer to the Ille-et-
Vilaine CERES.

As in many départements, the CERES in Ille-et-Vilaine existed
in fact long before it did in name. In 1966 E. Hervé and a small
group of student friends joined SFIO: coming from quite different
backgrounds, they had a shared purpose and a commonly-held
analysis. This was that Left unity (it was now the time of the
FGDS, in the wake of the 1965 unitary presidential campaign)[9]
could be developed further to take in the PCF, and that here lay
the key to reviving the SFIO, which was in Ille-et-Vilaine not so
much a degenerate apparatus as one that had never existed.
'Unité et rénovation' were thus the slogans on which the group
tried to mobilise. Hervé has recounted the hours spent trying to
set up branches, especially outside Rennes: it involved tracking
down old lapsed members, or trade-union contacts, or even the
village 'instituteur' and persuading them to create a branch. As
a result of this hard graft, the party began to revive: in 1968
the Hervé group received stimulus when before the birth of the
'new' Socialist Party they made contact with the Chevènement
group in Paris, now beginning to operate seriously as an organised tendency and poised to seize the Paris federation. The community of aims (unity and renovation) was obvious, and so was
the community of interests: Paris had the ideas and the theoretical
sophistication, but Hervé had the determination and effort and
was beginning to have the militants. Thus by Epinay, when the
federation had grown to some 200 members, Hervé secured a
massive vote for the CERES motion. The other left motion,
Poperen's, got a bare 5 per cent: clearly there was no substitute
for all the hard work which Hervé and friends had put in.

The early seventies were of course favourable to the rise of
Socialism in most of France. In Brittany, the decline of Gaullism,
the inability of centrism to do other than fall in behind Giscard
d'Estaing, the limited prospects of the PCF - all opened up possibilities for the development of a non-Communist Left, especially
given the context of increasing urbanisation and, on the cultural
level, a growing sympathy for Marxist and Socialist ideas in certain sectors of the Catholic Church and organisations close to it.
Thus the progress of the new PS was steady, as the popular part
of the old MRP electorate began to move over to it. From 200
members in 1971, the party had 500 by the mid-seventies, peaking
at some 1,200 in 1977 (today's figure is between 900 and 1,000).
In the municipal elections of 1977, PS mayors moved into the town

halls of 12 communes with over 1,000 inhabitants, including
Rennes and St Malo. Earlier electoral successes had come in 1973
when the party had three 'conseillers généraux': in 1976 came six
more (including the defeat of Fréville, still mayor at the time),
plus one in 1979 to give a total of 10 out of 49 in the département.
If national seats have so far eluded the PS, then both the Rennes
deputies' seats are winnable and Rennes-Sud should fall next
time. In the senatorial elections of 1980, L. Chopier was not far
off being elected. Now, during this period, at least until 1979,
CERES had a huge majority and exerted effective leadership of
the federation. While it is hard to say how much credit for this
growth can be attributed to the general factors outlined above,
it does seem reasonable to postulate that without the activist input
from CERES, results could have been much worse. In this context,
the political practice of the group within the federation merits
particularly close attention.

J.-M. Boucheron, now effectively the leader of the Rennes
CERES, divides the group's activity into two phases - before and
after the 1974 'assises'.[10] In the first phase, largely one of renovation, CERES was able to pull in militants who were mainly young
and often Catholic, on the strength mainly of its 'autogestionnaire'
discourse: CERES was, in Boucheron's words, 'the only one to
have any sort of political discourse'. With the arrival of the
Rocardian PSU, though, which was strong and organised locally,
as has been seen, CERES found rivals who could match them in
commitment and sophistication: thus ideological escalation set in.
The results of this polemic at national level are too well known to
merit comment here, but it should be pointed out that the Ille-et-
Vilaine CERES were always less sectarian than their Parisian
tutors. This political style, to which we shall return shortly, plus
external pressure in the shape of the 1977 elections, kept the
internal dissension much lower than in many other federations.
Thus at Nantes in 1977 Hervé got 72 per cent of the federation to
abstain in the final vote, thus manifesting a unitary will for the
party at large which, as he now admits, was optimistic. In the
end, centrifugal pressures proved too strong: the CERES was
split from 1977 onwards by the debate with the Pierret faction,
with the key figure of Hervé taking the side of the Vosges deputy.
At the same time, the Rocardian tendency, escaping from the
shelter of Mitterrand's ex-majority, showed its true strength, and
Mitterrand's own supporters surprised everyone by obtaining,
thanks to a rather heterogeneous coalition, a quarter of the federal
votes for the Metz congress in 1979. The Metz vote is indicative
of how the previously solid CERES bloc had broken up:

motion A	(Mitterrand)	25.4%
B	(Rocard)	35.5%
E	(CERES)	17.4%
F	(Pierret)	18.7%

In the resulting federal election, CERES lost the first secretaryship for the first time since Epinay. The new secretary, L. Chopier (motion A) is extremely and refreshingly untypical of most of the PS, and on the face of it, the exact opposite of CERES. How does one explain this sudden loss of power?

The root cause seems to lie in the political style of the CERES, which seems at once a source of strength and a weakness. The group always practised consciously what can only be called an ecumenical policy; placing party progress above that of its own tendency, it behaved very openly to other tendencies. No attempt was made to marginalise rivals, which is more than can be said for many federations where CERES has had the majority. The Ille-et-Vilaine CERES left its meetings open to all: it never had much of an internal structure (cf. its annual rotation of its correspondants - who are the links between federations and the Paris CERES - or its refusal of any regional or inter-departmental link-up), this being much to the distaste of Chevènement, according to E. Hervé. Moreover, the rule of proportional representation was even observed in the federal secretariat, i.e., anyone who wished to collaborate in the party's work could do so at the highest levels. A further example of this ecumenism is the absence of competition for electoral posts, especially winnable ones. Hervé had only 25 applicants for the 24 seats on his municipal list: none of the 12 PS mayors are CERES (Hervé was in 1977, of course). Of the 10 'conseillers généraux', only two are CERES, yet the tendency had an easy majority at the time of designation for all these posts. Such lack of greed is rare in a party where the practice is all too frequently to snatch anything winnable for one's own current.

In general the CERES placed a premium on militant work, as opposed to debate: and undoubtedly this trend was reinforced after 1977 when the best CERES activists found themselves heavily committed to the new challenge of town management, with its heavy drains on time and energy. It could be said here of course that the objective situation left CERES little choice but to be ecumenical: the huge tasks facing the party, the thinness of its resources and yet the vast progress waiting to be made - all this was bound to concentrate CERES' minds. This is true, but it plays down the subjective element, i.e., the deliberate choice of an open policy in the early years. After all the national situation facing the CERES leaders in Paris after 1978 might have been expected to concentrate their minds also: as it is, their choice at the Metz congress was sectarian and possibly suicidal. The choice of the original CERES core was crucial, and it is surely significant that the group in its essentials pre-existed the launching of a national CERES, thus ensuring a certain autonomy from the 'historic leaders' and their line. But an open policy also made the tendency more vulnerable, when attacks came.

Not that one can say that CERES has failed in Ille-et-Vilaine, however. The new secretary is extremely pragmatic, as befits that rarity among PS leaders, a practising farmer. Putting work in the town halls, associations and unions above ideological struggle

(he is dismissive of the whole notion of party currents), Chopier
wants to widen the party's appeal by its acts, not its discourse.
Having outmanouevred the PCF in St Malo and refusing to alienate
Catholics over issues like private schools, he has built a powerful municipal base in St Malo, and will probably soon be a senator.
But he is not just a burgeoning notable; his work in the farmers
associations and 'mairie' are what brings results for the PS. And
in this he is really very similar to the local CERES. Both these
and the ex-CERES, i.e., supporters of motion F, Boucheron and
Hervé, see the party's municipal work as the key to future
progress: undoubtedly running Rennes has imbued them with an
even more pragmatic frame of mind. Beneath the difference of
style that separates Chopier and Hervé, and beneath the Rennes/
St Malo rivalry, lies a continuity of analysis and action.

Perhaps this is the real historic contribution of CERES in Ille-
et-Vilaine. It has helped build a Socialist political base, with
excellent growth prospects, by adopting a dynamic, but non-
sectarian style. The cost of this might well be that the tendency's
own future locally will be less than brilliant - though this also
depends on factors extraneous to the département. It may also be
that CERES performance was not what the Parisian leaders would
have preferred. But of the tendency's contribution to building a
Socialist foundation in Brittany, there can be no real doubt.

The traditions of the Aude are as different from those of Ille-et-
Vilaine as one could wish. Political life has been sharply polarised
from the mid-nineteenth century onwards. The Second Republic
already saw sharp swings by an economically depressed peasantry
towards 'red' republicanism, and the imitation of the Paris Commune
at Narbonne in 1871 confirmed this trend. Well before 1900 a
Socialist base was established in Narbonne under the aegis of E.
Ferroul, mayor of the town for most of the period from 1888 till
his death in 1921. Culturally Ferroulist Socialism was based on the
classic anti-clerical sentiments always likely to find an echo in a
region where de-Christianisation had already progressed far;
sociologically, its core was the rather artisanal working class of
Narbonne, usually employed in activities dependent on the département's main economic function, wine-growing. But increasingly
after the wine riots of 1907, it spread out of the town among the
smaller wine-growers. Politically by now its main enemy was no
longer monarchism or even moderate republicanism, but Radical-
ism, which in the Aude existed under the aegis of the Sarraut
family with all the ambiguity and subtlety which characterise that
particular political culture South of the Loire. Wine-growing is
very much an enclosed culture with its own rhythms and logic,
as Guidoni, the CERES leader, remarks in his book on Narbonne.[11]
Thus Socialist penetration took time, and it was after the Second
World War that the countryside moved over massively to Socialism
and SFIO hegemony was achieved.

The material weight of 'audois' Socialism was and is impressive.
Long one of the biggest SFIO federations, it numbers today some

5,600 members in 145 branches, with one fifth of them involved in
agriculture. At the Epinay Congress of 1971 with its 3,000 members, it was the fifth biggest in France. Socialist penetration in
electoral terms is equally impressive, locally and nationally. In
September 1980 the party's two senatorial candidates were elected
with massive ease. All three deputies' seats have been comfortably
held for years, notwithstanding the slip-up at Castelnaudary in
1968. Of the 32 mayors in communes of over 1,000 people, 25 are
PS. The only real gaps in the list are Castelnaudary, where the
Gaullist mayor hung on by 400 votes in 1977 and Narbonne, to
which we shall return shortly. The 'conseil général' boasts 32
socialists out of 34 members.

More impressive still, albeit less visible, is the special structure
of 'audois' Socialism. It was always, as Guidoni observes, hierarchical.[12] The département has long been symbolised to the outside
world by the presence of a 'patron' who, without necessarily holding formal office, was the real decider inside the federation.
Ferroul began a long tradition in this respect, running through
Blum in the thirties down to such as G. Guille, the Courrières -
father and son - and R. Capdeville in more recent times. Their
authority has usually rested on a pyramid of 'conseillers généraux',
village mayors (often doubling as branch secretaries), ordinary
members and at the bottom the mass of voters/clients. Guidoni
speaks of 'the undisputed masters of the countryside, handing
out emoluments and doing favours, protecting village mayors and
distributing local authority grants'.[13] In fact, the author is
referring to the Radicals of the 1930s here; but the description
would not dishonour the PS of recent years.

In all logic such a system demands weak participation by the
party's grass-roots, if not to say an atomised acquiescence. This
was achieved by various means: systematic discouraging of debate in branches (sometimes by the simple expedient of not holding
meetings), reluctance to give members any political education,
packing branch votes with cards bought by the mayor or 'conseiller
général'. It should be stressed that this machinery does not mean
the rule of lazy notables; on the contrary, these latter work extremely hard to keep the favours of their clients. But needless
to say it is hardly in accord with the proclaimed policy of the
party.

Moreover, the Aude federation has always been primarily concerned to preserve its unity and strength, qualities which in the
discourse of its leaders are somehow seen as incompatible with
political debate. Such unitary feeling is encouraged by a strong
feeling of departmental patriotism and rivalry with neighbouring
départements like Hérault, which one detects in the remarks of
elected socialists, especially in the 'conseil général'. Ever since
Ferroul too, the 'audois' have always wanted to keep in line with
the Paris majority. Thus although Guille was briefly able to make
the federation delay joining the new party in 1969 and although
it voted against Mitterrand at Epinay, it swung over to him as
soon as his control seemed established and has persisted with its

loyalism down to Metz, where it gave him 70 per cent. What it would have done in the case of a firm, and therefore plausible bid by Rocard for the party's presidential nomination is a difficult question indeed.

As regards the presence of other Left elements in the départe-ment the position is clear. The PSU was never big, save for a very able core of militants at Carcassonne, where in a municipal by-election in 1970 it scored 15 per cent. Its absorption at the time of the 1974 'assises' was easy, partly because, most of its members being secularist, there was no 'clerical question' to cloud the issue as in some areas. The CFDT has only been in the Aude since 1970 and is still very weak. The PCF has some weight, but not too much as yet; it has a number of mayors and once had a deputy. The CGT has progressed steadily in the small and medium-sized firms in the towns. In an attempt to reduce the PCF threat the Aude Socialists have practised selective unity (e.g., at Carcassonne since 1959), but in fact the PCF's function vis-à-vis the PS is on the whole a positive one. It has just enough poten-tial to frighten the socialists, should it ever decide to go on the attack. The example of PCF growth in nearby Pyrénées-Orientales is a good illustration of what happens when the PS loses impetus, for whatever reason. Thus, if anything, the PCF presence prob-ably serves to strengthen the unanimist tendencies already at work in the party.

Socialism in the Aude thus emerges as subtly hierarchised, en-joying a massive share of local power and imbued with a unanimist ideology that subsumes internal debate to the cohesion of the apparatus and alignment with Paris. As such it has developed a capacity for absorption of different or rival cultures that is its most profound characteristic, if not its most visible one. Two examples will perhaps illustrate this digestive capacity. First, the occitanist regionalist movement, which was devoured by the PS practically before it started. Its cultural activities are financed by the 'conseil général'. PS members are encouraged to be active in its political organisations. The local party has even adopted the decentralising demands of occitanists: the first federal secretary, J.-B. Castilla, claims that his party invented the tag 'vivre, travailler, décider au pays'.[14] The result is that today there is no significant regionalist political presence in the Aude outside the PS. A second example is the arrival of the PSU Rocardians in 1974. Being obliged to take them into the majority, the local PS responded generously by offering them the federal secretariat for education and the most generous budget in France for such a post.[15] (Education is usually a post for which the tendencies fight with particular bitterness.) Clearly the party apparatus had every confidence in its ability to contain the virus of the modernising Left; and it did so easily enough.

All this suggests that prospects for a self-proclaimed revolu-tionary tendency like CERES were never likely to be high. How did the group challenge this classic example of what it would call 'a social democratic apparatus'?

The origins of CERES in the Aude date back to the sixties, in fact. A number of experienced activists were dissatisfied both with party organisation and, more seriously perhaps, the lack of national perspectives for the Left, given the SFIO leaders' hesitation about Left unity. Sociologically, or in terms of previous political itinerary, there is no reason to suppose that these members were different from the rest of the local party. Evidence for this widespread if unstructured dissatisfaction is shown not just by the CERES vote at Epinay but also by the presence of a persistent Poperenist vote (9.9 per cent in 1971, and an unusually high 8.5 per cent in 1973). Epinay in fact saw the beginnings of a CERES structure: R. Barailla speaks of having created the CERES in 1971.[16] But how did the tendency progress from there?

The answer is that they adopted from the start a very moderate stance, hence, in the Aude, a realistic one. Their efforts went into arguing, at branch and federal level, for Left union and also for making the party actually observe its own rules (i.e., branches to hold regular meetings, mayors to cease block purchase of cards, etc.). The main weapon at their disposal was the hard work of the activists, though an important outside stimulus quickly arose in the shape of a strong regional CERES structure, with regular meetings and exchanges between departmental leaders in Languedoc-Roussillon: the intellectual core of this would seem to be Montpellier, and the regional CERES publishes in its review 'Débat et Socialisme' a number of regional if not to say regionalist analyses. CERES strength in the Aude was never spectacular, but always respectable. Initially what the group did was to organise previously scattered dissidents on the basis of its minimal line of unity and party renovation. Thus between the Grenoble and Pau Congresses it seems to have picked up most of the Poperenists, no doubt disturbed by their leader's rush into the majority in 1973.

But CERES strength soon showed a peculiar feature, in that it was heavily concentrated in the east of the département, in the Narbonnais. There are several explanations for this. First, the presence of R. Barailla, ex-wine-grower and 'conseiller général' of Durban in the Corbières (the only CERES on the council, in fact): there is no doubt that this dynamic and charming personality has a great personal following, some branches in his area delivering 100 per cent votes for CERES motions. More significantly, perhaps, CERES was helped by the errors of its rivals, especially the late F. Vals, deputy and ex-mayor of Narbonne. In a way typical of Southern bosses, Vals held a whole pyramid of offices - deputy, mayor, member of the 'conseil général' and regional council, and even Euro-MP. As a result his presence and his efficacy in the constituency declined apace: in 1971 the PS lost Ferroul's 'mairie' in Narbonne to a man whom Vals had refused membership of the PS! One error compounded another as Vals' successor (he died halfway through his term of office), J. Antagnac, proved an unpopular deputy and another municipal failure, not managing to win back Narbonne in 1977.

This played into the hands of CERES who assiduously promoted against Vals, symbol of the old party, an incarnation of the new in the shape of P. Guidoni, a national CERES leader who had the advantage of being Narbonne born and bred. Eventually Guidoni won the party nomination for the 1978 elections and therefore the seat, despite a dissident candidacy from Antagnac. Since his arrival the CERES share of the federal vote has risen, which is the case only in one other federation in France. He will be expected to win back the town hall in 1983, which should permit some more modest growth for CERES.

However the mistakes of opponents, the intellectual vigour of CERES, the shrewdness of its moderate approach and even the arrival of Guidoni do not explain entirely the group's relative success in Aude. Crucial here was the role of the party apparatus. Clearly, established notables would have no symapthy at all for CERES; but this is not true of elements in the party which, while not sharing CERES' more advanced ideas, might none the less want to reduce the influence of 'notables' and to this end be ready for a limited alliance with either of the Aude minorities, CERES or Rocardians. In recent years it seems that just such a group has emerged within the Aude majority, centred on the present first secretary.

The process of loosening the grip of the elected office-holders is a delicate and slow one, but it has got under way: it is now established, for example, that no elected Socialist can be a member of the federal secretariat. But the reformers within the federation have not concluded an unconditional alliance with CERES to achieve their aims. In 1976-8, when the tendency was nationally in the minority, it came under some pressure in its Eastern strongholds, and more recently the local Mouvement des Jeunesses Socialistes has been effectively demobilised because it was felt that it was too close to CERES. What has happened in fact is that reformers and CERES have struck a geographical compromise, to quote a favourite CERES phrase. CERES will be left the Narbonnais, where their leader Guidoni has the weight to win back Narbonne and keep the PCF down: but they must remain there. Any attempt to spread unduly outside their territory will be met by a punitive expedition into their branches. Both sides understand this clearly, though it is never spelled out. Both sides clearly benefit: for the majority, the party as a whole reconquers the East, and internal balance is maintained inside the federation; while for CERES, apart from their success in spreading the idea of union and intra-party democracy (which is hard to measure), there is a guarantee of real influence even if limits are set to it. Clearly the future of such a compromise depends particularly on national trends within the party: but for the moment one can safely say that the Aude system has digested the CERES without too much disturbance.

Ille-et-Vilaine and Aude: a new département for Socialists, and a very old one. A small federation and a massive one. In one the CERES began as masters, in the other they came very much as suppliants. The differences seem vast. But underneath one is struck by the continuity and similarity of the CERES project. In neither case did dynamic cadres, armed with the analyses of Motchane or the 'Projet Socialiste' dominate a mesmerised public of activists, awaiting the right word. In both cases the way forward was a long march, where results were often quite modest and where compromise, either from choice or necessity, was the rule. Behind the rhetoric of Parisian ideologues, local reality was much more prosaic. But contradiction is the stuff of which the PS is made.

NOTES

I am most grateful to the Nuffield Foundation for the award of a Social Science Research Fellowship for several months, which has enabled me to do the fieldwork for this project. The British Academy has also very kindly contributed towards travelling expenses.

1   André Salomon, 'Le PS: mise à nu', Paris, Grasset, 1980, p. 255.
2   Ibid., p. 32.
3   Jean Poperen, 'L'Unité de la gauche, 1965-73', Paris, Fayard, 1975, pp. 274-5.
4   *Notes on Tables.* Table 7.1. This reflects dominant patterns of growth in the national economy over the past 20 years. Aude, with its absolute loss of population is clearly in a region of economic decline; whereas the growth in Ille-et-Vilaine clearly reflects the industrial development experienced by parts of the west. In both departments, the agricultural population is still very high (the national average is 9.3%); but decline has been faster in Ille-et-Vilaine than Aude. Although each department has a high percentage of its population living in 'rural' communes, this statistic obscures the presence of two large cities in Ille-et-Vilaine, whereas there is no real equivalent in Aude. Here the pattern is of large villages, with three medium-sized towns.
      Table 7.2. The indicative vote is taken in each federation before the party's national congress. Members vote in their branches on the different motions submitted, and these votes are collated at the federal congress, which mandates delegates for the national congress in proportion to the votes received by each motion (above a 5% threshold). The indicative vote is thus a fairly faithful photograph of members' opinions at that moment. Sometimes the final vote at the end of a congress differs from the indicative one because at congress the delegates of 2 or more motions have realised a 'synthesis', i.e., pooled their votes on the basis of a jointly agreed text.
5   The Poperists are the followers of Jean Poperen, ex-Communist and ex-leader of the PSU before joining the 'new' PS in 1969 at the Issy congress. Using a simple and accessible Marxist analysis, Poperen argued that the development of modern capi-

talism had created conditions for the emergence of a 'class-front', i.e., the political union of all wage-earners and other exploited categories (small peasants, etc.): the only political vehicle for this was unity of the Left parties on a common programme. At the Epinay congress Poperen's votes were cast against Mitterrand (as much for tactical reasons as for anything else), and he was in the minority of the PS till the 1973 congress, where he joined hastily with Mitterrand, as his own motion had barely scraped the minimum 5%. Since then, the tendency has had no official existence (i.e., it presents no motions to Congress on which its strength might be counted); but there are still Poperenist apparatuses in a number of federations, even if their members are all officially part of the Mitterrand tendency. They are held together by memories of past struggles, loyalty to the sympathetic and inspiring figure of Poperen and, no doubt, considerations of local power-bases. The relatively sudden eclipse of Poperenism after 1971 is probably due to (a) its leaders' own reluctance to promote their own tendency first and foremost, once the PS as a whole had taken on board enough of their own ideas, such as Left unity and the class-front and (b) the hard work and superior technique of CERES. For further information see an account by a Poperen loyalist Gilles Pudlowski, 'Jean Poperen et l'U.G.C.S.', Paris, Edns. Saint-Germain des Prés, 1975, pp. 162.

6   Interview at Rennes, 11 October 1980.
7   Interview at Rennes, 14 October 1980.
8   In Michel Rocard, 'Le PSU et l'avenir socialiste de la France', Paris Seuil, 1969, pp. 34-5.
9   The Fédération de la Gauche démocrate et socialiste was in-spired by Mitterrand's presidential campaign in 1965. It brought together under an electoral umbrella the SFIO, Radicals and political clubs represented in the Convention des Institutions Républicaines (CIR). Despite the electoral success of 1967, when FGDS and PCF stood down for each other on the second ballot, and despite the beginnings of talks with the PCF about a common programme of government in early 1968, the alliance was always a fragile one and never became the organic grouping that some of its founders had hoped for. It collapsed under the strain of the events of May 1968 and the recriminations resulting from this and the Soviet invasion of Czechoslovakia in August.
10 Interview at Rennes, 10 October 1980. The 'assises du social-isme' of October 1974 were an attempt to widen the basis of the PS in the wake of Mitterrand's presidential campaign of that year. It was hoped that as well as the PSU, many trade unionists from the CFDT and also many activists from non-political associations would join. The weekend of meetings was in fact organised from high up, with Mauroy, Rocard and Maire of the CFDT playing major roles. The results were ambiguous; if many Rocardians of the PSU followed their leader

back into the PS, many more PSU members boycotted that
organisation. Response from the CFDT was also disappointing.
In addition, if the assises did bring the PS some new blood,
it also brought it – in certain federations in particular – a
great deal of internal conflict. Mitterrand is known to have
regretted the whole operation in private.

11 Pierre Guidoni, 'La Cité rouge', Toulouse, Privat, 1978.
12 Ibid., p. 135.
13 Ibid., p. 180.
14 Interview with J.-B. Castilla, first federal secretary, at
     Carcassonne, 10 November 1980. 'To live, work and decide in
     the region'; this cry sums up the exasperation of provincial
     activists who see their regions as being exploited economically
     and oppressed politically by Paris. Economic decline and
     massive emigration have been the results of the situation.
     Very often such grievances are associated with a cultural
     affirmation of identity (Bretons, Corsicans, etc.). While the
     PS does not favour separation from France (as a small number
     of the above do), it does favour greater economic and political
     decentralisation, to the level of the region in particular.
     Hence it feels able to express the activists' cry with some
     conviction.
15 Interview with A. Melliet, Rocardian leader in Aude, at Car-
     cassonne, 11 November 1980.
16 Interview at Conques-sur-Orbiel, 13 November 1980.

INTERNAL POLITICS IN THE SFIO BEFORE AND

AFTER THE SECOND WORLD WAR

B.D. Graham

This chapter deals with the attempts which were made, in the period immediately following the Liberation of France in the Second World War, to change the doctrine and the organisation rules of the French Socialist Party, and examines how this was frustrated by the persistence of pre-war customs and ideas amongst the ordinary members of the party. The first section discusses the pre-war system of 'tendances' and the second the course of the revolt which led to the resignation of Daniel Mayer as General Secretary and to the installation of Guy Mollet in his place.[1]

In analysing these events, I shall use a distinction between three ideal-types of internal conflict, namely, factionalism, in which the main principle is the recruitment by leaders of diverse personal followings; sectarianism, involving disputes over philosophies; and sectionalism, in which conflicting groups are differentiated by a territorial, interest or social base. I shall argue that the pre-war pattern of 'tendances' was predominantly sectarian in character, and that the post-war revolt was predominantly factional with some sectarian characteristics.

THE PLAY OF 'TENDANCES' IN THE PRE-WAR SFIO

Founded in 1905 as the Parti socialiste (Section Française de l'Internationale Ouvrière), the French Socialist Party was essentially an amalgam of a number of earlier parties which had accepted unity without agreeing to a common view on all questions. As a result, the internal debates in the new party were persistent and intense, and the central leaders found the utmost difficulty in securing approval for clear and unambiguous statements of basic policy and in preventing determined minorities from gaining considerable power within the organisation. After the First World War, a serious conflict led finally to a division of the party at the Tours Congress of 1920, after which one group went on to become the French Communist Party and another proceeded to build another Socialist Party, under the old title of SFIO.

The reconstructed SFIO still provided considerable scope for internal debate and gave generous powers to its plenary bodies. Its main institutions were as shown in Table 8.1.

As revised to 1929,[2] the party's rules ('statuts') provided for the annual renewal of these bodies in the following sequence. In each département, the main administrative division in France, the party's branches would elect delegates to attend the congress of

Table 8.1

	Central Organisation	Departmental Federations	Local Branches
I. Executive and Administrative	Secretariat Bureau	Federal Secretariat Federal Bureau	Secretary Bureau
	Permanent Administrative Committee (CAP)	Administrative Committee	Administrative Committee
II. Plenary	National Council National Congress	Federal Council Federal Congress	Branch meetings

their Federation, and this congress would elect one delegate to the central National Council and one or more (the number depending on the size of the party membership in the département) to the National Congress of the party. The National Congress would elect the 33-member Permanent Administrative Committee (CAP), and this was authorised to appoint the members of a small bureau, in which the most important office was that of General Secretary. The National Congress was intended to be the main occasion for making policy decisions and the National Council (meeting at least every three months) and the CAP were to act for it between sessions. A similar relationship obtained for the congress, council and administrative committee in each of the departmental federations.

The philosophical basis of the party was more evident than its social basis.[3] The majority of its militants had been formed within regional Guesdist traditions, named after Jules Guesde, a leading Marxist thinker and activist at the turn of the century, and they were attached to a number of simple but very romantic ideas – that the Socialist Party should never lose touch with the mass of the people, that it should avoid accepting responsibility for the management of the bourgeois state, that it should keep alive the people's faith in the inevitability of revolution, that it should sustain the hope of re-uniting with the Communist Party for the sake of 'working-class unity', and that it should always be restlessly active in electoral and parliamentary politics. In Guesdist terms, adherence to these ideas – almost as the items of a creed – would ensure the 'moral unity' of the party, and those parliamentarians who showed signs of coming to terms with Centre parties, and of savouring the prospects of office, were treated with suspicion and scorn. 'Ministerialism' was the term used to describe an attraction to office, and it referred back to the controversies which had raged when Alexandre Millerand, a Socialist deputy, had accepted a cabinet post in the Waldeck-Rousseau government of 1899-1902.

The simple Guesdism of the party's ordinary members had a
remarkable timelessness. It did not provide a method of analysis
through which the flow of events could be interpreted to guide
action, and left the party's branch and federal leaders free to
employ, with considerable success, whatever strategies and policies seemed to them to be most appropriate in local politics. Far
from being a disadvantage, this combination of extreme moralism
and romanticism at one level with pragmatic activism at another
enabled the inter-war SFIO to adapt itself to a bewildering variety
of social settings, from the working-class communities in the
northern coal and textile towns to the peasant and small-town
communities of the centre and the south. Yet there was always
scope for groups of intellectuals within the party to provide re-
fined and systematic versions of the basic Guesdist faith, principally by offering theoretical interpretations of current party
policies and strategies. These intellectuals were the prophets of
the party, endeavouring to extend its horizons and anticipating
the moral consequences of apparently straightforward actions,
and they were readily accepted by the rank-and-file as 'the conscience of the party'. Although the origins of this belief are not
clear, the ordinary members were persuaded that the party's
survival depended upon minority groups being allowed to express
their views, and to explore their implications.

According to a party pamphlet published in the 1920s:

> The constitution of the new unified Party rests . . . on a
> democratic foundation.
> There is full freedom of thought for all, from the bottom to
> the top.
> There is freedom for each to have his own interpretation of
> the solutions to the problems which the Party encounters, free-
> dom to express it by speaking and writing within the Party, and
> an absolute right to seek to make it prevail. And, to ensure
> this freedom and this right, proportional Representation in all
> bodies of the Party secures for all intellectual persuasions ('les
> tendances d'esprit') the legitimate share of influence to which
> they are entitled by their respective strengths within the organ-
> isation.
> There is a duty for all to accept the sovereign decisions of
> National and International Congresses.[4]

As in this passage, 'une tendance d'esprit' originally signified a
body of ideas, but by the 1920s and 1930s the phrase had come to
mean a group within an organisation, such as a trade union or a
political party. The term was used quite freely, and was often
opposed to words such as 'fraction' and 'coterie'. Thus, writing
in 1938, one Socialist leader claimed that 'pivertisme' (after Marceau
Pivert):

> has never been, at least outside the Seine [Federation], other
> than 'une tendance' in the best sense of the word, that is to

say, a current of thought, a method of enquiry ['recherche'],
and not at all the cabal that they have wanted to make of it.[5]

This was obviously the ideal, but the 'tendance' noted in this
passage and its main rival had definite organisational characteristics - a leadership hierarchy; a nationwide web of connections,
sustained by ties of friendship and profession; and policy proposals covering the whole range of issues with which the party
was concerned. Nevertheless, these 'tendances' did express their
differences in philosophical terms, rather than in factional or
sectional terms, and this gave the party's internal affairs their
sectarian character.

The party's rules were sensitive to the claims of minority groups,
and one article stated that:

> Whenever agreement has not been reached, the minority will
> have the right to proportional representation at every level of
> party organisation - branch, federation, and CAP - and on all
> committees or delegations of these various bodies. (First para-
> graph of Article 19)

Thus, although the delegates to the National Congress were asked
to try first to agree on a single list of candidates for election to
the CAP, they were also permitted, failing agreement, to vote for
rival lists, seats being allocated according to the proportions of
votes obtained by each list.

A number of conventions grew up around the application of
these rules regarding proportional representation. When a National
Congress discussed 'la politique générale', the party's general
policies, it usually had before it a number of motions, which
tended to be lengthy statements combining a review of general
principles and perspectives with recommendations about what
policies the party should be following in public affairs. Each
motion was given a title: some were named after the person or
persons who had written them, others bore the title of the party
journal in which they had been published, and others were identified with particular groups within the party. If a Congress found
itself unable to agree on any one of the motions before it, all
would be referred to a Committee of Resolutions, whose task was
either to produce a single text or to present a selection of motions
for a vote.

These practices were closely related to that of instructing congress delegates about how to vote and what position to adopt at
meetings. The votes at the disposal of delegates were termed
'mandates' ('mandats'), and the number of mandates attaching to
a delegation was proportionate to the membership of the unit concerned, whether a branch (for federal congress or federal council
meetings) or a departmental federation (for National Congress and
National Council meetings). In the hope of influencing instructions
to delegates from preliminary meetings, the authors of motions
would distribute their texts beforehand, so that their supporters

in the branches and federations could rally support amongst un-committed members. Faced with a variety of motions, some meet-ings would try to achieve a united view, either by settling on one text in particular, or by drafting a compromise text, but others would simply vote on what proportions of the mandates should be given to each motion in contention. By the time of the National Congress a significant proportion of the mandates had usually been committed beforehand and it was usually necessary, after the routine exchange of views in open session, for the Committee of Resolutions to restrict itself to reducing the number of motions to be put to the vote. The final selection would perhaps include one motion representing the views of the central leaders and one or two others representing the views of the strongest of the minority groups. The places on the CAP were then distributed according to the proportions of the mandates gained by each motion, whose sponsors were treated as candidates for that body.

These conventions were an open invitation to organise 'tend-ances' and to compete for positions of influence in the party and, after a period of relative discipline and unity during the recon-struction of the organisation in the early 1920s, a variety of such groups began to form. The largest and most successful of these was the Bataille Socialiste, established in June 1927; it stressed the need for a close association between the party and the work-ing class and for respect for Guesdist principles, especially that of avoiding any entanglements with bourgeois politicians.[6] In this respect, it was exploiting rank-and-file uneasiness about the way in which the party, as a member of the Cartel des Gauches, had provided conditional support for a succession of Radical govern-ments in the period 1924-6.

In subsequent years, the possibility of co-operation with the Radicals continued to interest a section of the party's parliamentary group, but another serious opportunity did not occur until after the general elections of 1932, which weakened the Right and strengthened the Centre-Left in the Chamber of Deputies. At this time the question of Socialist participation in government was raised on at least two occasions, by Édouard Herriot in June 1932 and by Édouard Daladier in January 1933, but the policy condi-tions posed by the Socialists were not regarded as acceptable. Léon Blum, the leader of the parliamentary group, and Paul Faure, the General Secretary, were not openly challenged within the party because of their apparent willingness to talk terms with the Radicals, mainly because they were credited with a firm attachment to the principle of non-participation. Later, in 1933, Pierre Renaudel and several other Socialist deputies voted for the Daladier government's budget and for subsequent financial proposals, and a number of them were forced out of the party. They were called 'neo-Socialists' and their departure was interpreted as a victory for the Left within the party and as a defeat for 'ministerialism'.

However, the internal politics of the party were transformed between 1934 and 1936 during the events which led to the triumph of the Popular Front in the general elections of 1936. Following the street riots of 6 February 1934, the Socialists and the Communists held talks about ways of working together against what they considered to be the threat of a fascist insurrection, and in 1935 they linked up with the Radicals to form a Popular Front and to advance an ambitious programme of social and economic reforms. By this stage, many members of the Socialist Party were convinced that the long-awaited revolution was already underway and they therefore accepted the idea that their party should play a leading role in the Popular Front movement and in whatever government it might form. In the general elections of April-May 1936 the Popular Front parties between them won about 380 of the 618 seats in the Chamber of Deputies, and Léon Blum then formed a government composed mainly of Socialists and Radicals, the Communists having refused participation but offered support. The Blum government then carried through an extensive programme of reforms, including measures which established the Wheat Office, introduced a 40-hour working week and a system of collective bargaining in industrial relations, and provided workers with paid holidays.

Although he was considering further reforms, Blum found that he was facing a number of difficult decisions in financial policy and that the Radicals, who not only provided an important part of the government's majority in the Chamber of Deputies but virtually controlled the Senate, were reluctant to help with further radical legislation. Blum therefore announced in February 1937 that there would be a 'pause' in the government's progress, and he was criticised by some left-wing groups on this account and also for his government's refusal to sanction French intervention in the Spanish Civil War. In June 1937 he asked Parliament for special powers to pursue his financial policies: the Chamber gave its consent but the Senate rejected his proposal. Reluctant to press his case and thus provoke a crisis, he resigned from office. The Radical leader, Camille Chautemps, was then asked by the President to form a new ministry and the Socialists eventually accepted places in his government.

From this point on the coherence of the Popular Front began to weaken, and the SFIO's position became increasingly untenable. In January 1938 the withdrawal of the Socialists from the government precipitated another crisis, which ended with Chautemps forming a Radical ministry including two representatives of the Centre-Right. Some weeks later, uncertain that his financial policies would command support, Chautemps resigned again, and Blum was then able to form another government made up mainly of Socialists and Radicals. However, in April his request for special powers to implement his economic and social policies was turned down by the Senate, and he resigned office rather than lead an agitational campaign against the constitutional privileges of that body. Daladier then succeeded in forming a government composed of Radicals, Independent Socialists and some important figures from the Centre-Right, and proceeded at first as though his parliamentary support would come mainly from the groups of the Popular Front majority.

Throughout this period of ministerial crises, from June 1937 to June 1938, the SFIO's internal divisions became more and more acute. The central leadership attempted, with varying success, to rally support for the policy of keeping the Popular Front alive, partly to preserve the legislative gains of 1936, partly to provide a springboard for a further burst of reforms, and partly to avoid the alternative of a parliamentary majority based upon the Centre-Right. This policy was opposed by two 'tendances', the Bataille Socialiste group and the Gauche Révolutionnaire. By this stage, the Bataille was led by Jean Zyromiski, with moral support from the veteran Socialist, Bracke (A.M. Desrousseaux). Zyromski offered the party's members an activist philosophy which corresponded broadly with the classical Guesdist position and which also had 'populist' overtones. Zyromski's main theme was that participation in bourgeois politics would work only if the party became the political expression of a huge popular rally ('rassemblement populaire') and used the power of that rally to legitimate and strengthen its control of the state. He was also a zealous advocate of a close working relationship between the SFIO and the Communist Party and of a possible fusion between them. The other 'tendance', the Gauche Révolutionnaire, had been formed in October 1935 by Marceau Pivert and other colleagues after they had broken away from the Bataille group. Although they had supported the Popular Front government in 1936, by the middle of 1937 they had adopted a revolutionary position, arguing that constitutional action, while appropriate under certain conditions, would never destroy the political power of the bourgeoisie and that the party should therefore accept the ultimate necessity of abandoning legal methods and of appealing to the working class and its allies to take control of the state through a mass uprising.

Although these two 'tendances' were competing with each other, they had a common interest in forcing the party's central leaders to adopt a reformist position and to become, not the party's officers in authority, but the defenders of the theory that Socialist goals were best pursued within the framework of the Republic – to become, in other words, a 'tendance' like any other. Conversely, the interest of the leadership was to insist that they were simply acting to carry out previously agreed policies, to protect the achievements of the first Blum government, and to maintain order and discipline within the party.

The central leadership were able to hold their ground at the 34th National Congress at Marseilles in July 1937 but in 1938 their position became precarious. The decisive confrontation with the 'tendances' was expected to take place at the 35th National Congress at Royan in June, and both the Gauche Révolutionnaire and the Bataille Socialiste were intent on mobilising their resources for that occasion. However, the leadership gained an unexpected respite when Marceau Pivert and his lieutenants, having gained control of the Seine Federation, broke party discipline and were suspended from office for a time; when the federation's federal council opposed this action, the federation as a whole was dissolved

and a new one built in its place. This setback seriously weakened
the Gauche Révolutionnaire at the national level and prevented
Marceau Pivert from attending the Royan Congress. Subsequently,
he and his followers broke away altogether and formed a new
party, the Parti Socialiste Ouvrier et Paysan (PSOP).

At the Royan Congress, the debate on general policy was complex and inconclusive, but, at the request of the Committee of
Resolutions, Blum produced a compromise text which was accepted,
having drawn 58.6 per cent of the mandates against 20.9 per cent
for a Bataille Socialiste motion and 17.2 per cent for a Gauche
Révolutionnaire motion. One of the main features of the closing
debate was the readiness of prominent members of the party to
attack the system of 'tendances', which by 1938 had reached the
peak of their organisational development and influence. Even
Bracke, one of the early leaders of the Bataille group, felt com-
pelled to warn the party that the system for electing the CAP
'has led to what they mistakenly call the "struggle of tendances", but they're not tendances, they are clans! (Applause)
which find themselves facing each other'. He therefore argued
that the party's rules should be changed.[7]

However, throughout their difficult campaign to defend the
reformist strategy during this period, Blum, Faure and the other
central leaders were never forced to go beyond routine justifications of the party's participation in the Popular Front alliance.
The fundamental issues were often obscured at National Council
and National Congress sessions by the delegates' preoccupation
with immediate problems, and at no point were the central leaders
pressed to say where a series of policy decisions was taking the
party, and whether the party should revise its basic doctrines in
the light of its experience of government. The dissenting 'tendances', despite their ability to gather considerable support on
occasions, were not very effective in philosophical debate, and
failed to concentrate upon the central questions. As a result, the
Guesdist majority of the party were never confronted with the
contradiction between their party's successful participation in a
reforming government and their persistent faith that the SFIO
remained a revolutionary party opposed in principle to helping to
manage the bourgeois state. Even the Guesdists amongst the
central leadership, including Paul Faure and Jean Lebas (of the
Nord Federation), did not concede that either circumstances or
the party had changed, and they continued to see the party as a
moral community, sustained by a coherent and intact doctrinal
heritage and a settled myth of its own history.

Blum's place in this pattern was a curious one. As leader of the
party's parliamentary group, as Prime Minister on two occasions,
and as an expansive and gifted public speaker, he had won a
great deal of respect and affection, but it is clear that his intellectual endeavour, his consistent and sensitive attempt to lighten
and refine the party's revolutionary doctrines within the framework of humanitarian socialism, was appreciated by only a small
number of his colleagues, older men such as Vincent Auriol and

younger men such as André Philip and Georges Monnet. His distinction between the exercise of power, in which Socialists might
accept office within the existing regime, and the conquest of
power, aimed at effecting the creation of a Socialist order,[8] was a
subtle and constructive attempt to transcend the crude Guesdist
distinction between 'ministerialism', which was to be condemned,
and the straightforward capture of the state for revolutionary
purposes, which was held to be the final purpose of the party,
but this formulation was seldom taken up by people outside Blum's
circle. As an intellectual and a writer he was accorded a special
but isolated status, rather like that of a saint, to be listened to
with great respect but not to be taken seriously.[9]

CONFLICT WITHIN THE SFIO 1945-6

After the Royan Congress this game of 'tendances' was effectively
ended by a conflict over foreign policy questions, in which Blum
and his supporters, favouring preparation for war, were firmly
opposed by Paul Faure and his group, strongly attached to
pacifism. The high points in this protracted struggle occurred in
December 1938, when a special National Congress at Montrouge
adopted a motion endorsing Blum's views, and in May 1939, when
the 36th National Congress at Nantes ended in a virtual stalemate,
after Blum and Faure had agreed to frame a joint text. However, the divisions within the party continued to widen throughout
the months which followed the outbreak of the Second World War
and, after the Armistice, the fragile unity was finally shattered
by the events which accompanied the formation of the Vichy regime.
On 10 July 1940, at the special joint meeting of the parliamentary
deputies and senators which agreed to grant full powers to Marshal
Pétain, only a minority of the Socialists voted in the opposition.
    Between this vote and the reconstitution of the party at the end
of 1944, following the recovery of most of France by the Allied
armies, stretch the long years of the German occupation, of Vichy
government, and of the Resistance. Those who rebuilt the party
during the Resistance and after Liberation saw themselves as
acting in the tradition exemplified by Blum, whom the Vichy
authorities had made to stand trial at Riom to defend the record
of the Popular Front governments, charged with having failed to
prepare France for war, and who had later been interned in
Germany. Younger leaders had come forward, and the new General
Secretary, Daniel Mayer, set about reviving the party's organisation with as much speed as the conditions of that time allowed.
An extraordinary National Congress was held in Paris between 9
and 12 November 1944, and one of its most dramatic acts was to
expel from the party 85 of the Socialist parliamentarians (including Paul Faure) who had voted on 10 July 1940 for granting full
powers to Pétain or had been absent without good reason. This
was in essence an act of ritual purification and was inspired by
the same zeal which persuaded the Congress to change the party's

constitution in the interests of discipline and order. The rules
were altered to replace the CAP and the National Council with
a single executive body, the Comité directeur, consisting of 25
members to be elected by the delegates to the National Congress.
Article 19 was revised to restrict the use of proportional representation to the appointment of branch delegates to federal congresses and of federal delegates to the National Congress, and to
provide for the election of all executive bodies by a secret ballot
of the members of the relevant assembly (branch executive committee by branch meeting, and so on); it acknowledged that militants were entitled to form groups to make known and defend their
ideas within the party, but warned that such groups could not
exist legally as far as the party's constitution was concerned and
that they could not be allowed to take the place of the regular
bodies of the party.[10]

The incoming Comité directeur was asked to prepare provisional
versions of the rules and of the statement of basic principles for
consideration by the first ordinary post-war National Congress
and it requested Blum, who returned to France from captivity in
May 1945, to produce preliminary drafts. The revised set of rules
was then considered by the Comité directeur, and the final text
provided for an organisational framework which resembled that
of the pre-war party in many respects but which strengthened
the powers of the central executive and reduced the scope for the
play of 'tendances' at the national level. The provisions of the
new Article 19 were modified and expressed in two articles, 17
and 18, the latter stating that: 'There is complete freedom of
discussion within the Party. But no permanent grouping of a per-
suasion ['groupement permanent d'affinités'] can be tolerated in
it.'[11]

In drafting the new charter, the Declaration of Principles',
Blum produced a fresh and coherent text differing significantly
from the founding Charter of 1905, which it was intended to
replace. In the 1905 statement, the founding groups had proclaimed:

> their common desire to found a party of class struggle which,
> even when it utilises for the workers' advantage the secondary
> conflicts of the propertied classes or finds itself accidentally
> combining its action with that of a political party to defend the
> rights and interests of the proletariat, will always remain a
> Party of fundamental and irreducible opposition to the whole of
> the bourgeois class and to the State, which is its instrument.

Linked with this clear rejection of 'ministerialism' was their advocacy of an aggressive method of political action:

> the Socialist Party, while pursuing the realisation of the immed-
> iate reforms demanded by the working class, is not a reformist
> party, but a party of class struggle and of revolution ['lutte
> de classe et de révolution'].

By contrast, Blum's Declaration did not state directly whether
or not the Socialist Party should co-operate with other parties
and it also toned down the references to class relations, as in the
following extract:

> The transformation of society entails the substitution for the
> regime of capitalist property of a regime in which the natural
> wealth, along with the means of production and exchange, will
> become collective property and in which, as a result, classes
> will be abolished. This transformation, carried out in the
> interest of all men, can be accomplished only by the workers
> themselves. Whatever the means used in its realisation, it in
> itself constitutes the Social Revolution.
> It is in this sense that the Socialist Party has always been
> and continues to be a party of class action ['action de classe']
> and of revolution.[12]

By asking Blum to prepare this text, the Comité directeur had
demonstrated that it intended to give him a central place in the
intellectual life of the party and that it was willing to recognise
him as an authority in matters of doctrine and party philosophy.
As General Secretary, Mayer identified himself strongly with
Blum's views and Blum himself willingly accepted the responsibility
of moral leadership. He and his colleagues considered that the
party had been transformed by its part in the Resistance movement, and that it had broadened its scope to represent the hopes
of thousands of men and women who now wanted to build a new
Republic and to realise a programme of generous economic and
social reforms. In one respect, the draft Declaration was an expression of faith in the ability of the SFIO to transcend its origins,
and to leave the moorings of its early Guesdist doctrines; indeed,
Blum's text was as much an implicit rejection of Guesdism as a
positive statement of the ideals of humanitarian Socialism. A great
deal depended, therefore, upon whether the older members of the
party, now returning to branch life and to local politics after a
lapse of four years, would accept this redefinition of the party's
purpose or whether they would attempt to defend the 1905 text as
a sacred document which should not be varied.
There was a reasonable prospect that both the revised rules and
the draft Declaration would gain approval. The remnants of the
old 'tendances' had little resistance to offer; their former leaders
were no longer able to stand up for them (Zyromski had joined
the Communist Party during the war, and Marceau Pivert had not
yet been readmitted to the party) and their old communication
networks had fallen into decay. There were also a number of other
equally important issues to be settled, such as whether steps
should be taken to increase the unity of action between the SFIO
and the Communists and whether the party should affiliate with
particular Resistance organisations and continue its association
with the Christian Democrats.
The draft rules and Declaration were eventually printed in a

special brochure and were considered at the federal congresses
which were held in the summer of 1945 in preparation for the 37th
National Congress, which was arranged to take place in Paris between 11 and 15 August 1945. As might have been expected, the
drafts were severely criticised at the federal congress of the Seine
Federation in July, when a number of speakers expressed a preference for the 1905 Charter and for the former rules, demanding
that the National Council should be restored and that the central
executive bodies should be elected by proportional representation.[13]
Similar points were also made by delegates from several federations
when the drafts came before the National Congress on 11 and 12
August; some speakers defended the 1905 Charter, claiming that
the adoption of the proposed changes would affect the party's
basic orientation ('it would be a slide towards the Right', claimed
one delegate).[14] Speaking towards the end of the debate, Blum
claimed that the essential principles of Marxism had been retained in
the Declaration, and he indirectly defended the absence of any
reference to the issue of 'ministerialism' in his text by asserting that:

> Today there is no longer anyone in the proletarian world, the
> labouring world, or the Socialist or Communist world who claims
> that the evolution of capitalism and of the parties of the workers
> and the proletariat are independent of the political forms of the
> society in which we work.

He went on to insist upon the interdependence of Socialism and
Democracy and he referred to the opposition between reform and
revolution contained in the 1905 text, influenced by the debates
of its time:

> I do not distinguish between two species of Socialism, one of
> which is revolutionary and one of which is not. There is but
> one Socialism and this Socialism is in itself and in essence re-
> volutionary.[15]

Despite this spirited defence of the draft proposals, they were
not submitted for the approval of the Congress, which simply confirmed the powers vested in the Comité directeur by the extraordinary Congress of November 1944 and increased its size to 31
members. The federations were invited to submit to the incoming
executive any recommendations for amending the draft rules and
the Declaration, in order that an agreed version, or alternative
versions, could be submitted to an extraordinary national assembly,
to be held before 1 March 1946.[16] The new Comité directeur accordingly appointed a Commission des statuts and this body met on
five occasions in December 1945 to review the drafts in the light
of comments and proposals by the federations. Blum's Declaration
won general approval, but the Commission amended the text to
signify the party's attachment to the principle of secular schooling
and to change the wording of the contentious passage quoted
above, so that it read:

> The Socialist Party is an essentially revolutionary party: its
> end is to achieve the substitution for the regime of capitalist
> property of a regime in which the natural wealth, along with the
> means of production and exchange, will become collective
> property and in which as a result classes will be abolished.
> This transformation, carried out in the interest of all men, can
> be accomplished only by the workers themselves. Whatever the
> means used in its realisation, it in itself constitutes the social
> revolution. It is in this sense that the Socialist Party has always
> been and continues to be a party of struggle and of class action
> ['de lutte et d'action de classe'], based on the organisation of
> the labouring world.[17]

Having considered the draft rules, the Commission recommended
the retention of the Comité directeur but proposed that this body
should remain in permanent contact with the party as a whole by
convening, at least once every three months, a conference consisting of one representative from each federation. In a concluding
observation, it justified the ending of proportional representation
in the party's executive bodies on the grounds that it would avoid
returning to 'the struggles of "tendances" whose bitterness had
jeopardised the very existence of the Party before the war'.[18]
As requested by the 37th National Congress, the drafts thus
amended were finally referred to a national assembly, which met
in Paris on 24 February 1946. Still strongly opposed to the proposed changes, the Seine Federation at its federal council expressed
the view that the old statutes should serve as the basis for discussion; that the National Council should be re-established; that
minorities should be represented by proportional representation
on executive bodies; and proposed a new text for the Declaration
of Principles and the preamble to the rules for consideration by
the assembly.[19] However, the delegates to the national assembly
proved unwilling to follow this lead and adopted Blum's Declaration,
having effected some minor amendments and having replaced the
composite phrase 'un parti de lutte et d'action de classe' with the
less ambiguous 'un parti de lutte de classe' in the disputed paragraph. In the same spirit, the assembly decided to restore Article
1 of the old rules, which stated that the party was based on the
following principles:

> The national and international understanding and action of
> workers, the political and economic organisation of the pro-
> letariat and of the labouring world in a class party for the con-
> quest of power and the socialisation of the means of production
> and exchange, that is, the transformation of capitalist society
> into a collectivist or communist society.

At Mayer's suggestion, it converted the proposed conference of
federal representatives into a National Council, to be convened by
the Comité directeur every three months and whenever necessary,
and attributed to it the functions of supervising the Comité directeur

and of checking that the party's principles and statutory rules
were respected and that Congress decisions were carried out.
With these exceptions, the amendments made to the draft rules by
the assembly were minor in nature. It rejected a motion to restore
proportional representation and therefore the claim that minority
interests should be projected into the Comité directeur.[20]

By this time, however, the position of the Mayer leadership was
far from secure, mainly because they had been blamed for the
party's general strategic difficulties in post-war politics. After
Liberation, the SFIO had given its support to General Charles de
Gaulle, whose Provisional Government contained a number of ministers recruited from political parties, including Communists and
Christian Democrats as well as Socialists and Radicals. This support was justified partly on patriotic grounds and partly on the
grounds that the Provisional Government could be expected to
carry out the radical economic and social policies set out in the
programme which the National Council of the Resistance (CNR) had
adopted in March 1944. In the general elections of 21 October 1945,
the Communists, the Socialists and the Mouvement Républicain
Populaire (MRP), a Christian Democratic Party formed in November
1944, together gained a clear majority of seats in the first Constituent Assembly. Although the Communists would have preferred
an alliance with the Socialists alone, negotiations led finally to the
three major parties accepting representation on the coalition
ministry which de Gaulle formed on 21 November, within the framework of a pre-Constitution. Known as tripartisme, this combination
of parties aroused the resentment of several sections amongst the
SFIO's rank-and-file, especially after de Gaulle's resignation as
President in January 1946 and the appointment of Félix Gouin, a
Socialist, as his successor.

In defending tripartisme as an arrangement which was necessary
to provide France with a new constitution and to carry out a programme of economic recovery and reform, Blum, Mayer, Gouin
and other leaders of the SFIO were obliged to reach back to the
reformist arguments of the 1936-8 period. They claimed, in effect,
that the party had a duty to defend and strengthen the republican
tradition, and to share in the responsibilities of government during a time of trial, if only for a limited period. They also held out
the hope that the tripartite government would carry out important
reforms, but although the Gouin ministry was responsible for
legislation enabling the state to nationalise the principal gas and
electricity concerns, the Bank of Algeria, various insurance companies and several coal mines (in addition to those brought under
public control at the end of 1944) it was unable to prevent a steady
rise in prices and a fall in living standards.

Within the SFIO, opposition to the party's participation in government was justified on a number of grounds. In the tradition of the
Gauche Révolutionnaire, some members argued that the party
should pursue a revolutionary course and that it should leave the
government for that reason, while pro-Communist groups, in the
manner of the Bataille Socialiste, proclaimed the necessity of break-

ing with the MRP and joining with the Communists and the progressive Radicals within a new Popular Front, around which a rally of the people could be formed. Much more ominous, however, was the revival of the more elemental objection that the SFIO should never undertake any course of action which might weaken its ties with the working class, that it should not participate in the management of the bourgeois state, and that it should never disavow its revolutionary heritage. Stimulated partly by the scattered resistance to Blum's 'revisionist' Declaration, this return to the unqualified Guesdism of the 1920s and 1930s represented the most serious challenge to the leadership's policies.

Associated with this general pattern of dissent were a number of more specific grievances about the party's electoral tactics and organisational policies. Thus, federations in areas where the main local opponent was the MRP, as in the west, were often persuaded that tripartisme entailed an unjustified electoral constraint, and that a break with the Christian Democrats would leave them free to champion the cause of secular schooling and to question the political role of the Church. On the other hand, the alliance with the Communist Party was resented by federations such as Nord and Bouches-du-Rhône, which were engaged in the gruelling day-to-day battle with the Communists in trade unions and local authorities. In organisational affairs, the central secretariat was the subject of a number of often contradictory complaints; Mayer has recalled that he was criticised on the one hand for being away from Paris too often and on the other for not having visited a sufficient number of federations to arrange meetings. He also aroused resentment by sending to federal secretaries (who were sometimes deputies as well) a circular setting out the names of those parliamentarians who had been absent from meetings of the party's parliamentary group.[21]

In one respect, the central leaders saw themselves as puritans, setting new standards of discipline and purposefulness for the militants, but this was a difficult course to pursue in the context of tripartisme. The correction of error could cause resentment not only in the federation affected, but generally within the region to which it belonged, as happened in Languedoc, following the action of the Commission nationale des conflits in removing from office three members of the bureau of the Tarn Federation because of the formation of a Comité d'entente with the local Communists.[22] At the national level, in November 1944, the extraordinary Congress had not hesitated to expel from the party those parliamentarians who had voted for granting full powers to Marshal Pétain on 10 July 1940 (or had been absent without good reason on that occasion) but this sanction was often resented by branches for whom a banned member had been a respected and loyal representative before the war,[23] and the expulsion of Paul Faure must have been a particular cause of grievance amongst militants for whom he had been the main figure in the struggle against the neo-Socialists in 1933 and in the pacifist movement of 1939-40. It was also difficult for the central leaders, preoccupied with the inter-

minable constitutional and political disputes in Paris, to maintain
confidence amongst the members in the provinces, and according
to the writer of a pamphlet published by the Isère Federation in
March 1946 'our militants feel unarmed and helpless before the
formidably orchestrated propaganda of the other big parties'.
Having reviewed the resources available to the Communist Party
and the MRP, he complained that:

> Our party, lacking money and permanent officials, and having,
> most often, only one political weekly with a small print-order
> and a small distribution, is considerably handicapped by com-
> parison with its 'competitors'.
> Our supporters know and feel this.
> THEY SUFFER FROM A GREAT INFERIORITY COMPLEX.[24]

By the spring of 1946 it was obvious that these diverse resentments and grievances could be drawn together within a dissident
movement, providing that the sectarian groups (the intellectual
heirs to the pre-war 'tendances') could be persuaded to moderate
their doctrinal demands so that the philosophical justification for
any combined revolt could be cast in the vague and general terms
of simple Guesdism. The distrust of the game of 'tendances' was
still strong amongst the provincial federations and it was evident
that any attack against the central leaders would have to be
directed by a leader from a provincial unit rather than one from
the Seine Federation, the recognised home of sectarianism. The
main candidate for this role was Guy Mollet, the secretary of the
Pas-de-Calais Federation; he had played an important part in the
Resistance movement in northern France and after Liberation he
had been appointed Mayor of Arras. He first made his mark in the
party's affairs at the 37th National Congress in August 1945, when
he had spoken out in favour of a proposal that the Socialist ministers should withdraw from de Gaulle's government. Mayer's
motion advising against this course of action was approved by
7,625 mandates out of a total of 10,633, but fully 2,916 (or 27.4
per cent) were registered in favour of Mollet's recommendation.[25]
  The extent of the hostility towards tripartisme within the party
was revealed at the extraordinary National Congress at Montrouge
between 29 and 31 March 1946.[26] The ostensible purpose of the
gathering was discussion of the party's programme and strategy
for the general elections to the new National Assembly whose insti-
tution was expected to follow the approval of the draft Constitution
by the referendum scheduled for 5 May. The resolutions produced
by the federations for the Congress, and the speeches made at
the sessions themselves, contain a bewildering variety of views
and formulations, but three main complaints stand out: first, that
the leadership had failed to equip the party for what had proved
to be an exacting competition with its partners in the alliance;
second, that both the MRP and the Communist Party were unsuit-
able allies in any case; and, third (from a different point of view),
that the party should break away from the MRP and strengthen its

ties with the Communist Party and the Confédération générale du travail (CGT), the principal trade union organisation. Mayer and his colleagues did not try to deal with these complaints directly but offered what may be described as a 'strategy of separation', by encouraging the delegates to build on the hope that the coming elections might enable the SFIO to increase its size greatly and to become once more, as in 1936, the major base of government and the arbiter of party alignments.

On the first day of the Congress, Mayer suffered a reverse when a procedural motion was carried against his advice by 2,882 mandates to 1,439 (with 133 abstentions and 31 absent), but he eventually won support for his electoral policy that the party should present its own lists of candidates in the elections, which were to be conducted (like those of 21 October 1945) within the framework of a proportional representation system. In the discussion of the programme, Mollet spoke with considerable assurance, implying that the Socialist ministers had lost touch with the party's basic values; he declared that it was not sufficient for them to be good administrators:

> it is necessary that they should at the same time be Socialist militants acting in government, surrounding themselves with Socialist militants [Applause] in such a way that they would not be just the administrators of a dying capitalist regime, but men preparing for the Socialist regime which is about to be born.
>
> In a word, we must affirm our revolutionary conception tirelessly and energetically.[27]

Events did not rescue the Mayer leadership from its dilemma. The draft Constitution produced by the first Constituent Assembly was supported only by the Socialists and the Communists and was rejected at the referendum of 5 May 1946 by a No vote of 52.82 per cent. As a result, the long-awaited general elections, eventually held on 2 June 1946, were used for the election of a second Constituent Assembly, and once more the Communists, the Socialists and the MRP found themselves holding a majority of the seats. Preparations were then set in train for forming another tripartite government to take over from the Gouin ministry. When the first meeting of the reconstituted National Council of the SFIO was held on 9 June 1946 to take stock of the situation, Mayer recommended that the party should continue to accept governmental responsibilities within the framework of tripartisme but that it should not bid for the presidency or the major portfolios. A motion against participation was defeated by 3,375 mandates to 939 (with 171 absent) and the Council then resolved to authorise the Comité directeur and the parliamentary group to enter into discussions with the MRP and the Communist Party. It also adopted an oral resolution relinquishing claims to the presidency, to the ministries of National Economy, Finance, Food and Labour, and to any body charged eventually with the fixing of prices.[28] Thus, the party chose to continue its policy of participation with a severely limited

responsibility. In the end, Georges Bidault of the MRP was elected
as the next President, and formed yet another tripartite ministry
on 23 June 1946.

The focus of party activity now became the 38th National Congress, which was to be held in Paris between 29 August and 1
September 1946. A group of Parisian intellectuals decided that it
was essential to identify a person who could challenge Mayer for
the General Secretaryship and, considering that the provincial
federations would have reservations about supporting a candidate
from the Seine Federation, they agreed on the need to select 'un
camarade de province' for this role. Pierre Commin was entrusted
with the responsibility for enquiries, and the result was an agreement to support Guy Mollet.[29] A number of the Parisians (Yves
Dechézelles, Henri Barré, Léon Boutbien, Jean Rous and Pierre
Rimbert) joined with Mollet in preparing a resolution for consideration by the congresses of the federations in the period leading
up to the National Congress.

In the first section of their text, they argued that the alleged
decline of the party, indicated by its electoral setback in June
1946, could be explained in doctrinal terms. In an apparent appeal
to the 'moral unity' ideal of the Guesdist tradition, they presented
Marxism as a 'doctrine of action' rather than a dogma, and then
drew the following contrast:

> we consider that all attempts at revisionism should be condemned
> especially those which, being based upon a mistaken conception
> of humanism, enabled our adversaries to believe that the Party
> was neglecting the struggle of classes, this fundamental reality.
> It is this weakening of Marxist thought in the Party which
> has led it to neglect the essential tasks of organisation, propa-
> ganda, and the penetration of the popular masses in order to
> confine itself to parliamentary and ministerial action. . . .

From this moral failing had stemmed other failings, such as that
of not pressing hard enough for such reforms as the programme
of nationalisations and of not taking a definite position on the
problems of wages and prices. They asked the National Congress
to break with this 'political line' by refusing to adopt the annual
review, the 'rapport moral', of the Comité directeur. In their
'Policy of Rectification', they again placed the emphasis on doctrine by prescribing a return to moral certainty:

> Recent historical experience not only fails to contradict the
> fundamental ideas of Scientific Socialism in any way, but it
> shows that only the offensive action of the working class can
> promote social progress and safeguard liberties.

They claimed that doctrinal work should be concerned with enrich-
ing Marxism with the lessons drawn from the struggle against
fascism, and adjusting it to the circumstances of preparing workers
for management and not sweetening it by a more or less camouflaged

return to utopian Socialism. The resolution also contained proposals for new domestic and international policies and advocated
a more robust relationship with the party's political neighbours.
It therefore proposed a firm stand on the issue of secular schooling to reveal 'the paternalistic and reactionary basis of the doctrine of the MRP' and, in dealings with the Communist Party, a
reaffirmation of its interest in achieving the political unity of the
working class combined with a message that this objective could
not be realised so long as the national Communist parties did not
free themselves from their 'political and intellectual subjection to
the Russian State' and did not practice true working-class democracy. They concluded by calling for a 'profound reform' of the
party's organisation.

By framing their resolution in this way, Mollet and his fellow
signatories had skilfully highlighted the essential difference between Paul Faure and Daniel Mayer as far as party doctrine was
concerned. As General Secretary before the war, Paul Faure had
concentrated his energy not so much on making the party aware
of changing circumstances as on sustaining the faith of the rank-
and-file members that their party was acting in accordance with
its founding Charter, and that it would remain a party of the
working class, of class struggle, of political revolution, and of
peace. At the same time, he had insisted that a Socialist had to
be an activist, a realist and a hard fighter. Even during the
Popular Front period, he was not drawn beyond the practical
justifications for participation in government. When he became
General Secretary, Mayer had adopted the very different approach
of trying to bring doctrine into line with the practice of a party
which could not avoid governmental responsibility and which had
to broaden its social base by attracting middle-class support if
it was ever to outdistance its rivals. Blum, freed from the duties
of parliamentary leadership, was able to help in this enterprise
by returning to the fundamental questions of Socialist philosophy
which Eduard Bernstein had broached at the turn of the century.
It was this break with the past, and this essay in revisionism, to
which the Mollet text was alluding.

The federal congresses were also asked to consider another
resolution, named after its principal sponsor, André Philip, which
also suggested that changes were needed. However, it did not
propose the rejection of the 'rapport moral' and it dealt more with
issues of policy and strategy than with doctrine. Drawing attention to the economic damage which France had suffered during the
war, it stressed that the party's policies were appropriate for
dealing with the resultant problems but complained that the party
had, by its day-to-day behaviour, 'given the impression of not
responding directly enough to the concrete aspirations of the
people'. It declared that too many of the party's activists 'restricted themselves to general and vague speeches', that 'they haven't
stopped preaching a revolution which has already started' and
that they had ignored achievements which the party had inspired,
such as the nationalisations:

Instead of appearing to be a modern party, preoccupied with
all aspects of the life of the citizens . . . the idea has been
created that the party is an outmoded type, confined within a
powerless revolutionary declaration or solely concerned, like
the Radicals of yesterday, with electoral affairs.

It acknowledged that the SFIO should distinguish itself from the
Communists and the MRP and stressed the need to contrast 'the
verbal socialism of the MRP and the totalitarian socialism of the
Communist Party' with the Socialism, at once humanist and revolutionary, of their own party. In this respect, this resolution was
a subtler statement of the 'strategy of separation' advocated by
Mayer earlier in the year and, despite its critical tone, it was
basically in harmony with the doctrinal and strategic views of the
central leaders. Its signatories were drawn from the moderate
wing of the parliamentary party and included three members of
the Comité directeur - Philip, Augustin Laurent of the Nord
Federation, and Gaston Defferre of the Bouches-du-Rhône Federation.

Along with a third resolution, presented by the sixth branch
of the Seine Federation, the Mollet and Philip resolutions were
printed in a pre-Congress issue of the 'Bulletin intérieur'.[30]
They were widely debated at federal congresses; the majority of
those reported in 'Le Populaire' (the central newspaper of the
party) voted for the rejection of the 'rapport moral', and there
were indications that the Mollet resolution was attracting more
support than the Philip resolution. At some stage, Mayer invited
the principal signatories of the Mollet text to meet him, and about
twenty of them did so. Mayer told this group that he would not
stand for re-appointment as General Secretary if they would withdraw their demand that the 'rapport moral' should be rejected. He
then retired from the meeting, which decided against accepting
his offer, the majority having taken the view that unless the
'rapport moral' were rejected there would be nothing to stop a
similar policy being followed by another General Secretary.[31]

On the first day of the National Congress, 29 August, the tide
of feeling ran strongly against the central leadership.[32] The attack
on revisionism was pressed home by Jean Rous and Pierre Rimbert,
while other speakers suggested that the central organisation was
not assertive enough and called for changes in the party secretariat and its working methods. In his address, Mollet alleged
that the party's failure in tripartisme had been one of policy:

our Party has too often figured as a mediator when we wanted
it to figure as an arbitrator. So much so that a section of the
public has begun to visualise the Socialist Party as a group
situated between a party which claims to be on our left and
another which is certainly on our right.

He advocated more attention to the party's relationship with the
working class: 'If the middle classes . . . become proletarian, it's

for them to come to Socialism and not for Socialism to go to them'.

In defending the record of his administration, Mayer pointed out that there had been no alternative to *tripartisme*, because a Communist-Socialist government would not have been possible and because the MRP had been a more suitable ally than the Radicals, given the backwardness of the latter in social policy.[33]

From the beginning of the dissidents' campaign, Blum had singled out the sectarian groups as his main opponents and had concentrated upon the doctrinal issues. He defended his own position in a skilful essay entitled Notes sur la doctrine, which was published in 'La Revue Socialiste' in July 1946[34] and reprinted in 'Le Populaire' on 25-26 August, just before the National Congress. Its central theme was that one of the meanings which Marx had attached to the term 'class struggle' was that the social revolution, although a logical necessity of history, would be realised only by an application of the human will, and that, in preparing for revolution, the proletariat had to rely on its own efforts in promoting class solidarity and in organisation, propaganda and educational activities. Thus, in Blum's view, the organised proletariat and Socialist parties were obliged to assume responsibilities in the management of capitalist states in the pre-revolutionary period and to pursue their ultimate objective, the conquest of power, within the framework of capitalist society.

He returned to these themes in his speech to the delegates on the opening day of the Congress, as he attempted to discover the basis of the difference between the leadership and its critics. He claimed that the party's doctrine, combining the thought of Marx with that of Jaurès, did not need rectification, and defended his formulation of it in the new Declaration of Principles, while acknowledging the special character of that text. Nor would he concede that there could be differences over the general tactics of the party:

> In a country which has universal suffrage, political action necessarily signifies parliamentary action and parliamentary representation. And when a political party has grown sufficiently for its parliamentary group to have the majority or to become a necessary part of any possible majority, the problems of political action become the problems of power.

He suggested that the cause of the confusion lay in members' fear - of the Communists, of the electors, of comrades who would or would not appoint them as candidates, of opinion, and of failure.

> You invoke the necessity for renewal. But, more than anything else, you are afraid of novelty, you are nostalgic for everything which can bring you closer to the party which you knew and to which you belonged formerly. You miss the old CAP, an institution so absurd that it can only be understood, like all other absurd institutions, in historical terms. You did not rest until you had restored the National Council from its ashes. You are

engaged in resuscitating everything that the Party condemned
after Liberation: the 'tendances' and the fractions along with
the rest. Although the 'tendances' which demand the rejection
of the 'rapport moral' are not homogeneous, they make full use
of the classic procedures of 'tendances', such as the circulation
in the federations and in the branches of texts which are drawn
up before the Congress and which bring together representative
signatures. You have re-established the imperative mandate
which the first draft of the new rules prohibited.

He concluded by affirming that a vote for the Mollet resolution
would be 'a species of moral alibi to relieve your bad conscience'.[35]
    However, the issue had been largely determined by the decisions
of the preceding federal congresses, and the 'rapport moral' was
rejected by a substantial majority, the detailed figures being as
follows:

38th National Congress, 29 August 1946	Mandates	Per cent of Total
For acceptance of the *rapport moral*	1,365	30.4
Against	2,975	66.3
Abstentions	145	3.2
	4,485	

Although the large Nord Federation gave 91 per cent of its mandates for the 'rapport', five other strong federations (Bouches-
du-Rhône, Gironde, Pas-de-Calais, Seine and Seine-et-Oise)
voted for rejection, and only 21 of the 97 federations represented
at the Congress gave a majority of the mandates cast for adoption.[36] Following this outcome, Mayer and the other leading
officials of the party submitted their resignations.
    On 30 and 31 August, the debate on general policy provided a
further opportunity to discuss questions of strategy with direct
reference to the Mollet and Philip resolutions. Philip built his
address around the argument that French society was already
changing from capitalism into a new economic and social order,
and that whether this order would be Democratic Socialist in
character or a 'kind of authoritarian and technocratic collectivism'
on National-Socialist or National-Communist lines would depend on
the extent to which the Socialist Party accepted governmental
responsibilities. He implied that the governments of tripartisme
could not have been avoided and claimed that the MRP was preferable to the Radicals as an ally, given the economic and social
conservatism of the latter party. However, he criticised both the
MRP and the Communist Party and foreshadowed the possibility
that a purely Socialist government might be formed on the basis
of a tripartite parliamentary alliance.
    Mollet, who spoke later, agreed that capitalism was undergoing

changes of a socialist nature but warned of the danger of a
reaction, in which event the Socialist Party should be prepared
to seize and hold political power. He argued that the task of
the Socialists in power was not to repair the capitalist system
but 'to furnish the working class with springboards for its future
action'. Although he excluded the possibility of union between the
SFIO and the Communist Party so long as the national Communist
parties were not freed from their political and intellectual subjection to the Russian state and did not practice working-class
democracy, he claimed that the two parties could act together
under special circumstances.[37]

Had the Mollet and Philip resolutions been put to the vote, the
result (judging from the votes taken at the preceding federal congresses) would probably have been a majority for the Mollet text,
but when they were referred to the Committee of Resolutions the
Molletistes apparently chose to help in drafting a compromise resolution. They had already scored a success in decisively influencing the rejection of the 'rapport moral', and thus in forcing the
resignation of Mayer and his colleagues, and it was not in their
interest to engage in further confrontations. The coalition of
interests which they had constructed could not be expected to
hold together beyond a certain point, and there was nothing to be
gained by so punishing their rivals that they became a permanent
opposition. The result was a text whose structure differed significantly from those of the rival resolutions. It expressed pride in
the party's contribution to post-war achievements and policies,
referred cryptically and relatively blandly to the opposed doctrinal
themes which had been developed by Philip and Mollet in the preceding debate, and criticised the MRP, the Radicals and the Communists. While acknowledging that the composition of the Constituent Assembly had necessitated a coalition, it represented
such arrangements as unsatisfactory and declared that, failing
the formation of a purely Socialist government, the party did not
envisage its members participating in a coalition government in
future without a prior agreement on a minimal programme of precise measures responding to the aspirations of the working class.[38]
When the text was submitted to the open session on 1 September
it was adopted unanimously.

By this stage, the establishment of a new executive was well
underway. In the election of members of the Comité directeur,
federal delegates were asked to record their votes on ballot papers
containing a list of 60 or so candidates arranged in alphabetical
order; each delegate was entitled to cast 31 votes (equivalent to
the membership of the Comité) without indicating preferences. The
electorate consisted of delegates from 93 federations and 385 papers
were completed, 29 of which were declared invalid. When the
results were announced, as a ranked list of successful candidates,
Philip was placed first, Mayer third, Mollet seventh, and Augustin
Laurent nineteenth.[39] According to Jacques Fauvet, 16 of the 31
places were held by Mollet's friends.[40] On 4 September the new
Comité met to elect its officers and it appointed Mollet to be General

Secretary, by 16 votes to the 14 cast for Laurent, and Yves
Dechézelles, one of Mollet's lieutenants, to be Administrative
Secretary. However, the Molletistes did not exclude the old
leadership from the Bureau, which contained not only Mollet,
Dechézelles, Arrès-Lapoque (Propaganda Secretary) and Léon
Boutbien (Deputy Treasurer) of the new guard, but Mayer,
Robert Verdier, Laurent and Victor Provo (Treasurer) of the old.[41]

Thus, the main result of the great revolt had been a change of
leadership rather than a radical change of strategy or doctrine.
Despite the intensity of the exchange of rhetoric before and during the National Congress, the essential statements of both sides
had retained an element of ambiguity. Blum had restricted himself
to yet another refinement of the distinction between pre-
revolutionary and revolutionary politics, between the exercise
and the conquest of power, and between class action and class
struggle, but he had not broached the most fundamental question
of all - was the SFIO still committed to the achievement of a political as distinct from a social revolution, or was it prepared to
accept that a Socialist society could be brought about through
parliamentary and governmental action alone? Although Mollet's
supporters amongst the Parisian intellectuals had been explicit
about their own faith in revolutionary Marxism, he had confined
himself to a cautious defence of the SFIO's past commitments to
class action on the grounds that the bourgeoisie could not be
trusted and that the electoral support of the middle classes was
unreliable. For Mollet, the SFIO had always been and would always remain a party of the proletariat, in spirit at least, whereas
Blum, Mayer and Philip were prepared to acknowledge, with varying degrees of reluctance, that the SFIO had not only to win the
allegiance of the middle classes but also to accept certain of their
values as well, especially their political liberalism and their attachment to individual freedom and to social as well as economic reform.

The central issue had been whether the revision of doctrine
could have been carried out without destroying the moral basis of
the party. For Mollet and his supporters, the stability of doctrine
was necessary to sustain the faith and loyalty of the ordinary
militants, and for continuity in action over time. They did not
believe that the process of revision, once commenced, could ever
be arrested short of a complete convergence with the doctrines of
economic and political liberalism, and the consequent alienation of
the party's traditional supporters. The revisionists, on the other
hand, claimed that good faith within the party depended upon a
close and honest correspondence between the party's general
philosophy, the doctrine derived from that philosophy, and the
programmes and policies which it had proclaimed as its goals
within the framework of constitutional politics. In their view, the
moral integrity of a party was achieved only when an organic
relationship existed between all three elements. In the last resort,
however, the 38th National Congress of the SFIO had avoided a
resolution of this underlying conflict of views about the moral
nature of the party and had chosen Mollet as its guide because he

too was prepared to proceed as though a choice could be avoided, while the SFIO remained revolutionary in theory and revisionist in practice.

NOTES

1 This article is partly based on material collected in 1958-60, partly on further research in 1977 during the tenure of a Nuffield Fellowship, and partly on subsequent visits to Paris. I am grateful for the financial assistance provided by the British Council and the Australian National University in the former period and by the Nuffield Foundation and the University of Sussex in recent years. My thanks are also due to the Office Universitaire de Recherche Socialiste (Paris), whose library is an invaluable source of information on the history of the SFIO, to M. Pierre Rimbert of OURS who gave me the benefit of his detailed knowledge of this period, and to Mr Philip Williams, Dr Robert Dowse, my friends and colleagues at the University of Sussex, and the members of the Conference for their criticisms and suggestions about matters of interpretation.

2 The rules were adopted by the First National Congress of April 1905 and were amended by the second session of the Eighth National Congress in November 1911, by a National Council meeting in July 1913, by another National Council meeting in November 1925, and by the Twenty-Sixth National Congress in June 1929. They were not further amended until the extraordinary National Congress of November 1944.

3 This paragraph draws upon the excellent article by Donald Noel Baker, The Politics of Socialist Protest in France: The Left Wing of the Socialist Party, 1921-39, 'The Journal of Modern History', XLIII, 1, March 1971, pp. 2-41.

4 J. Ferretti, 'Ce Qu'est le Parti Socialiste', Number IV in the series, 'Pour les Elections Législatives de mai 1928', Paris, Librairie Populaire, 1928, p. 49.

5 Maurice Deixonne, 'La Vérité sur la Scission de Royan', Aurillac, Imprimerie du Cantal, 1938, p. 8.

6 See Baker, The Politics of Socialist Protest in France, pp. 3-9.

7 Parti Socialiste (SFIO), '35e Congrès National', Royan, 4-7 June 1938, 'Compte rendu sténographique', Paris, Librairie Populaire, n.d., p. 597. On the SFIO's internal politics in 1937-8, see Nathanael Greene, 'Crisis and Decline: The French Socialist Party in the Popular Front Era', Ithaca, New York, Cornell University Press, 1969, ch. 4, pp. 185-224.

8 On this question, see Joel Colton, Léon Blum and the French Socialists as a Government Party, 'The Journal of Politics', XV, 4, November 1953, pp. 517-43.

9 Cf. the comment by Colette Audry, 'Léon Blum ou la politique du Juste', Paris, René Julliard, 1955, p. 60.

10 See Parti Socialiste (SFIO), 'Les décisions du Congrès National

extraordinaire des Cadres des Fédérations Socialistes recon-
stituées dans la résistance', 9-12 November 1944, Paris, pp.
5-6 and (for the rules as amended) pp. 22-31.

11 Parti Socialiste (SFIO), '37e Congrès National', Paris, 11-15
August 1945, 'Projet de déclaration de principes et de statuts',
p. 6.

12 See Projet de déclaration de principes (Blum's text) and the
Déclaration commune des organisations socialistes adoptée le
13 Janvier 1905 (the 1905 text) in ibid., pp. 3-4 and 11-12.

13 See 'Le Populaire' (Paris), 31 July 1945, p. 2; 'Le Monde'
(Paris), 31 July 1945, p. 5.

14 'Le Populaire', 12-13 August 1945, p. 3; 14 August 1945, p. 2.

15 Speech of 12 August 1945, reproduced as Le Socialisme Maître
de l'Heure, in 'L'Oeuvre de Léon Blum', VI, 'Naissance de la
Quatrième République; La Vie du Parti et la Doctrine Socialiste;
1945-1947', Paris, Albin Michel, 1958, pp. 65-78, quotations
from p. 68. See also Blum, Notes sur la doctrine, 'La Revue
Socialiste', 3, July 1946, pp. 257-61.

16 Parti Socialiste (SFIO), '38e Congrès National', Paris, 29
August-1 September 1946, 'Rapports', Paris, Librairie du
Parti, n.d., pp. 9-10.

17 'Bulletin Intérieur du Parti Socialiste (SFIO)' (Paris), 9,
December 1945, pp. 9-14, quotation from p. 11.

18 Ibid., p. 10.

19 'Le Populaire', 19 February 1946, p. 2.

20 Although this assembly was held in secret, a fair indication of
its proceedings, and the division lists for ballots, were published in the 'Bulletin Intérieur', 11, February-March, 1946,
pp. 3-10. See also 'Le Populaire', 26 February 1946, p. 1.

21 See Daniel Mayer, 'Pour une histoire de la Gauche', Paris,
Plon, 1969, pp. 309-10.

22 On the case, see 'Bulletin Intérieur', 11, February-March
1946, pp. 2 and 11. The issue was raised by the Gers Federation at the extraordinary National Congress at Montrouge,
which approved the proposal of a special committee that the
sanctions should be lifted ('Le Populaire', 2 April 1946, p. 1).

23 In August 1946 the General Secretariat of the party, noting
the increasing number of requests for the reintegration of
parliamentarians, drew the attention of branches to the danger
of responding favourably to such requests and defended the
resolution of the 37th National Congress of August 1945 ratify-
ing the expulsions ('Bulletin Intérieur', 15, 1 August 1946,
p. 15).

24 Parti Socialiste (SFIO), Fédération de l'Isère, 'Ripostes . . .',
by Alix Berthet, Grenoble, March 1946, pp. 3-4.

25 See B.D. Graham, 'The French Socialists and Tripartisme
1944-1947', Canberra, The Australian National University
Press, 1965, pp. 95-6. In this study, I distinguished between
the opposition offered to the Mayer leadership by anti-
participationist and progressive factions, which broadly correspond to the revolutionary (in the Gauche Révolutionnaire

tradition) and the pro-Communist, popular rally (in the Bataille Socialiste tradition) groups in the present article. However, I have now revised my interpretation of the party's internal conflicts in 1945-6 in several respects.

26 On this Congress, see ibid., pp. 162-8.
27 Minutes of the Extraordinary National Congress, Montrouge, 29-31 March 1946, p. 123, cited in Graham, 'The French Socialists and Tripartisme', p. 167.
28 See ibid., p. 182.
29 Interview with M. Pierre Rimbert, Paris, 17 April 1980.
30 'Bulletin Intérieur', 15, 1 August 1946, pp. 1-15.
31 Mayer, 'Pour une histoire de la Gauche', pp. 310-12.
32 On this Congress, see Graham, 'The French Socialists and Tripartisme', pp. 197-219. Several of the translated quotations given below are from this source.
33 For the debates of the first day, see 'Le Populaire', 30 August 1946.
34 Pp. 257-61 in that source.
35 Blum, Discours au XXXVIIIe Congrès in 'L'Oeuvre de Léon Blum', VI, pp. 276-88. However, note that this speech was delivered on 29 August and not on 1 September, the date given in this source (p. 276 n).
36 'Bulletin Intérieur', 18, August-September 1946, p.6.
37 For the closing stages of the debate, see 'Le Populaire', 1-2 September 1946.
38 Ibid., 3 September 1946, p. 4.
39 'Bulletin Intérieur', 18, August-September 1946, p. 6.
40 'Le Monde', 3 September 1946, p. 3.
41 'Bulletin Intérieur', 19, October 1946, p. 1. See also Graham, 'The French Socialists and Tripartisme', pp. 212-13.

Joy Bound and Kevin Featherstone

The election of François Mitterrand as President of France, in May
1981, has attracted widespread attention to the developments
within both the Parti Socialiste (PS) and the Parti Communiste
Francais (PCF), aimed at gauging future policies. Of course, with
a Socialist in the Élysée, the focus of the French party system
has shifted ground. How closely the two parties might work together or influence each other is as yet unclear, but the most
relevant starting point for any future projections as to likely
policy attitudes lies with an analysis of their standpoints in the
recent past. The following discussion of attitudes towards the
European Community will follow this rationale.

The accession to power of François Mitterrand represents a
break with the predominance of the Centre-Right for the foregoing
23 years. For the whole of the previous history of the Fifth
Republic, French interests abroad have been directly represented
by Gaullists or have been strongly influenced by the late General's
shadow. Even for the Left, the peculiar phenomenon of Gaullism
has had its impact, both in terms of debate and of strategy.

The European debate has produced a unique cleavage within the
French party system that at one level cuts across conventional
ideological lines, in that both the PCF and the Gaullists oppose
current schemes aimed at transcending the nation-state. The fact
that this 'nationalism' stems from widely divergent ideologies is
indicative of the theoretical problems provoked in relating Leftist
principles with capitalist integrative notions. Nor are such contradictions on the Left solely a French phenomenon: in general,
throughout Western Europe a commitment to left-wing ideology is
a less than accurate predictor of attitudes held towards European
integration. Amongst Socialist parties, there is a clear contrast
to be drawn between, for example, the fervent support of the
Belgian Socialists and the policy of withdrawal adopted in 1980 by
the British Labour Party.[1] For the Communists, a distinction can
be similarly drawn between the support for accession shown by
the Spanish PCE and the opposition to entry adopted by the Greek
KKE (exterior CP). It is thus not only in France that the European
issue has proved problematic.

In terms of party strategy, the European issue in France also
plays an illustrative role in that it highlights the manner in which
the development from the SFIO to the PS has taken place. The
differences of European policy between the Fourth and Fifth Republics reflect the transition from the moderate governmentalism
of the fifties to the ideological renaissance of the seventies.

Similarly, the attitude of the Communists reflects the changes in the party's image over the same period: from the aggressive Stalinism of the 1950s to the co-operation with the Socialists and their allies in the 1970s, and more recently to their return (before Mitterrand's election) to non-co-operation with the rest of the Left and their emphasis on a patriotic resistance to supra-nationality. Moreover, for both the Socialists and the Communists, the approach adopted towards the European policy-area has been seen as indicative of the progress made towards unity within the heart of the French Left.[2]

To the outside observer, then, a discussion of the attitudes of the French Left towards European integration should not only help to clarify the nature and significance of the internal debate within France, but also to suggest parallels within the wider European context. The discussion below will first examine the attitudes held within the PS, and will then focus on the position of the PCF. Finally, the themes of the two sections will be considered together in the conclusion.

THE PARTI SOCIALISTE AND THE EUROPEAN COMMUNITY

As has already been indicated, the following section will seek to clarify the attitudes held towards the European Community within the PS. Before turning to a contemporary analysis, however, it is instructive to make comparison between the position of the PS in the 1970s and the SFIO in the 1950s, at the start of the moves towards European integration.

At one level, the contrast lies in the differences of context. The fifties experienced the anti-Communism of the Cold War and a party system in France revolving around pivotal Centrist forces, both of which led the SFIO to participate frequently in government. The seventies, however, were years of détente and support for a regrouping of the Left designed to finally break the hold of the Gaullists and Giscardians over the reins of government. Between the two periods lies also a difference in the perceived image of external allies. In the earlier period, the political rehabilitation of West Germany prompted SFIO fears over the new nation eclipsing France, and the party thus sought safeguards within the operation of the European Coal and Steel Community and were later totally divided as to whether to accept a European Defence Community resting on a Franco-German axis. By contrast, the SFIO's rather idealistic regard for Britain prompted it repeatedly to seek the participation of her northern neighbour, and the onset of the Cold War led the party to recognise the importance of American support for Western Europe. In the seventies, however, Britain had finally been admitted to the European Community and acted as a rather weak partner; and relations with the USA and West Germany were now more likely to be related to the threat of multinational capitalism, as well as the danger of France being subsumed underneath an American umbrella.[3]

But the differences of attitude between the SFIO, and the PS must also be explained in terms of a more internal development within French Socialism, and one that has played a more basic role. The creation of the PS itself represents the culmination of a disillusionment with the moderate governmentalism and coalition manoeuvrings of the SFIO – termed Mollétisme after the party's Secretary-General – which prompted moves to establish a new party with a more leftist approach, and one that sought an alliance with the Communists as an alternative to the parties of the Centre. From this transition, stems a more radical policy on questions of European integration. In the fifties, the SFIO took up a stance in favour of a Social Democratic Europe – in the main a capitalist Europe with greater public involvement and one in which the interests of French workers were protected. The SFIO had thus supported, with some reservations, the proposals for Marshall Aid, NATO, ECSC, Euratom, and the EEC. By contrast, the PS now emphasises a fundamentally different conception of Europe: one that is based on a radical domestic project and one that seeks to create a 'Europe of the Workers', though the PS has recently both supported direct elections to the European Parliament and has pro-posed rather tough conditions for the enlargement of the European Community.

The fundamental contrast between the attitudes of the PS in the 1970s and the SFIO in the 1950s is thus one of a leftward shift in the party's own self-image. The ideological renaissance within the PS has taken place in the context of external events helping to foster such a development. The debates that have occurred within the PS, on Europe, have divided the party rather more than they divided the SFIO. In consequence, congressional motions and policy statements have appeared with greater ambiguity and have seemed more conditional upon the party's wider strategy. The aim here, then, is to examine these more recent attitudes of the 1970s, in order to assess the current position of the PS.

When President Pompidou held a referendum on the question of the enlargement of the EEC in April 1972 (to admit Britain, Denmark and Ireland), the PCF recommended their supporters to vote 'no' and the PS recommended that the electorate abstain from voting. Both parties regarded the holding of a referendum as a manoeuvre by Pompidou, designed partly to emphasise the differences among the parties of the Left and partly to restore his own prestige as the heir to de Gaulle. In recommending an abstention, the Social-ists were regarded as having compromised their own pro-integrationist stance to accommodate the more critical approach of the PCF, and so maintain left-wing unity. In the event, almost 40 per cent of the electorate did not bother to vote, which was the highest abstention rate of any referendum held under the Fifth Republic.[4] Afterwards, Marchais for the PCF commented that, 'In refusing to accept a "no" position for the Union of the Left, the groups of the non-Communist Left have prevented a blow sustained by M. Pompidou from being a complete rout.'[5] Mitterrand saw it

differently however: 'it seems to me', he said, 'that the status
of the PS has increased and that, if I cannot say who has won in
this affair, I know very well who has lost. . . . These results
place the Socialists in a strong position when they come to discuss
with the PCF, or any other party, the future of the Left.'[6] With
the high rate of abstention, it did indeed seem that the Socialists
had more accurately judged the mood of the electorate.

With the approach of the 1973 legislative elections, both the PCF
and the PS had become more interested in a closer understanding
and after three months of difficult negotiations both parties signed
the 'Common Programme of the Left', together with a nationally
binding second ballot electoral pact. The programme outlined a
general agreement on the principles that would guide them when
dealing with the EEC in government. It stated two basic objectives:
first, they would, 'participate in the construction of the EEC, in
its institutions, in its common policies seeking to free it from the
domination of monopoly capital, democratising its institutions,
supporting the workers' demands by orientating Community objectives in the direction of their interests'; and second, they would
seek to preserve at the heart of the Common Market their liberty
of action for the realisation of their political, economic and social
programme'.[7] The PS and certainly its pro-EEC elements, regarded
the programme as a clear affirmation that a left-wing government
would take a constructive approach to questions of European
integration, and an indication that the Communists had been forced
to compromise on their own previous antagonistic stance. Others
were more sceptical, though, and emphasised the vagueness of
such rhetoric.

The PS held an 'Extraordinary National Congress' in December
1973 at Bagnolet, to elaborate further on its own European policy
and to produce a policy document that would form the basis of the
party's long-term approach. However, the party came away with
a motion to which there have been two divergent interpretations.
As Huntzinger has noted, 'the Europeanists saw it as a formal
ratification of their propositions while the sceptical and conditional
Europeans saw the rough draft of a concept critical of the EEC,
and the proposition of conditional participation in the Common
Market enterprise. This can be called the Bagnolet misunderstanding.'[8] Entitled, 'A Europe on the march towards Socialism' it sought
'the construction of an independent, open and Socialist Europe'.
Though it failed to give the precision it claimed as its objective,
Mitterrand did manage to rally 80 per cent of the delegates behind
it, which was perhaps a more basic party aim.

Early in 1976 the PS was faced with a more concrete issue: direct
elections to the European Parliament. The earlier intra-party conflict resurfaced but Mitterrand sought firmly to resolve the question by stating that:

The European Parliament exists. This debate has been resolved
ever since the signing of the Treaty of Rome. Such is reality.
Therefore, it is not a question to-day of taking a position for or

against the Parliament, but of knowing how it will be elected.
At the present time the existence of the European Parliament is
nowhere being called into question. Election by universal suffrage will give it the authority and prestige of which it is now
deprived and will clearly establish in public opinion the European
idea which has up to now been fuzzy. A decision was made in
December 1973 at Bagnolet . . . For socialists, a large scale
political policy must be substituted for the economic power of
grand capital . . . Europe will either be Socialist or she will not
be, and it is now appropriate to pave the way for the massive
entry of workers into the European institutions and the intellec-
tualisation of the struggle.[9]

On 1 February 1976 the PS Comité directeur voted by 97 votes
to 34 in favour of direct elections to the European Parliament.
In the same month, however, the party distinguished its support
for European integration from that of the liberal centre, by declar-
ing its opposition to the recommendations of the Tindemans Report
on European Union. The Tindemans Report, explained the PS,

. . . begins from a concept which does not correspond to the
economic and social reality of Europe, and its propositions are
extremely insufficient insofar as the institutional aspect takes
an exaggerated precedence over the very substance of the Union
and on the will of a Europe which to-day is very far from existing. In reality, this Report corresponds both to the political
position of the man who wrote it and to the present state of
Europe. On the whole, the Tindemans Report expresses a
favourable attitude toward the Europe which has failed and
admits that it is in no position to propose another.[10]

This ideological rejection of the Tindemans Report was followed,
in May 1976, with a speech by Mitterrand that elaborates further
on the party's mainstream attitude.

Europe is, first, the Common Market. We must begin with what
we have at our disposal. This Europe is part of our heritage.
Even if it is contestable, American, capitalist, full of red tape,
annoying, devoid of meaning, we must take it as it is and try to
initiate from this point a different approach without making a
tabula rasa. The Common Agricultural Policy has failed because
of world capitalism which has passed into another phase of its
expansion. It has failed because of the absence of a common
monetary policy. It has failed because of de Gaulle. The danger
to-day is of an American or Atlantic Europe. The time for
Europeans is ripe. Notably West Germany now considers Europe
as a means and not as an end. Only Socialism is capable of
returning elan, vitality and creativity to Europe.[11]

Mitterrand thus sought to combine the traditional notions of
Europeanism with the new critique of the PS. In doing so, he

attacked the USA (to appeal to the Left) and West Germany (an appeal which echoes SFIO debates in the 1950s) and at the same time criticised de Gaulle and talked of 'true' Europeans. The old-style SFIO support for Europe had thus been tied much more closely to current socialist critiques.

In October 1978, the PS Comité directeur published its manifesto for the European elections, entitled, 'Socialists for a Europe of the Workers'. With respect to the Community's institutions, the manifesto declared that, 'The objective of the Socialists is, firstly, to assure, within the framework of the existing treaties, a better democratic control of Community life and a much stronger participation by working people in the elaboration of its decisions. The European Assembly must, in particular, assure that overall control is maintained over directives that now escape the control of national parliaments. For this reason, the Socialists are not hostile to an enlargement in terms of certain Community competences.' Thus whilst not openly advocating Treaty amendments, the PS did appear to give cautious support to a more active and democratic functioning of the Community institutions.

On enlargement of the Community, however, the PS were concerned to protect French domestic interests. They advocated a reform of the CAP to give special help to the products affected by enlargement, and the establishment of a system of minimum prices checked at the national frontiers. In addition, they called for a reinforcement of the Community's regional policy and the facilitating of greater public intervention to protect living standards. Finally, as a last precaution, the PS proposed that new member states should have to progress from one transitional stage to the next on the basis of the performance achieved, not on the basis of the time elapsed during these periods. The attractions of the French agricultural vote had clearly superseded any 'Communautaire' inclinations the party might hold in this sphere.

In the 1979 European elections, the PS started the campaign with the opinion polls accrediting them with 29.5 per cent of the vote in mid-April 1979, but they eventually finished with only 23.5 per cent of the actual vote (21 seats), or 1.2 per cent less than in the previous national elections of 1978.[12] During the campaign, the Socialists lumped their old Communist allies with the Gaullists, calling their opposition to Europe 'nationalist-poujadism', whilst within the PS itself friction developed as a result of the reluctance of CERES (a left-wing party faction) to be identified with a pro-EC stance, particularly when the PCF was conducting such a nationalist campaign. However, the low turnout in the elections of slightly over 60 per cent probably had a greater impact on the PS vote than did any image of party in-fighting.

Shortly before the European elections, the PS had held its party congress in Metz in April 1979. The motions submitted to the Congress highlighted three distinct positions on European policy: those identified with Mitterrand, Michel Rocard, and CERES.[13] Of the three, the CERES motion was the most hostile towards the EEC. It aimed at an independent campaign in the European elections,

with an homogeneous list of candidates which excluded left-wing
Radicals such as Michel Crépeau. It was against any extension of
the powers of the European Parliament and any further moves
being made towards European integration. It supported, amongst
other things, greater control of multinational companies and a
selective raising of external tariff barriers. It also sought increased co-operation between Europe's left-wing parties and it
strongly opposed any enlargement of the Community. Moreover,
CERES attacked any idea that existing EEC institutions could be
used to develop Socialist policies and was very critical of the
common document signed by the Socialist parties of the Nine for
the European elections.

The position of Rocard, interestingly, has shown a tendency to
emphasise the European dimension to policy much more. Previously,
Rocard's contempt for the Community had been quite open,[14] but
his change of heart was presumably intended to bring him into
line with his own supporters, who tend to be pro-EEC, and to
avoid a breach with Mauroy.

Consequently, Rocard's motion to the Metz Congress provided a
bridge between his own previous hostility towards the EEC, and
his present strategic concern to appear interested in European
action so as to increase his support within the party. The new
formula was that of working at the European level to combat the
businessman's Europe, and the Europe of American imperialism
by building a working people's Europe.

Against a background in which Mitterrand's supporters sought
an alliance with CERES largely against Mauroy/Rocard, the Mitterrand motion at Metz once again represented the centre position of
compromise. The motion, after reaffirming its commitment to direct
elections to the European Parliament, went on to state that,

> Although favourable . . . to the reinforcement of the powers of
> control of the European Assembly, the Socialist Party does not
> intend to see the competence of this Assembly expanded at the
> expense of national parliaments. . . . There is no way that the
> present Common Market - the market of 'big capital interests'
> - can be acceptable to us. We want, rather, a Europe of working
> people.[15]

The wording suggested a more strident, independent tone than
had the manifesto in October 1978. The Mitterrand motion at Metz
eventually received the largest support, and given the PS system
of internal democracy, his supporters now dominate the Comité
Directeur.

In January 1980, a PS National Convention at Alfortville adopted
a 'Socialist Project for France in the 1980s', which sought to present the guidelines for party policy for the new decade.[16] It stated
as one of its four priorities, 'A France independent and open to
the world.' The Project seemed noticeably to move the party to
accommodate a new wave of concern to defend the French national
interest. It declared that:

Against the 'mondialisme' of the present Head of State, which is merely an alibi for multinational capitalism, the Socialist Party affirms that, pursuing the inspiration of Jaurès, love and respect for one's homeland are at the heart of a true internationalism. . . . 'To live, to work, to decide within the country', this is the cry which best summarises, without doubt, the pain of men uprooted by the crises and it is not an appeal to isolation or retreat . . .

The Project went on to give further recognition to the problems that a leftist government in France might face in the Community:

Without doubt, the perspective of socialism is not the hallmark of the [Rome] Treaty, but it is as well to establish that it is the scope of multinational capitalism which has made prevail a conception of the Community which is almost exclusively commercial. Indeed, the realisation in France of a socialist project will be a shock within our European environment, which will cause it to be less marked by liberalism and Atlanticism. Engaged in the construction of a socialist society, France will contribute to the democratisation of the Community, she will utilise the institutions to favour the convergence of the social struggles against unemployment, for the reduction of the working period, for the control of the multinationals, for the defence of liberties and the extension of democracy.

The Project also outlined the party's refusal to accept regional economic disparities, its desire to see a more thorough common agricultural policy geared to the structural problems of the industry, and its rather tough safeguards for French workers and producers affected by Community enlargement, (as in the October 1978 European manifesto).

The Project concluded its discussion on Europe by stating that its, '. . . course implies that the rule of a necessary unanimity for the revision of the Treaty of Rome remains the law. As long as Europe, in effect, remains largely dominated by capital, the preservation of our room for manoevre and similarly its extension, will remain an imperative of the Socialist plan.' The PS was thus maintaining the commitment to its Socialist policies, in the face of a greater recognition of the specific needs of France.

By the start of the 1980s, the PS was, then, committed to seeking greater democratic participation in the Community institutions; a more active European Parliament though not one that took power away from the national parliaments; rather tough safeguards for French workers, industries and regions affected by the enlargement of the Community; common action with EC partners against unemployment and for the reduction of the working period; and common policies to control the activities of multinational companies. The party had thus developed a more vigorous European policy than its SFIO predecessor, and one that was more distinctively Socialist.

Precisely how distinctive the party's European policy actually
is, and what is the party's attitude to specific short-term issues,
is set to be tested by government office with the election of
François Mitterrand as President of the Republic, in May 1981.
For the first time in its history, the PS provides the incumbent
in the Elysée and is now at the helm of French foreign policy-
making. As soon as he took office, the actions of President
Mitterrand received widespread attention as observers, both at
home and abroad, sought to plot the likely new course for France.
Mitterrand immediately called fresh parliamentary elections for
June 1981, and in the meantime appointed a provisional government. He named Pierre Mauroy as his Prime Minister, and together
they appointed Claude Cheysson as Foreign Minister and André
Chandernagor as a junior minister with special responsibility for
European affairs. At this stage, Mitterrand's cabinet did not include any Communists, though he had found room for Jacques
Delors (Finance) and Michel Jobert (Trade) who had both previously served Gaullist prime ministers, and he had also appointed
four members of the centrist MRG. After the impressive victory
of the Socialists in the parliamentary elections, in which the party
leapt ahead to 37.5 per cent of the vote, much of it at the expense
of the PCF, the Socialists bargained with the Communists from a
position of strength, the like of which it had never known before.
For largely tactical reasons of forcing the PCF to accept some degree of collective responsibility for government policy, Mitterrand
appointed four Communist ministers. This was little more than a
token participation, however, for the Socialists were now in the
ascendancy and had the opportunity to govern according to their
own inclinations, ultimately able to rely on their own National
Assembly majority.

The appointment of Claude Cheysson indicated a positive attitude
towards European integration, as Cheysson had previously been
an EEC Commissioner in Brussels in charge of the Community's
policy towards the developing countries. Whilst there, he had
established a reputation as a strong supporter of the Third World,
and this experience was seen to complement Mitterrand's own desire
to develop closer links with such countries. Whilst Europeanists
could be pleased with Cheysson's appointment, they were also
left to speculate, however, on the outcome for European policy of
the divergent influences of pro-integrationists such as Maurice
Faure and Michel Crépeau (both MRG ministers), and of others
such as Michel Jobert (a former minister in a Gaullist cabinet),
Jean-Pierre Chevènement (of CERES), and the PCF ministers led
by Charles Fiterman.

During his election campaign, Mitterrand had talked of his
attitude on certain issues connected with the European Community.
As to his general approach to Community politics, Mitterrand
repeatedly stressed his preference for a multilateral, rather than
any bilateral, strategy. 'The Europe of the Common Market', he
explained, 'is a Europe of ten equal partners, and the right of
each is an equal right to that of all the others.' In terms of an

objective for this broader-based strategy, Mitterrand also declared that 'Europe today needs a spirit, an ideal, a conviction.'[17]

Indeed, 'Europe is a voluntary affair; of course interests are at
stake, but there must be a common will to make Europe a political,
economic, social and cultural force. In that way, [it] will represent a communal force, internationally. This is already happening
in commercial matters, but it should be extended to other fields,
otherwise Europe will inevitably split up.'

In stressing the need for a multilateral approach, the implication
was that the close personal relationship that had previously existed
between Giscard d'Estaing as President and Chancellor Schmidt of
West Germany would not be continued with the same amity.
Mitterrand had said during his campaign, that 'It is necessary to
draw closer links between France and West Germany', but, 'it is
not a question of a Paris-Bonn axis.' The end of such an axis,
which had underpinned the development of the European Community for so many years, would indeed represent a turning-point
in French policy towards Europe.

Whilst the prospects for Franco-German relations seemed to have
worsened, the British government was optimistic that Mitterrand
would be willing to improve the understanding between Paris and
London. Though Mrs Thatcher headed a right-wing Conservative
government, she hoped that Mitterrand would be more accommodating to British interests in the Community's agricultural and budgetary policies. Such optimism was based on the opinion that
Mitterrand was less dependent than Giscard d'Estaing had been on
the agricultural vote. During his election campaign, however,
Mitterrand had been highly critical of his predecessor's policy
towards Britain. He had stated his desire to see all existing Community members remaining within the alliance, but he also commented that, 'I would simply like to see our diplomacy being more
vigilant so far as Great Britain is concerned, which was not the
case during the fishermen's or sheep-farmers' disputes. With
respect to agricultural prices, although better, the Government
was still not vigilant enough.'

In his television debate with Giscard d'Estaing, Mitterrand
attacked his opponent for having failed over the fisheries dispute:
'I think you have not been firm enough, that happens to you quite
often', he said.[18]·Earlier in the campaign, he had also commented
on the deal over Britain's budgetary payments: 'We would have
felt less resentment at the snub shown to M. Giscard d'Estaing
over the concession to Great Britain of 15 million francs, if we
had not previously treated the latter so easily and cavalierly.'
Whilst such statements might be regarded as mere electioneering,
there would seem to be grounds for caution when predicting a
more accommodating attitude being shown from Mitterrand, once
'essential' French agricultural and budgetary interests are at
stake. None the less, the British government could find themselves
rather more pleased with President Mitterrand's attitude towards
the need for a more vigorous regional and social policy within the
Community, which dates back to earlier policy statements from the

PS during the 1970s, as was shown above.

Mitterrand showed a similar concern for French interests, when discussing the possible enlargement of the European Community to include Spain and Portugal. In his television debate, Mitterrand explained that, 'As far as Spain and Portugal are concerned, I voiced my opinion before 1979 when I put forward various preconditions to the accession of Spain and Portugal to the EEC. At the time, Giscard d'Estaing was strongly opposed to my views: he thought it was absurd to refuse immediate access to Spain and Portugal. I am glad to see that common sense has prevailed since and that the President now agrees with me.' Mitterrand thus reaffirmed his commitment to the rather tough conditions for entry laid down in his party's manifesto for the European elections, which were noted above.

Whilst Mitterrand was being cautious about enlargement, he was enthusiastic for a more positive approach towards the Third World. 'Bearing in mind', he commented, 'that the Community exports 40 per cent of its goods to Third World countries, I would say that we are missing a great opportunity to develop our industries and gain some economic expansion that could be achieved by operating a courageous, intelligent and generous policy towards the Third World.' Clearly, the appointment of Claude Cheysson is in line with such a development.

More immediately, the Mitterrand administration faced a run on the franc which had started even before it had taken over from Giscard d'Estaing. Premier Mauroy made it clear that his government would do all it could to safeguard the European Monetary System, and proved his determination by introducing severe foreign exchange controls to keep the franc within the margin allowed for under the EMS. Whilst Mitterrand and Schmidt had an early meeting in Paris, both the Bank of France and the Bundesbank were intervening to hold up the Franc, which helped to curb speculation that the Mauroy government would be forced to devalue.

Within the alliance of Western European Socialist parties, Mitterrand's election inevitably represents a turning point. For the first time under the Fifth Republic, the foreign allies of the PS now have a Socialist President to work with, and Mitterrand's election will lead to expectations as to the diplomatic impetus he will give to the Atlantic and European alliances. Whilst Mitterrand's relations with the West German SPD government are not particularly close, his relations with the British Labour Party have been reserved and distant. French Socialists are typically sceptical as to the ideological inclinations of their German counterparts, but the policy of withdrawal from the European Community adopted by their British neighbours will inevitably cause difficulties for Anglo-French foreign policy co-ordination, in addition to any likely divergences over the Common Agricultural Policy. It might well be that the British and French Socialists will develop a greater degree of compatibility in their domestic policies than they will in their external policies. By contrast, the Mitterrand leadership enjoys good relations with its other European allies; notably those in Italy, Spain, Greece and the Benelux countries. Indeed, their Mediterranean partners form a Southern alliance more understanding of the French political environment and the implications of the Socialists operating alongside a well-established Communist Party. Generally within Western Europe, the ability of Mitterrand to make a distinctive impact on foreign policy as a Socialist President may well be dependent upon the degree of compatibility existing between the PS and its kindred parties in other European states. Such a relationship would also indicate how far it is possible to talk meaningfully of a 'European Socialism'.

More immediately, the ability of Mitterrand to implement the policies prepared during the years of opposition, will be affected by the position of domestic political parties. Of major importance will be the attitude adopted by the French Communist Party. The foregoing discussion has outlined the nature of the PS debate over Europe as it has developed since the early 1970s, and has considered the likely shape of policy to be pursued by President Mitterrand. For an analysis of the corresponding position of the Communists, the discussion now turns to examine their policy development with respect to Europe, before concluding with a consideration of the position of the Left in general.

THE PCF AND THE EUROPEAN COMMUNITY

The discussion which follows attempts to outline the major developments in the French Communist Party's attitudes towards European integration, and to relate them to the national and international contexts in which they occurred. Little attention is paid to specific policy issues, except in so far as they highlight particular changes in the PCF's analysis of the European Community. Rather, emphasis is laid on the ideological development of the French Communist Party during the Fifth Republic and how this has been reflected in its stand on Europe.

Post-war political life in France was largely dominated by issues concerning West European integration. Marshall Aid, the European Coal and Steel Community and the European Defence Community all took their toll in the frequently bitter internal disputes of the parties. The French Communists, however, suffered little. The PCF's antagonism towards West European integration of any kind was a fundamental aspect of its very essence as a party which embodied the interests of the nation and of the working class, and as a party which defended the interests of the Soviet Union.

The degree of hostility shown towards West European integration has varied over the years from the virulent denouncement of the United States' (and, by extension, West Germany's) hegemonic intentions of the 1950s, to the more subdued and more co-operative approach of the 1970s. In this respect, the period from 1958 is of particular interest, highlighting these changes in attitude, but also testifying to a certain continuity.

More importantly, European integration (in the form of the European Community) touches upon and indeed affects all three of the determining axes of the PCF's policy-making process.

The first of these is the connection with the Soviet Union or, in PCF terms, support for proletarian internationalism, generally understood by outsiders to mean the defence of Soviet foreign policy aims. Thus, in supporting the initial Soviet condemnation of the EEC as merely an economic base for NATO, and thereby a further threat to peace in Europe, the PCF could claim to be acting in the interest of the working classes internationally.

The second determining axis of PCF policy-making is the maintenance of internal party organisation. For this a uniting, or mobilising, factor is required, usually taking the form of a vision of socialism based on the Soviet model. Thus, the analysis of the EEC as an anti-Socialist entity provided the basis of party cohesion, a common enemy around which the party could unite.

The third element of the policy-making process involves the party's situation in the national context and the demands made on it by the national political system. If under threat, or weakened in any way, then the PCF traditionally calls on the appeal of nationalism to strengthen its position. French Communists were quick to use the opportunity provided by the creation of the EEC, and especially by the transfer of sovereignty envisaged in the Treaty of Rome, to exploit the appeal of popular nationalism. The emphasis on the loss of sovereignty continues to be the major element of the PCF's anti-EEC stance, and electorally at least, would seem the most successful aspect. Other demands have been equally salient, however, not least the chosen strategy of left-wing unity.

Three purposes were thus served by the PCF's opposition to the European Community. Party activists were united around a common objective. Nationalist sentiments were championed to great effect. And this nationalism, expressed through opposition to the EEC, was reconciled with proletarian internationalism. All three criteria for policy-making were fulfilled. Hence the importance of the European Community for the PCF. Any substantial change in favour of the EEC could upset the delicate balance of the policy-making process.

The PCF initially regarded the EEC as the product of a military-political alliance, designed to serve as an economic base for NATO. Created in 1949, NATO became, after the breakdown in 1954 of plans to establish a European Defence Community, the means whereby West Germany was rearmed, West Germany becoming a full member in 1955. The PCF had compaigned vigorously against this development, seeing it as a threat to peace in Europe. The inclusion of an economically strong and American-backed West Germany in the EEC increased the PCF's fears, both with regard to peace and to France's economic position within the Community.

The Community was also regarded as the quintessence of the policy pursued by (primarily American) monopoly capitalists aimed at further subjugation of the working class. The EEC was the incarnation of three supreme vices in the eyes of the French

Communists; it was at one and the same time anti-national, anti-Socialist and anti-Soviet Union. The PCF analysed the Common Market as an attempt on the part of European capitalism to resolve all its inter-imperialistic contradictions, but these very contradictions contained the seeds of destruction of the Community of the Six.[19] This theme still forms the cornerstone of the PCF's critique of the EEC. At this early stage in the development of European integration, however, the thesis maintained that the union was kept from falling apart only by shared anti-Soviet sentiments. The anti-national character of this policy was crystallised for the PCF in the abandonment of national sovereignty envisaged by the Treaty of Rome.

The PCF rejected the argument put forward by the members of the EEC that prosperity was assured for all who participated. It was argued by the PCF that no matter what the size of such an economic community, misery, unemployment and falling living standards would be inflicted upon the French working class. They maintained that French industry, already weak in comparison with other countries (especially West Germany) could not withstand the fierce competition which would of necessity take place within the EEC.

The above analysis of the EEC was faithful to that adopted by the Soviet Union in the '17 Theses' published by the Institute of World Economy and International Relations in 1957.[20] The '17 Theses' highlighted the monoplistic nature of the EEC, American domination via the resurgence of West German imperialism in both economic and political terms, thus threatening East-West relations and directly challenging the Soviet Union. But above all, the EEC was seen as a major step towards the destruction of capitalism and its own destruction was unavoidable and imminent. This analysis re-emerged during the debate surrounding direct elections to the European Parliament in the late 1970s.

The PCF's 1958-59 position proved the cause of some embarrassment in 1962/63. The obstacles to the functioning of the Common Market were quickly overcome. Neither the deficit in the French balance of payments nor the shock of German competition jeopardised the construction of Europe or France herself, as predicted by the Communists. De Gaulle, although hostile to any notion of integration or supranationality, accelerated the success of the Common Market with regard to French interests, initially through economic measures taken in 1958 and the early 1960s to render the French economy more competitive, and subsequently through his veto of Britain's application for entry to the EEC. This meant that there was an almost complete lack of reaction in French public opinion to the PCF's anti-European campaign, thereby rendering its action sterile.

Other Communist parties (for example in Belgium and Italy) who had experienced a similar lack of response in their own countries conducted a reappraisal of the situation, concluding that the new strategy should be to work from within the EEC rather than attacking from the outside.[21] The Soviet Union too was forced to reap-

praise the situation. Under the aegis of the Institute of World
Economy, a conference grouping Marxist specialists from 22
countries, was held in Moscow in September 1962 with the object of
redefining the Communist analysis of the EEC. Subsequently, the
Institute published the '32 Theses',[22] which were in fact a compromise between the differing opinions put forward at the conference.

The PCF's opposition to Europe at this conference was total.

What is Europe? A geographical reality that stretches from the
Atlantic to the Ural mountains. An economic and social reality
composed of capitalist countries and socialist countries. Europe
is thus a geographical whole yet divided politically. To declare
oneself to be a partisan of 'Europe' thus has no sense, for one
cannot be for or against a geographical fact and neither can
one support two opposed social systems simultaneously.[23]

The EEC was seen as a response to the objective need for the
extension of markets and openings characteristic of the economics
of the period. This objective need, as well as the tendency towards
the internationalisation of economic life, found its source in the
scientific and technological revolution and in the generalised
spread of automation and new methods of production. But the response furnished by the Common Market to these objective tendencies of economic development was 'abnormal and reactionary'.
The Common Market's aims of sharing the capitalist world market
did not (and could not) resolve either inter-imperialist rivalries
or the contradiction between the rise in productive forces and
the monopolistic framework in which they were forced to develop.
Nor did it resolve the essential contradiction of the contemporary
world between socialism and capitalism. Thus, in the final analysis,
the EEC offered only the prospect of an intensification of the
contradictions already tearing apart the capitalist world. Again,
it is interesting to note the renewed emphasis placed on this
analysis in the late 1970s.

The PCF was faced with a dilemma however. It was reluctant to
recognise the objective fact of the internationalisation of productive
forces and to denounce the form in which this objective fact was
incarnated: the EEC. If the former were recognised then the latter
would have to be acknowledged. To acknowledge the EEC would
mean the PCF giving a framework to the working-class struggle
that was not its own but one imposed upon economic life by the
monopolies. On this point the PCF differed from the Institute's
analysis. The Institute rather ambiguously called for the co-
ordination of the working-class fight on a European level, thus
recognising (somewhat tentatively) the reality of the EEC. The
PCF maintained that the workers' struggle should take place in
each individual country, thereby refusing categorically to recognise the EEC.

To speak of a 'people's Europe' under the conditions of the

capitalist Common Market is a deception with the aim of covering up the reality of the Europe of the trusts. . . . The people's
Europe will cease to be a utopia only when each of the European
nations succeeds in ending the domination and exploitation of
the monopolies in their own countries.[24]

The PCF then, was quite steadfast in its opposition to the EEC,
refusing to recognise it, and in this respect deviating from the
Soviet line. The Soviet Union had now come to view the EEC as
an 'objective reality'. It was recognised that the EEC was there
to stay and that more benefit could be derived from working with
it than against it. Although this was only grudgingly accepted,
the new line could be defended by pointing to the objective
factors of the internationalisation of the means of production and
changes in technology, both of which could be used to further
the cause of the revolution.
Within the Socialist camp, economic progress had been consolidated and, moreover, socialism had triumphed in Cuba. Within
the EEC, de Gaulle had effectively prevented any moved towards
supranationality. More importantly, his very presence constituted
a barrier to any further American infiltration of the Community
through his veto of British entry. There was thus a greater
equilibrium between the two power blocs which led the Soviet
Union to re-evaluate the nature of her political and economic
relations with the capitalist world.
If, according to the Soviet Union, the only way in which the
imperialist world could combat the new strength of the Socialist
camp was by military force, then the answer was to pursue a
policy of peaceful coexistence.[25] And in so doing, the original
analysis that the EEC was a militarily aggressive and essentially
provisional organisation became untenable. The EEC was now an
economic 'reality', though not a political one.
Europe, as noted earlier, was not, in the early 1960s, a serious
policy issue in French political life. Generally, France, and the
French, were doing well out of the Common Market, and de Gaulle
ensured that France's honour was well safe-guarded. The PCF,
having adopted an (albeit tentative) alliance strategy with the
Socialists, was anxious to play down acute points of divergence,
European policy being (and remaining) one of the most acute.
However, the candidature of the Centrist (and pro-European)
Lecanuet in the presidential election of 1965, forced the European
issue to the forefront of public opinion and the PCF had to clarify
its own position, whilst taking care not to offend the sensibilities
of its pro-European Socialist allies.
Their position on Europe now became more subtle. The fundamental hostility towards the EEC remained but the implication was
that it could be used for ends other than those for which it had
been conceived. Charles Fiterman, writing in April 1966,[26] recognised the need for international economic organisations as a response to the internationalisation of economic life. He contested,
however, the capacity of the bourgeois capitalists successfully to

construct such organisations, given capitalism's propensity for conflict in the quest for increased profits. It was not, he continued, within the framework of bourgeois monopolist domination that a democratic, people's Europe could be built. The framework had to be provided by the working classes of Europe, for with the disappearance of the exploitation of one man by another would disappear the main obstacle to the reconciliation of nations.

This was a task that should be undertaken immediately, without having to await the advent of Socialism in each country.[27] But there was no concession to the notion of supranationality. Fiterman reasserted the belief that 'the interest of the working class is intimately linked to the national interest' and the national interest lay in national independence. This formula was valid for France and for every other country, with international relations only destined for success if national independence were accepted as the basis of those relations.

In April 1968 Fiterman announced that the PCF was in favour of taking common action with other Socialist forces within the EEC with the aim of democratising its institutions and revising the Treaty of Rome to this end. He also called for the representation of trade unions within the Community institutions, and for the admission of Communist deputies to their rightful place in the European Parliament.

Here, then, we see formulated the basis of current PCF thinking on Europe, the turning point coming in the mid-1960s and attitudes being well defined by 1969.

It is one thing to recognise the existence of the Common Market which we do because it is an objective fact and because the French economy is committed to it to such an extent that to withdraw from it would do us great harm. But it is quite another thing to think of following the present policy of the European Economic Community which is inspired exclusively by the interests of monopoly capital. The question now raised by all the democratic forces in Western Europe is to give to European organisation a new social and economic content which conforms to the interest of the popular masses.[28]

The period 1958-69 is thus characterised by a major shift in the PCF's attitudes towards European integration which may be related to three major developments; first, the change in international circumstances, and especially the strengthening of the Socialist camp, which led to the new policy of peaceful coexistence or the relaxation of the Cold War. France played a major role in this policy. De Gaulle was considered in a particularly favourable light by the USSR, because of the independent foreign and defence policies he pursued. The Western Alliance, after France's withdrawal from NATO, lacked a united front, which could only favour the Soviet Union.

The second development was linked to the Communist world's change of analysis of the nature of capitalism, and more specifically to the PCF's realisation that Thorez's 'absolute pauperisation' theory (re-emphasised in the mid-1950s) was no longer tenable. This theory maintained that the purchasing power of workers in capitalist countries, particularly in France, was constantly declining.[29] But now it was recognised that the capitalist system had the capacity, albeit contradictory and limited, to develop productive forces and increase, albeit in a relative and necessarily insufficient way, the standard of living of the working class. This could no longer be denied and was reflected in a much more realistic attitude towards the EEC.

The third, and perhaps the over-riding development, was the formulation during the 1960s of the alliance strategy with the Socialists, a strategy dictated by the PCF's electoral humiliation of 1958 and the need for the Party to reassert itself as a legitimate force in French political life.

The PCF's acceptance of, and indeed commitment to, the EEC can be gauged from a statement made in its programme, 'Changer de Cap' published in 1971:[30] 'The Party is aware that France could not, without serious damage, unilaterally break the ties created by the existence of the Common Market.'[31] Despite increasingly public hostility towards the EEC, this view still holds true. Withdrawal from the Common Market is out of the question. Again, several international developments during the early 1970s could serve to explain this position. Détente was flourishing, opening the doors of co-operation between the EEC and COMECON. This seemed to be a move in the direction towards what might be termed the 'other' Europe – the Europe of peace and co-operation, a 'Europe of the Workers' which the PCF had championed since the early days of European integration. The advent of Willy Brandt to the Chancellorship in West Germany was welcomed as putting an end to the ambitions of revanchist forces in West Germany.[32] His Ostpolitik with the effective recognition of the East German state brought hopes of a peaceful solution to the German problem. Republican China's admission to the United Nations weakened American domination. Again, the balance of force was tipped in favour of the Socialist camp, and as a consequence, criticism of the EEC was maintained at a low level.

Within France, the PCF had to contend with a new, reinvigorated Socialist Party, under the leadership, after 1971, of François Mitterrand, the man who led the non-Communist side of the 1960s alliance with the PCF. This posed a new challenge to the PCF. During the 1960s it had been the dominant partner of the alliance. Faced with an ideologically revitalised and large Socialist Party, the mid-1970s situation could be very different.

The arguments surrounding the 1972 referendum and the setting-up of the Common Programme were discussed earlier in the chapter. Suffice to say here that the PCF and the PS went into the referendum divided, and emerged relatively unscathed. Both parties had asserted themselves vis-à-vis each other, and both had shown the extent to which they were prepared to make concessions for the sake of unity. Judging from the content of the Common Pro-

gramme of Government (finally signed in June 1972), the PCF
had shown itself to be the stronger of the two, especially in
economic matters.[33]

As far as the EEC was concerned, post-referendum, any differences between the PCF and the PS were very definitely kept
well hidden. For the PCF at least, this was a second-rate area of
contention. The breakdown of the Common Programme, however,
and the decision to hold direct elections to the European Parliament in 1977 threw a new light on the debate. This was definitely
a no-holds barred confrontation, the main subject of attack being
the PS, with the accusations of 25 years previously constituting
the leading blows. The fundamental attack on the PS came after
legislation allowing for direct elections had been passed by the
National Assembly. On 6 June 1977, the PS signed the 'Project for
an electoral programme of the Union of Socialist Parties of the
EEC'. Little was said about this in the Communist press until
October 1977, after the breakdown of negotiations on the up-
dating of the Common Programme.[34]

Great emphasis was laid on the 'social-democratisation' of the
PS, and on the incompatibility of the Programme of the Socialist
Parties of the EEC and the Common Programme, the former being
classed as a supranational document, outlining a programme of
crisis management. This marked the start of a campaign openly
hostile to the EEC, although the PS gradually ceased to be a prime
target. The PCF saw in the direct elections campaign the opportunity to reassert itself independently of the PS, and again become
the real defender of French interests, the only party to provide
a challenge to the Right.

The campaign witnessed the resurgence of themes which, although constant in the PCF's analysis of the EEC, had been toned
down quite considerably during the 'friendship' days of the later
1960s and the early to mid-1970s. West Germany was again singled
out for attack – the EEC was dominated by West Germany industry
and capital, all of which was directly responsible for the ailing
state of French industry, and West German domination of the
Common Agricultural Policy was seen as responsible for the decay-
ing state of French agriculture. PCF election publicity proclaimed
that a vote for any other party would be a vote for Helmut Schmidt
and West German domination of France.

There was a resurgence of the nationalist theme, which went
hand in hand with the anti-German campaign. The French people
must decide their own fate – sovereignty should reside in the
National Assembly, not in Brussels or Strasbourg.[35]

More importantly, the PCF's economic analysis assumed a
slightly different aspect, somewhat reminiscent of its analysis
during the early years of European integration. Emphasis was now
placed on the inevitability of the collapse of the Common Market,
because of its internal contradictions. The whole exercise of direct
elections was seen as a last ditch attempt by monopoly capital to
save itself – further integration would lead to increased centralisation and concentration and would thereby defend profit, the

raison d'être of the monopolies. As a result, a tendency to remove any obstacles that act as a brake on transnational centralisation and concentration had developed, including harmonisation of the fiscal and monetary policies of the individual states.

This development, however, is analysed by the PCF as contradictory – capitalist competition is becoming more intense and the monopolies are using the diversity of the individual nation states (and the aid accorded to them by each of the individual states) against their competitors. This means that integration is proceeding in the heart of a deepening crisis. The monopolies and multinationals need the Common Market, but they are in fact destroying it with each move towards further integration, by playing one state off against another.[36] This very closely resembles the analysis put forward in 1958, the implication being, now, as then, that West German and American trusts can be the only beneficiaries of such a policy.

The resurgence of the nationalist theme is also very reminiscent of PCF attitudes in the early days of European integration, when the party emphasised the need for each of the European nations to end domination and exploitation in their own countries before a 'people's' Europe could emerge. This is not to suggest that the PCF has ever abandoned the notion of the national road to Socialism. But this theme was, during the 1970s, submerged to a very great extent by the alliance strategy pursued both nationally and within the context of the EEC. However, one must be careful not to over-emphasise the place of Socialism in the PCF's current anti-EEC campaign. The threat posed by the Common Market is not to Socialism, but to France. All recent PCF literature on the EEC, and indeed on the situation in France, stresses this point.[37]

As noted in the introduction to this section, any change of attitude favourable to the EEC could have detrimental effects on PCF policy. It should be emphasised therefore that, although a distinct change in favour of the EEC did take place, the party's fundamental hostility to the monopolistic nature of the Community remained throughout. The PCF still believed that the collapse of the EEC was inevitable, but this belief was overlaid by the 'state monopoly capitalism' thesis which maintained that capitalism had stabilised (albeit temporarily) and that the EEC (or monopoly integration) had played a major part in this.

Thus, agreement could be reached with the PS on the basis of their shared aim of eliminating the monopolistic character of the Community, at the European level, in conjunction with other 'democratic' forces. This did not imply that the 'struggle' had moved from the national to the European arena. Both levels were now appropriate. And either level could be emphasised according to the demands of the national political context.

Once it became clear that the PCF was no longer the major beneficiary of the alliance strategy with the PS, no time was lost in finding reasons for withdrawing from that alliance. The breakdown of negotiations on the up-dating of the Common Programme in September 1977 was thus inevitable. Other arguments perhaps reinforce the sense of inevitability surrounding the split in the Union of the Left. One maintains that the PCF, in common with the PCI, decided, after the crisis had set in in 1974, that it was not interested in managing the capitalist crisis. Also, the Soviet Union, now quite favourably placed as regards trading concessions from the capital West, no longer had any immediate interest in seeing Communist-led governments in Western Europe, as this would 'simply substitute awkward dependents for troubled enemies, which is never sound strategy'.[38]

Whatever the real reason, the current leftward move of the party was to be expected after the collapse of the Union of the Left. There was no other direction in which to move. The PCF needed to re-establish its credibility as the party of change, and to reaffirm itself in its opposition role. This it has traditionally asserted in its ultra-nationalist defence of French interests, and, given the present economic and international conjuncture, the best possible forum for this is the European forum.

The argument runs as follows. The French bourgeoisie, in its traditional collaborationist policy with the German bourgeoisie, is, through the structure of the Common Market, milking France of all her resources, material and human, in the pursuit of profit. Hence the PCF's opposition to the enlargement of the European Community, which could only further aggravate the crisis in France, to the detriment especially of French agriculture, and which would serve only to increase the profits of these bourgeois elements.

During the period of 'success' of the EEC this position would have been untenable. The only challenge to a successful Common Market was through a united anti-capitalist campaign, grouping the working classes of all the countries involved and potentially involved. In this respect, it was the duty of the PCF as the avant-garde of the French working class to lead the fight, and this it did. However, the changed economic circumstances of Western Europe, with the renewed emphasis on the inevitable and indeed imminent collapse of the system, validates the current argument that only within the national context can 'change' be achieved.

It would seem that the French Communist Party has come full circle with regard to the problems posed by European integration. We have witnessed the re-enactment of, and the restatement of, its attitudes of 20 to 25 years ago. The election of Mitterrand to the Presidency of the Republic casts a new light on the European question, however. Ideologically, any renewed co-operation with the now governing Socialists can be accommodated within the 'state monopoly capitalism' thesis, outlined earlier. On a more practical level, the PCF is faced with two major problems (apart from its falling electoral support), neither of which have confronted it before during the Fifth Republic.

First, there is no guarantee that France, under Mitterrand, will maintain the 'special' relationship with the Soviet Union, whereby France effectively acts as a brake on any further integration of the Western alliance. Mitterrand's avowed preference for a multilateral approach to Community affairs could lead to greater political co-operation within the Community, which, in the Soviet view, would constitute a threat.

The second problem is perhaps of more immediate consequence. As a partner in government (albeit very junior) the PCF will become involved in the formulation of policy with regard to the Community. The PCF will have to undertake some quick thinking here, as it has not so far brought forward any concrete policy proposals. The majority of Communist statements on Europe are of a highly critical and ideological nature unconcerned by the practicalities and difficulties of government. Broadly speaking, the PCF would agree with the CERES proposals for the European Community, outlined in the earlier section. But it is as yet far from clear how influential the CERES faction will be within the new government. And it is certainly unclear how welcome Communist support for CERES proposals, of whatever kind, would be.

Should the PCF feel uncomfortable in government, as is perhaps likely, then the question of European integration would provide the perfect grounds for resignation. The PCF has never compromised its position on Europe. It has simply chosen to emphasise or de-emphasise its views according to internal and external circumstances. Should it become the focus of renewed emphasis, then it will be for the traditionally noble reason of safeguarding the integrity of France. The appeal of this will be far greater than any argument over the number or rate of nationalisations.

CONCLUSION

The preceding discussion outlines the changes and developments in the attitudes of the French Left towards European integration. Clearly, the issue has been of major importance with regard to the state of relations between the PS and PCF. With a Socialist government now in power, it may assume an even greater significance.

Superficially, there would seem to be no immediate areas of contention that could break the newly formed alliance. As outlined in the section on the PS, the Socialists have moved sufficiently close to the Communist line for the latter to be content for the time being, at least. Opposition to enlargement of the Community, to the extension of the powers of the European Parliament, to the use of majority voting, indeed, opposition to any move in the direction of supranationality in the foreseeable future is common to both parties. Both vigorously support proposals for a more egalitarian social policy, greater workers' participation in the Community's institutions and, of course, both parties vociferously defend the interests of French agriculture.

Ideologically (although again at a superficial level) the PS and the PCF are closer than before in their analysis concerning the domination of the EEC by the multinationals, and the need to eliminate monopoly capitalism, thereby creating what they both refer to as the 'Europe of the Workers'. That the PCF sees the 'party' playing a very major role in this 'Europe of the Workers' may be of long-term significance. But doubtless the PS would expect to have undermined Communist strength within France by the time a 'Europe of the Workers' became a reality.

Of more immediate interest is the fact that despite the agreements that can and will be made with regard to certain European issues, fundamentally, the PS is committed to the idea of 'Europe' within the Atlantic Alliance, and the PCF is not. The Communists constantly advocate the dissolution of the power blocs, and claim to be working towards that end, the first goal being, of course, the dissolution of the Atlantic Alliance. Conflict could therefore well arise, should the Mitterrand government seek closer ties with the Atlantic Alliance, in line with the new President's stated desire to maintain the French defence capability as a warning to the Soviet Union.

For the time being, however, within the national context the Socialists have the upper hand, which necessarily circumscribes the PCF's room for manoeuvre. Moreover, the PCF in the short term will doubtless be concerned with a re-examination of its recent strategy, given the impressive electoral victories of the Socialists. None the less, the still substantial Communist presence in France (and the potential support to be won over from them) will continue to exert pressure on the Mitterrand government for tougher action on Community issues, as will the pre-eminence of the Gaullists on the Right. Indeed, should Mitterrand fail to deliver the goods, then the PCF will be in a strong position to make electoral capital out of his failure for they will clearly seek to present themselves as the true left-wing defenders of French national interests.

Not untypically for left-wing political parties in Western Europe, the attitudes of the PCF and the PS towards the development of the European Community have thus displayed both the theoretical and the tactical dilemmas involved in reconciling basic left-wing values, such as a desire for greater international co-operation, with the actuality of a capitalist integration process. In such a context, the danger of finding utility in chauvinistic electoral appeals is all the greater, given the basic difficulty of defining the appropriate left-wing response to the kind of integration pursued. In the new political situation created by the 1981 elections, the student of French politics can be confident that the ramifications of this ideological dilemma will continue to be felt, and that in the rivalry between the two parties of the Left, few opportunities will be missed for exploiting any electoral advantage to the full. Their respective attitudes in the past would not suggest otherwise.[40]

NOTES

1   See K. Featherstone, Socialists and European Integration:
    the attitudes of British Labour MPs, in the 'European Journal
    of Political Research', forthcoming. The literature on theories
    of regional and international integration is extensive, but for
    the present purposes we refer to support for integration in
    the definition suggested by E.B. Haas, 'The Uniting of
    Europe', Stanford University Press, 1958.
2   See C. Bruclain, 'Le Socialisme et l'Europe', Paris, 1965, p. 11.
3   See B. Criddle, 'Socialists and European Integration', for an
    examination of the SFIO's attitudes; also E.B. Haas, 'The
    Uniting of Europe'.
4   The abstention rate was 47% of the electorate. See J. Frears,
    'Political Parties and Elections in the French Fifth Republic',
    London, 1977, p. 97.
5   'Le Monde', 25 April 1972.
6   Ibid.
7   See 'Le Programme Commun de Gouvernement', Paris, 1978,
    p. 116.
8   J. Huntzinger, The French Socialist Party and Western Rela-
    tions, in W.J. Feld (ed.), 'The Foreign Policies of West
    European Socialist Parties', London, 1978.
9   'L'Unité', January 1976.
10 Quoted by J. Huntzinger, p. 79.
11 Quoted by J. Huntzinger, p. 80.
12 For an analysis of the European elections in France see:
    'Revue Politique et Parlementaire', 881, July-August 1979;
    and, 'European Journal of Political Research', March 1980,
    8, 1. For a discussion of the preceding legislative process
    see V. Herman and M. Hagger, 'The Legislation of Direct
    Elections to the European Parliament', Farnborough, Gower,
    1980.
13 We are indebted to David Lowe's unpublished paper, The
    French Socialist Party: the Congress of Metz and its reper-
    cussions (1979).
14 See M. Rocard, 'Parler Vrai', Paris, 1979 and M. Rocard,
    French Socialists and Europe, in 'Foreign Affairs', 55, 3,
    1977.
15 D. Lowe, The French Socialist Party.
16 See 'Projet Socialiste Pour La France Des Années 80', Paris,
    Club Socialiste du Livre, 1980.
17 Campaign statements here taken from 'Le Monde', 8 May 1981,
    and earlier issues.
18 For text of replies given in television debate, see 'Le Monde',
    7 May 1981.
19 G. Frischmann, Périls du Marché Commun et Contradictions
    Européennes, 'Cahiers du Communisme', 34, 1958, p. 1641.
20 For a full account of the '17 Theses' see Bernard Dutoit,
    'L'Union Soviétique face a l'Intégration Européenne', Lausanne,
    1964, pp. 183-207.

21 On the PCI see Donald Sassoon, The Italian Communist Party's European Strategy, 'Political Quarterly', 1976, pp. 253-75.

22 For a full account of the '32 Theses' see Dutoit, L'Union Soviétique, pp. 211-35.

23 H. Claude, La Révolution Européenne, 'Economie et Politique', 100-101, 1962, p.20.

24 H. Claude, La Fausse Querelle de l'Europe, 'Economie et Politique', 95, 1962, p. 3.

25 On this see R. Pinto Lyra, 'Le Parti Communiste Français et l'Intégration Européenne', Université de Nancy, 1974, p. 112.

26 Charles Fiterman, Les Communistes, l'Europe et la Nation Française, 'Cahiers du Communisme', 42, April 1966, p. 35.

27 Ibid., p. 36. This marked the PCF's adoption of the position put forward in the '32 Theses'.

28 Waldeck Rochet, 'L'Avenir du Parti Communiste Français', Paris, 1969.

29 See Maurice Thorez, La Situation économique de la France - mystifications et réalités, 'Cahiers du Communisme', 31, 3 March, 1955, pp. 259-79.

30 PCF, 'Changer de Cap - Programme pour un gouvernement démocratique d'union populaire', Paris, 1971.

31 'Changer de Cap', p. 224.

32 'L'Humanité', 8 October 1971.

33 The sections in the Common Programme dealing with the economy resemble very closely those of the PCF's programme 'Changer de Cap' of 1971.

34 See for example, 'L'Humanité', 4/26 October 1977 and 'France-Nouvelle', 3 October 1977.

35 Comité Central du PCF, 'Pour une France Indépendante, une Europe Démocratique: Vingt propositions pour l'Europe'.

36 D. Debatisse et al., 'Europe-La France en Jeu', Paris, 1979.

37 For example, D. Debatisse et al., 'Europe-La France en Jeu'; 'Pour une France Indépendante'; Anicet le Pors, 'Marianne à L'Encan', Paris, 1979.

38 See Neil McInnes, 'The Communist Parties of Western Europe', London, 1975, pp. ix/x.

39 See 'Le Monde', 11 August 1981.

40 Although the chapter is largely a joint venture, Kevin Featherstone is responsible for the discussion on the PS, and Joy Bound for that on the PCF. Kevin Featherstone would like to record his thanks to David Hanley and David Lowe for unpublished material on the PS Congress at Metz. Joy Bound extends her thanks especially to Mike Newton, Michael Watson and George Squires for their most useful comments on earlier drafts of the section on the PCF. Her thanks also to Gérard Strieff and Daniel Debatisse of the PCF's European section for the highly stimulating interviews they accorded her.

APPENDIX

THE FRENCH LEGISLATIVE ELECTIONS OF 1981

First Round (15 June figures)

Electorate	36,257,433
Votes	25,508,800 (70.35%)
Abstentions	10,748,633
Valid votes	25,141,190

Party	Candidates	Votes	%
Extreme Left	(508)	334,674	(1.33)
Communists	(483)	4,065,540	(16.17)
Socialists & Left Radicals	(532)	9,432,362	(37.51)
Other Left	(130)	183,010	(0.72)
Ecologists	(174)	271,688	(1.08)
RPR ⎱ UNM	(299)	5,231,269	(20.08)
UDF ⎰	(280)	4,827,437	(19.02)
Other Right	(148)	704,788	(2.08)
Extreme Right	(170)	90,422	(0.35)

FRENCH LEGISLATIVE ELECTION RESULTS OF 1981

Second Round (322 seats)

Registered Voters:	25,730,576
Votes:	19,178,322
Abstentions:	6,552,254 (25.5%)
Valid Votes:	18,665,922

	Votes	%
Extreme Left	–	–
Communist Party	1,303,920	6.98
Socialist Party & MRG	9,152,082	49.00
Other Left	139,460	0.74
RPR ⎱ UNM	4,184,323	22.04
UDF ⎰	3,427,101	18.36
Other UNM	371.004	1.98
Other Right	88,032	0.47
Ecologists	–	–
Others	–	–
Extreme Right	–	–

1981 Assembly: Second Round Result in Seats (491 in total)

	1978	1981
Communists	86	44
Socialists plus MRG	116	285
Other Left	2	4
RPR	151	84
UDF	122	64
Other Right	12	8
(Plus Polynesia and Wallis)		

UNM	= Union pour la nouvelle majorité (the Right-wing coalition)
RPR	= Rassemblement pour la République
UDF	= Union pour la démocratie française
MRG	= Mouvement des radicaux de gauche (Left Radicals).

NOTES ON CONTRIBUTORS

David S. Bell is a Lecturer in Politics at the University of Leeds and a Visiting Fellow at SERC, Sussex University.

Joy Bound is a Lecturer in Political Science at the University of Wales, Aberystwyth;

Philip G. Cerny has been a Lecturer in Politics at the University of York since 1970, and is currently Visiting Research Associate at the Center for European Studies, Harvard University;

Kevin Featherstone is a Lecturer in Political Studies at the University of Stirling.

Vladimir Claude Fišera is Reader in Politics in the School of Languages and Area Studies at Portsmouth Polytechnic.

B.D. Graham is Professor of Politics at the University of Sussex.

David Hanley is the author of numerous articles on French politics and is the co-author of 'Contemporary France: Politics and Society since 1945', London, Routledge and Kegan Paul, 1980.

Jolyon Howorth is Senior Lecturer in French Studies at the University of Aston in Birmingham.

Peter Jenkins is a Lecturer at Stockport College of Technology.

Neill Nugent is Senior Lecturer in Politics at Manchester Polytechnic.

Ella Searls is a Lecturer in the Department of Politics at the University of Newcastle-upon-Tyne.

Michalina Vaughan is Professor of Sociology at the University of Lancaster.

advanced capitalism 24-9
Afghanistan invasion 79, 82, 101
agricultural areas see Aude; Vilaine
agriculture 33, 169, 183
Algeria 31, 47, 108-9
Almond, A. 46, 51
Antagnac, J. 133-4
anti-communism 16, 31, 76
anti-egalitarianism 52-9
anti-nuclear movement 113
anti-semitism 57, 63
'Après-Demain' 54
Apter, D.E. 48
Argenteuil resolution 91, 99, 101-2, 107
Aron, R. 65, 68
Assises de Socialisme 111-12
Aude, CERES in 123-37
Auriol, V. 145
authority, legitimation of 46-8
'autogestion' 108-9, 111-15, 128
Autonomous Socialist Party 109

Baccou, P. 56, 67
Bagnolet misunderstanding 168
Barailla, R. 133
Barjouet, A. 105
Barré, H. 155
Barre, R. 28, 38, 45, 59, 72
Barrillon, R. 45
Bataille Socialiste 142, 144-5, 151
Belgium 165, 176, 178
Bell, D.S. 192
Benoist, A. de 53, 55-8, 62, 66-8
Bernstein, E. 156
Beullac, C. 55-6
Bidault, G. 155
biologism 58-9
bipolarisation 34, 115
Blanc, J. 15, 17
Blum, L. 131, 142-64 passim; Declaration 147-50, 152, 158
Bobigny resolution 99-101
Bodin, L. 104
Bonapartism 28, 31, 36
Bouchardeau, H. 6, 83; in presidential election 83, 114, 116, 119
Boucheron, J.-M. 128
Bound, J. 165, 189, 192

Bourdet, C. 109, 116, 119
Boutbien, L. 155, 161
Bracke (Desrousseaux) 144-5
Brandt, W. 182
Bretagne et Démocratie 127
Britain 165-7, 175
Broeck, M. van dem 53, 66
bureaucracy 27

cadre parties 24, 48
'Canard Enchaîné, Le' 109
cantonal elections 44, 75, 95, 115
CAP see Permanent Administrative Committee
Capdeville, R. 131
capitalism: advanced, and Gaullism 24-9; changes in 159-60; monopoly 187; state monopoly, and intellectuals 92-3
Cardoze, M. 102
Castilla, J.-B. 132, 137
Catholicism 113-16; see also religion
Cayrol, R. 119, 126
central parties see Mouvement des radicaux de Gauche, Mouvement Republicain Populaire, Section Francaise de l'Internationale, etc.
Centre Alliance, proposed 72-4, 80
CERES (left wing party faction – earlier SFIO) 5, 77; in Aude and Vilaine 123-37; congresses 133, 135; and EEC 170-1, 173, 186; press 133; and Parti Socialiste 76-7
Cerny, P.G. 1-2, 24, 48-51, 192
CFDT (union) 5, 111, 114-17, 126-7, 132, 136-7
CGT see Confédération générale de travail
Chaban-Delmas, J. 37, 42-5
Chandernagor, A. 173
Chapuis, R. 112, 118
Chautemps, C. 143
Chevènement, J.-P. 123, 127, 173
Cheysson, C. 84, 173
Chinaud, R. 16, 22
Chirac, J. 2, 47, 114; on 'convergences' 74; as leader of Gaullists 36-47; loss of supporters 83, 87; in pres-

idential elections 24, 28, 44, 83, 87;
    as prime minister 11, 36-8; writings
    51
Chopier, L. 128-30
Christen, Y. 67
Christian Democratic Assembly 151
Christianity *see* Catholicism; religion
CIR *see* Convention des Institutions
    Républicaines
class: alliances and PCF 89-107; and
    political strategy 90-2; relations 148,
    156; struggle 158-9
Club de l'Horloge 52, 56
CNR *see* National Council of the Res-
    istance
'collective labour' 92
COMECON 182
Commin, P. 155
Common Agricultural Policy 33, 169,
    183; *see also* European Economic
    Community
Common Programme (PCF, PS and MRG)
    71, 75, 79, 91, 93, 111, 168, 182-4
communists *see* Eurocommunism; French
    Communist Party
Comte, G. 55, 58
Confédération générale du travail 97,
    126, 132, 154
conflict: in SFIO 146-62; in UDF 16-17
congresses: CERES 133, 135; PCF 90-
    100, 103; PS 76-7, 111, 124, 128, 136,
    168, 170-1; PSU 110, 112, 115; SFIO
    131, 144-64; UDF 18
conservative revolution 53-4
Convention des Institutions Répub-
    licaines; 127, 136
'convergences' 74
Craipeau, Y. 109, 118
creativity 59, 90
Crépeau, M. 83, 171, 173
Criddle, B. 118, 188
'Critique Socialiste' 113
'Croix, La' 112
Cuba 180
cultural power 52-68, 90; *see also*
    intellectuals
Czechoslovakia 136

Dabezies, P. 44
Daladier, E. 142-3
Daniel, J. 80, 87, 114, 118
Darwinism 58
de Gaulle, C.: and Algeria 31; and
    EEC 32-3, 39, 165, 167, 178, 180;
    and foreign policy 2; and president-
    ialism 10-12; and Soviet Union 181;
    his writings 49, 51; *see also* Gaullism
'Débat et Socialisme' 133
Debré, M. 37, 39, 43, 45, 83
Dechartre, P. 44
Dechézelles, Y. 155, 161

defeat of Left 71-2
Defferre, G. 73, 75, 157
Delors, J. 45, 173
Denmark 167
Depreux, E. 109
'deproletarisation' 98
Desrousseaux, A.M. 144-5
dominance, legacy of, and Gaullism
    32-6
Duclos, J. 103
Dumézil, G. 61, 67
Duverger, M. 10, 22, 48

Ecologist Party 83, 85, 116, 190
ecology 113-15
economic and social perspectives of
    Gaullism 45-6
economists, new 59-60
education, selective 55-6
EEC *see* European Economic Community
elections *see* cantonal; European Econ-
    omic Community; legislative; munic-
    ipal; presidential; senatorial
electoral machine, need for 12-13
'Eléments' 55, 59, 66, 68
elitism 52-9
Ellenstein, J. 96, 101-2, 106
Engels, F. 91
'entryism' 52
étatism 25, 57, 76; *see also* state
Euratom 167
Eurocommunism 80, 94
European Coal and Steel Community
    166-7, 176
European Defence Community 166,
    176-7
European Economic Community: and
    CERES 170-1, 173, 186; elections
    43, 83, 98, 114, 168-70, 183; and
    Gaullism 32-3, 39, 165, 167, 178,
    180; and Left 165-89; and PCF 165-8,
    176-86; and PS 166-76, 185, 187
European Monetary System 175

Fabre, R. 72
Faisceaux nationalistes européens 57
FANE *see* Fédération d'action nationale
    et européenne
fascism 57
Faure, M. 173
Faure, P. 55, 142, 145-6, 152, 156
Featherstone, K. 165, 188-9, 192
Fédération de la Gauche Démocratique
    et Socialiste 111, 125, 127, 136
federation, UDF as 20-1
Ferroul, E. 130-1, 133
FGDS *see* Fédération de la Gauche etc
Fifth Republic: class and political strat-
    egy 90-2; Constitution 10; and Gaul-
    lism 29-32
'Figaro-Magazine' 55, 58, 66-7

Fišera, V.C. 3-5, 108, 118, 192
Fiszbin, H. 98-9, 106-7
Fiterman, C. 173, 180-1, 189
FNE *see* Faisceaux nationalistes euro-
péens
FNRI *see* National Federation of Independent Republicans
foreign policy: Gaullist 2, 34-5, 39,
46; ND 61; PCF 176-8, 182-3, 185;
PS 166-7, 175-6; SFIO 146
Foucarde, J. 15, 17-18
'France Nouvelle' 97
Frederikson, M. 57
Frémontier, J. 97, 106
French Algerian Secret Army 47
French Communist Party 1-4, 89-107;
alternative strategies 78-80; in Aude
and Vilaine 125-7, 130, 132, 136;
class and political strategy 90-2;
congresses 90-100, 103; crisis of
intellectuals 95-104; and EEC 165-8,
176-86; in elections 83, 105, 190-1;
foreign policy 176-8, 182-3, 185;
hostility to 16, 31, 76; isolationism
75; liberalisation 78-9; and Mitterrand
173, 182, 187; and MRG 87; press
79, 97, 99, 101-2, 106, 109; and PS
73, 77-87, 100, 103, 112, 183, 186-7;
and SFIO 144, 152-60; state monopoly capitalism and intellectuals 92-3;
and Union du Peuple de France 93-
100; and working class 79, 89-100,
105-6; *see also* Common Programme
Front Autogestionnaire 113-14; *see also*
'autogestion'
front de classe 103, 106

Garaud, M.-F. 43
Garaudy, R. 83, 91, 104-5
Garcia, J. 98, 103
Gauche Révolutionnaire 144, 151; *see
also* Left
Gauchon, P. 56
Gaullist Party (RPR) 10; after de
Gaulle 36-9; and capitalism, advanced 24-9; economic and social perspectives 45-6; and EEC 32-3, 39,
165, 167, 178, 180; in elections 85,
190-1; and fifth republic 29-32; and
foreign policy 2, 34-5, 39, 46; and
institutional power 41-2; legacy of
dominance 32-6; legitimation of authority 46-8; and party system 42-5;
problems 26-9, 36-8; prospects 40-8;
and PS 74; and SFIO 151; and UDF
73; and working class 33, 36-7; *see
also* de Gaulle; UDR
Germany 53-4, 166, 170, 175-80, 182-5
Giscard d'Estaing, V. and Giscardians
2; and Chirac 39; economic policies
86; and EEC 17, 174-5; marketing

techniques 12; and Mitterrand 80-2,
174-5; and party politics 9-23; and
presidential elections 12-13, 21-2,
36, 41, 80-1, 83, 87; and president-
ialism 9-14, 35; and press 84; rise
of 14-20; and UDF 10, 15-22; his
writings 72
Goffard, S. 102
Gollet, P. 113, 118
Gouin, F. 151, 154
Graham, B.D. 5, 138, 163-4, 192
Granier, G. 116, 119
GRECE *see* Groupement de recherche
et d'études etc.
Greenstein, F.I. 50
Groupement de recherche et d'études
pour la civilisation européenne 52-9,
63, 65-8
Guesde, J. and Guesdism 139-40, 144-
5, 148, 152-3, 155
Guidoni, P. 130-1, 134, 137
Guille, G. 131

Haby, R. 56
Hamon, H. 109, 117
Hamon, L. 44
Hanley, D. 5, 123, 192
Hayward, J. 50
Hercet, G. 112-13, 118
Herriot, E. 142
Hervé, E. 126-30
Hincker, F. 95, 102, 106
Hitler, A. 53
Howorth, J. 3-4, 89, 106, 192
'Humanité, L'' 79, 99
Huntzinger, J. 168, 188
Huxley, A. 60

ideology, PCF 90-100, 103
Ille-et-Vilaine 123-37
independent left-wing strategy 74-5
Independent Republicans 11, 14, 16,
18, 21
INSEE 94, 106
institutional power and RPR 41-2
intellectuals: left-wing 55, 89-90, 95-
104, 140, 155; right-wing 55-7; and
state monopoly capitalism 92-3; *see
also* cultural power
Ireland 167
isolationism of PCF 75
Italy 176, 178

Jaurès, J. 158, 172
Jenkins, P. 3-5, 108, 192
Jobert, M. 44, 84, 173
journals *see* press
Judaism 57, 62-3; *see also* religion

Krivine, A. 112, 118

labour *see* working class
Lajoinie, A. 79
Lattre, A. de 50
Lauarmet, J. 15
Laurent, A. 157, 160-1
Laurent, P. 93, 107
Lebas, J. 145
Lecanuet, J. 16-19, 23, 180
Left 71-119; and EEC 165-89; in elect-
    ions 78-9, 83-6, 190-1; intellectuals
    55, 89-90, 95-104, 140, 155; strat-
    egies of 71-88; *see also* French Com-
    munist Party; Mouvement des
    Radicaux de Gauche; Parti Socialiste;
    Section Française de l'Internale etc.;
    Unified Socialist Party; Union de la
    Gauche
Le Guen, R. 97
legislative elections: 1936: 82, 125,
    142-4; 1945: 125, 151; 1946: 154-5;
    1958: 74, 105, 125; 1962: 105; 1967:
    43, 105, 125, 136; 1968: 34, 43, 105;
    1969: 103; 1973: 43, 75, 82, 125,
    168; 1974: 82, 86; 1978: 20, 42, 71,
    74, 82, 95-6, 103, 113-14, 125; 1981:
    21, 42, 44, 71, 83-6, 103, 108, 113-
    15, 190-1
legitimation of authority 46-8
Lejeune, M. 15
Leninism 97, 110
Le Pors, A. 116
Lévy, B.-H. 62
liberal-democratic legitimacy 28
liberalisation of PCF 78-9
liberalism 58-9
'Liberation' 111, 118
Ligue Communiste 110, 112
Lip factory occupation 108, 111-12
LO *see* Lutte Ouvrière
local organisation in UDF 19-20
Lutte Ouvrière 83, 110, 114-15

Maffre-Baugé, E. 98
majority 10, 47
Mallet, S. 100, 105, 109
MAN *see* Mouvement pour une alter-
    native non-violente
Marchais, G.: on discontented 96; and
    EEC 167; on Marx 89; and PCF 93-4,
    97, 105, 107; and presidential elect-
    ions 4, 80-1, 83, 86, 103; to Soviet
    Union 79; and Union de la Gauche 85
Marchand, J.-P. 101
Marest, L. 102
Marmin, M. 66, 68
Marshall Plan 29-30, 167, 176
Martinet, G. 109
Marx, K. and Marxism: and CERES
    123, 127; and ND 60; and PCF 89-97,
    139; and SFIO 139, 149, 155, 158
materialism, condemned 59-62

'Matin, Le' 114
Mauroy, P. 4; and EEC 6, 171; as
    prime minister 44, 84, 173; and PSU
    116, 136; and reconciliation 76-7
Mayer, D. 138, 146-64 *passim*
mayoral elections 43
Mazauric, C. 102
Mendès France, P. 108
Messmer, P. 37
Micberth, M.-G. 56
Michel, J.-P. 126
middle class 158-9
Millerand, A. 139
'ministerialism' 139
Mitterrand, F.: cabinet 84, 173; and
    EEC 167-76, 185-6; and Giscard 80-
    2, 174-5; and Metz congress 128;
    and PCF 173, 182, 187; personality
    76; and Poperen 136; presidency 6,
    24, 39, 44-8, 84, 173; and presi-
    dential elections 3-4, 11, 78, 80-7,
    93, 112, 114, 136-7, 165; and Union
    de la Gauche 75-7
'mode rétro' 53
Moissonnier, M. 101, 104
Mollet, G. 109, 138, 153-61
'Monde, Le' 55, 66-7, 84, 114, 164
Monnet, G. 146
monopoly capitalism 92-3, 187
Mousel, M. 112, 116-19
Mouvement de Liberation du Peuple
    109, 127
Mouvement Démocrate et Socialiste
    Française 15
Mouvement des Jeunesses Socialistes
    134
Mouvement des radicaux de gauche 30;
    in Aude and Vilaine 125; in elections
    85, 93, 173, 190-1; and PCF 87; and
    PS 74-5, 84-6, 190-1; and SFIO 153;
    see also Common Programme
Mouvement pour une alternative non-
    violente 113
Mouvement Républicain Populaire 30,
    125, 127, 151-2, 157-9
MRG *see* Mouvement des radicaux de
    gauche
MRP *see* Mouvement Républicain Pop-
    ulaire
multinationals 186
municipal: councils 80; elections 44,
    75, 95, 98, 113, 115, 127-9, 133
Murville, D. de 110

National Assembly 10-12: *see also* leg-
    islative elections
National Council of the Resistance 151
National Federation of Independent
    Republicans 14, 31
NATO *see* North Atlantic Treaty Organ-
    isation

Naville, P. 100, 109
ND *see* Nouvelle Droite
NDF *see* Nouvelle Droite Française
non-partisan image 13
North Atlantic Treaty Organisation 29,
34, 39, 167, 177, 181
'Notre Europe' 57
'Nouvelle Critique, La' 97, 106
Nouvelle Droite 1-3; cultural power and
political influence 52-68, 90; press
55, 57-9, 65-8
Nouvelle Droite Française 56
'Nouvelle Ecole' 55, 66-7
Nouvelle Gauche 109
'Nouvel Observateur, Le' 114
Nugent, N. 3, 192
Nungesser, R. 43

OAS *see* French Algerian Secret Army
ODJ *see* Organisation de défense juive
OEEC *see* Organisation for European
Economic Co-operation
oil crisis 38
oligarchy, modernising 28, 48
Organisation de défense juive 63
Organisation for European Economic
Co-operation 30; *see also* European
Economic Community
Ornano, M. d' 43
ouvriérisme 89, 95, 98; *see also* work-
ing class

Paris 103-4, 107, 114, 124, 127
Paris Federation 98-9
Parti des Forces Nouvelles 56
Parti des Socialistes 111
Parti Socialiste 1, 3, 5; alternative
strategy 75-7; in Aude and Vilaine
125-6, 129, 131-2, 135-6; and CERES
76-7; congresses 76-7, 111, 124, 128,
136, 168, 170-1; and EEC 166-76,
185, 187; and elections 40, 83, 85,
190-1; foreign policy 166-7, 175-6;
internal politics 138-64; and MRG 74-
5, 84-6, 190-1; and MRP 127; and
PCF 73, 77-87, 100, 103, 112, 183,
186-7; post-war 146-62; press 114;
pre-war 138-46; and PSU 84, 111-17;
public debate in 76; and RPR 74; and
SFIO 71, 91, 125, 165-7; and UDF
72-3; *see also* Common Programme
Parti Socialiste Ouvrier et Paysan 145
party system: and Gaullism 42-5; and
Giscard 9-23
Passeron, A. 44, 51
PCF *see* French Communist Party
PDS *see* Parti des Socialistes
Permanent Administrative Committee
139, 141-2, 147, 158, 170
Perrault, G. 102
'personalism' 41

Perspectives et Realités 15-16
Pétain, H. 146, 152
Peyrefitte, A. 43, 45
PFN *see* Parti des Forces Nouvelles
Philip, A. 146, 156-7, 159-61
Philipponneau, M. 127
Piaget, C. 111-12
Pinton, M. 16-19, 23
Pisani, E. 33
Pivert, M. 140, 144-5, 148
Plunkett, P. de 66
pluralism 40-1, 50
Policy differences in UDF 17
political influence of ND 52-68
polls, public opinion 72-3, 78, 80, 87,
114
Pompidou, G.: death 25, 37; and EEC
6, 167; and Gaullists 10-11, 32, 35,
37, 42, 45; and presidential elect-
ions 12
Poperen, J. 109, 114, 123, 135-6
Popper, K. 62
'Populaire, Le' 157-8, 163
Popular Front 142-6
'populism' 144
Portelli, H. 13, 22
Portugal 175
Poulantzas, N. 105
power: alternative pathways to, by
Left 72-5; institutional 41-2
PR *see* Perspectives et Realités
presidential elections 35; 1962: 12, 42;
1965: 37, 73, 136; 1969: 34, 74-5;
1974: 36, 43, 75, 93, 114; 1981: 13,
21-4, 28, 42-3, 71, 79-83, 87, 103,
108, 114, 116, 119, 173; 1988: 44
presidentialism 9-14, 16, 35
press: CERES 133; Communist 79, 97,
99, 101-2, 106, 109; ND 55, 57-9,
65-8; non-Communist 95; PS 54, 114;
PSU 108, 111-13; SFIO 157-8, 163
problems of Gaullism 26-9, 36-48
proletariat *see* working class
prospects of Gaullism 40-8
Provo, V. 161
PS *see* Parti Socialiste
PSOP *see* Parti Socialiste Ouvrier et
Paysan
PSU *see* Unified Socialist Party

Quilès, Y. 97, 101, 106

racism 54, 57
Radicals *see* Mouvement des radicaux
etc.
Ralite, J. 4, 102, 107
Rassemblement du Peuple Français 30-
1, 44
Rassemblement pour la Republique *see*
Gaullist Party
recession 28, 38-9, 58

referenda 42, 167, 182
religion 53, 57, 61-4, 113-16
Renaudel, P. 142
'Révolution' 97, 101-2
'revolutionary class' 90
revolutionary nature: of PCF 79; of
    PSU 110
'Revue Socialiste, La' 158
Right 7-68, 190-1; *see also* Gaullist
    Party, Giscardians, Nouvelle Droite
Rimbert, P. 155, 157, 162, 164
Rocard, M. and Rocardians 132, 134;
    and EEC 170-1, 188; in presidential
    election 4; and Metx congress 128;
    and PSU 108-18; and reform 76-7;
    and third force strategy 73; and
    unions 5, 136
Rotman, P. 109, 117
Rous, J. 155, 157
RPF *see* Rassemblement du Peuple
    Français
RPR *see* Rassemblement pour la Répub-
    lique

Salan, Gen. 31
Salomon, A. 123, 135-6
Saunier-Sëité, A. 55
Schain, M.A. 49, 51
Schmidt, H. 174-5, 183
Schreiber, J.-J. Servan 15, 73
Schwarz, W. 119
scientism 58-65
Searls, E. 1-2, 22, 142
sectarianism 138
Section Française de l'Internationale
    Ouvrière (later CERES) 30, 76; in
    Aude and Vilaine 5, 125-7, 130-1;
    congresses 131, 146-64; and EEC
    165-7, 170; foreign policy 146; and
    Gaullism 151; and intellectuals 89;
    and MRG 157-9; and MRP 157-9; and
    PCF 144, 152-60; post-war conflict
    146-62; press 157-8, 163; pre-war
    tendances' 138-46; and PS 71, 91,
    125, 165-7; and PSU 109-11; and
    working class 157-8
sectionalism 138
senatorial elections 75
Servan *see* Schreiber
Service d'Action Civique 47
SFIO *see* Section Française de l'Inter-
    nationale Ouvrière
Socialist parties *see* Left
sociobiology 58-9
'Sofres' poll 72-3, 87-8
Soisson, J.-P. 14, 17-18, 23
Soviet Union 79, 82, 177-81, 185-6
Spain 165, 175-6
Stalinism 58, 78, 166
state: monopoly capitalism and intel-
    lectuals 92-3; role of 25, 27-9, 38;

    see also étatism
    strategies of Left 71-88

'tendances' in SFIO 138-46
territorial conflicts 16-17
Thatcher, M. 174
third force strategy 72-4
Third World 175
Thorez, M. 182, 189
Tindemans Report 169
Tornikian, J. 97, 106
totalitarianism, condemned 62-4, 68
Touraine, A. 57, 62, 67, 100
'Tribune du Communisme' 104
'Tribune Socialiste' 108, 112, 118
Trotskyism 110, 112

UDF *see* Union pour la Democratie
    Française
UDR *see* Union des Democrates pour
    la République
UDT *see* Independent Republicans
UGICT (federation of managers, engin-
    eers and technicians) 97
UGS *see* Union de la Gauche Socialiste
Unified Socialist Party 1-5, 108-19; in
    Aude and Vilaine 125-6, 128, 132,
    135; congresses 110, 112, 115; in
    presidential elections 83; press 108,
    111-13; and PS 84, 111-17; and
    SFIO 109-11; and working class 110-
    11
Union de la Gauche Socialiste 71-86
    passim, 109-15, 167, 185
Union des Démocrates pour la Répub-
    lique 33-4, 36-8, 41, 44
Union du Peuple de France 93-100
Union of Left *see* Union de la Gauche
Union pour la Démocratie Française 10-
    11, 41, 43-4; conflict in 16-17; con-
    gress 18; in elections 21-2, 85, 190-
    1; as federation or party 20-1; and
    Giscard 10, 15-22; local organisation
    in 19-20; and PS 72-3; reasons for
    the formation of 14-18; and RPR 73;
    structure of 18-20; *see also* Giscard-
    ians
Union pour la nouvelle majorité (RPR
    and UDF) 22, 190-1
Union pour la Nouvelle République 31,
    33, 41-3, 45
unions *see* CFDT, CGT
United States, attitudes to: by Left
    166, 170, 176-7, 182; by Right 60-2,
    67-8
UNM *see* Union pour la nouvelle maj-
    orité
UNR *see* Union pour la Nouvelle Rép-
    ublique
UPF *see* Union du Peuple de France

Vallant-Couturier, P. 90
Vals, F. 133-4
Vaughan, M. 1-3, 52, 192
Verba, S. 46, 51
Verdier, R. 161
VGE *see* Giscard d'Estaing
Vial, P. 56-7, 65-8
Vichy 146
Vilaine, CERES in 123-37
'volontarisme' 123

wars, impact of 29-30, 146
white-collar workers 33, 89, 94

women 116
women's movements 112-13, 118
working class: and Gaullism 33, 36-7;
   new 90, 92-4, 98, 103, 109; and
   PCF 79, 89-100, 105-6; and PSU 110-
   11; and SFIO 157-8

Ysmal, C. 7, 119

Zyromiski, J. 144, 148

index compiled by
Ann Hall